$15-

D1249162

Patronage
The Crown
and
The Provinces

In Later Medieval England

Patronage
The Crown
and
The Provinces

In Later Medieval England

Edited by Ralph A. Griffiths

ALAN SUTTON
HUMANITIES PRESS

First published in Great Britain in 1981
by Alan Sutton Publishing Limited
17a Brunswick Road
Gloucester GL1 1HG

First published in the United States of America in 1981
by Humanities Press Inc.
Atlantic Highlands
New Jersey 07716

ISBN 0-904387-45-3 Alan Sutton
ISBN 0-391-02096-X Humanities Press

BRITISH LIBRARY CATALOGUING IN PUBLICATION DATA

**Patronage, the crown and the provinces in later
  medieval England.**
  1. Great Britain - History - Lancaster and
  York, 1399-1485
  2. Great Britain - History - Henry VII, 1495-
  1509
  I. Griffiths, Ralph Alan
  942.04   DA245

  ISBN 0-904387-45-3

Typesetting and origination by
Alan Sutton Publishing Limited
Photoset Bembo 10/11
Printed in Great Britain by
Redwood Burn Limited
Trowbridge & Esher

Contents

List of Abbreviations

Unless otherwise stated, the place of publication of cited works is London

AN	Archives Nationales, Paris
BIHR	*Bulletin of the Institute of Historical Research*
BJRL	*Bulletin of the John Rylands Library*
BL	British Library, London
BN	Bibliothèque Nationale, Paris
CCR	*Calendar of Close Rolls*
CChR	*Calendar of Charter Rolls*
CFR	*Calendar of Fine Rolls*
CIM	*Calendar of Inquisitions Miscellaneous*
CIPM	*Calendar of Inquisitions Post Mortem*
CP	G.E. Cokayne, *The Complete Peerage*, ed. V.H. Gibbs *et al.* (13 vols., 1910-59).
CPR	*Calendar of Patent Rolls*
DNB	*Dictionary of National Biography*
DRO	Devon Record Office, Exeter
EconHR	*Economic History Review*
EETS	Early English Text Society
EHR	*English Historical Review*
HMC	*Historical Manuscripts Commission*
PPC	N.H. Nicolas (ed.), *Proceedings and Ordinances of the Privy Council of England* (7 vols., RC, 1834-37)
PRO	Public Record Office, London
RC	Record Commission
RP	*Rotuli Parliamentorum* (7 vols., RC, 1832)
RS	Rolls Series
SR	*Statutes of the Realm* (11 vols., RC, 1810-28)
TDevonA	*Transactions of the Devonshire Association for the Advancement of Science, Literature and Art.*
TRHS	*Transactions of the Royal Historical Society*
VCH	*Victoria History of the Counties of England*

Classes of documents in the Public Record Office

Chancery

C1	Early Chancery Proceedings
C30	Receivers' Accounts
C47	Miscellanea
C49	Parliament and Council Proceedings
C53	Charter Rolls
C54	Close Rolls
C61	Gascon Rolls
C67	Supplementary Patent Rolls
C76	Treaty Rolls
C81	Warrants for the Great Seal, Series I
C85	Significations of Excommunication
C139	Inquisitions Post Mortem, Series I, Henry VI
C219	Writs and Returns of Members to Parliament
C258	Writs of Certiorari, Tower Series Files

Court of Common Pleas

CP40	Plea Rolls

Exchequer

E101	King's Remembrancer, Various Accounts
E163	, Miscellanea
E358	Lord Treasurer's Remembrancer, Miscellaneous Accounts
E364	, Foreign Account Rolls
E403	Treasury of Receipt, Issue Rolls
E404	, Warrants for Issues

Court of King's Bench

KB9	Ancient Indictments
KB27	*Coram Rege* Plea Rolls

Prerogative Court of Canterbury

P.C.C.	Registered Copies of Wills

Privy Seal Office

PSO1	Warrants, Series I

Special Collections

SC6	Ministers' and Receivers' Accounts
SC8	Ancient Petitions

Introduction

This collection of essays had its origin in a symposium held at the University College of Swansea in July 1979. This symposium was the second such meeting to take place on the initiative of Professor Charles Ross and to be devoted to the history of late-medieval England. The first resulted in a successful volume which Professor Ross edited as *Patronage, Pedigree and Power in Late-Medieval England* (Gloucester, 1979). Those who took part in the second venture were mainly former postgraduate students of history of the University of Bristol or the University College of Swansea, augmented by several others, who, in one way or another, had become closely connected with them. Once again, the principal object was to encourage younger scholars to make more widely available the results of their researches, and to this end no rigid commission was imposed on those offering papers, though, in preparing this volume for publication, two major themes suggested themselves as being common to almost all the essays: the links between the crown and the provinces of the realm, and the pervasive importance of patronage in English society and politics during the fourteenth and fifteenth centuries.

Historians of late-medieval England have in the past been powerfully attracted — for impeccable historical reasons and because of the well organised and enticing nature of the surviving national archives — to the king, the court and the government offices at Westminster. They have been, to use K.B. McFarlane's happy phrase, the 'King's Friends'.[1] Of course, dioceses and individual bishops have long been popular subjects for study, not least because episcopal registers are still to be found in diocesan registries or county repositories.[2] But a more decisive shift in late-medieval English historiography has taken place in the last generation or so with more sophisticated and concerted studies of the aristocracy, their estates and their 'connection', particularly among the gentle classes; though it is still the rare student who is able to reassemble, with any claim to completeness, the private archive of a late-medieval magnate.[3] Most of these latter investigations, moreover, have taken as their focus the administrative headquarters of bishops and magnates — Lambeth and Canterbury in the case of a statesman-archbishop like Henry Chichele, or Westminster and the Savoy palace in the case of John of Gaunt. The provinces of the realm have figured in these studies mainly in so far as they were territorial dioceses ruled from Durham, Wells or other, or they contributed to the administrative and economic structures of a highly centralised seignorial organisation like that of Mortimer or Stafford. To some extent, this has been inevitable: there is a dispiriting paucity of surviving records from late-medieval towns (though, as Rosemary Horrox here shows, these are by no means negligible), and archives of individuals and families below the ranks of the nobility and gentry are rarer still. Past emphases in historical writing also owe much to the intractable nature of certain categories of royal documents which, when fully mastered, might well take the historian into the shires of the kingdom. It is for this reason that R.L. Storey's exploitation of the records of the court of king's bench, with their reflection of the state of public order in the realm, offer such a fruitful avenue whereby the English provinces can be examined in their own right.[4] Ailsa Herbert here follows in his footsteps to greater depth in Herefordshire and the Welsh borderland, and so too in part does Martin Cherry in Devon and the west country more generally.

The relationship between the crown and the provinces was direct, immediate and crucial in a state as relatively compact and centralised as late-medieval England. The annual appointment of sheriffs and escheators, the frequent though irregular nomination of J.Ps. and commissioners for a variety of other tasks, and the installation of constables in royal castles scattered through the length and breadth of the kingdom — all these occasions provided the king and his ministers with an opportunity to determine events in town and countryside. Local lords, knights, esquires and other worthies were relied on frequently for these purposes, yet many of them also received fees from the royal household and therefore could be regarded by the king as a corps of dependable servants.[5] Others were lawyers or courtiers who had little or no prior connection with their new bailiwick, but whose presence in the localities inspired in the crown a confidence that its interests would be rigorously safeguarded. By such means, the king's influence on events that occurred at a distance from Westminster was reasonably assured.[6] And well it needed to be, for, as C.A.J. Armstrong demonstrated some years ago, it took well nigh a week for messages to be carried from Newcastle upon Tyne to London and almost as long for news of Edward IV's death at Westminster to reach Ludlow; meanwhile, as Charles Ross reminds us below, unfounded or malicious rumour could attempt its insidious worst.[7] In the later middle ages, therefore, good channels of communication of a personal kind were essential for effective government by the king and his officials resident in London and the south-east.

The immense private domains which the Lancastrians and Yorkists enjoyed at the time they seized the crown (and which Henry Tudor acquired in 1485) gave new and significant dimension to their royal estate. Many were the servants and administrators who henceforward moved easily from the private lands of kings to the public service of the crown in all parts of the realm.[8] The royal family might also be at the monarch's disposal, for (to quote B.P. Wolffe) 'A well-endowed royal family was an essential attribute of effective kingship'.[9] Barely studied though it has been, the estate (in the broadest sense) of the prince of Wales encompassed authority and property in those distant parts - notably Cornwall and Chester, not to speak of Wales itself - which were least sensitive to the wishes of Westminster. And a well-stocked family like that of Edward III or Henry IV could be expected, in the most favourable circumstances, to buttress the practical power of the crown where their lands and interests were predominant.[10] Even more valuable in this respect was the queenly estate, for Anne Crawford's assessment of the consorts of the fifteenth century pictures their domestic and estate organisation as an extension of the royal household and court; whilst among the dowers of queens were broad acres situated in several parts of the country, and an English-born queen like Anne Neville was a considerable heiress with private interests to place at the disposal of her husband.[11] Some queens, like Margaret of Anjou and Elizabeth of York, travelled especially widely, taking the face of majesty where the king might never go; others like Elizabeth Woodville, took a close interest in estate and business management; and yet others could exploit, as did Queen Margaret in the late 1450s, the regional influence which position and property afforded them.

On a broader front, kings and their ministers had to mould influential opinion, communicate their views more widely in town and country, and, in a society where sedition often bred violence, correct rumour and falsehood where they flourished. Charles Ross's essay illustrates the growing need for an effective method of propaganda and the increasingly novel methods — administrative, parliamentary and other — whereby it could be disseminated throughout the realm. In the crises of the fourteenth and fifteenth centuries, the rulers of England appreciated the importance of shaping popular opinion and the potentiality for doing so, even over large distances, that the spread of education and literacy created. The relationship between the crown and the subject would never be quite the same again.

This relationship was defined by obligations which practical necessity, custom and statute had framed during the course of the middle ages. The most fundamental of these obligations, the touchstone of successful rule, were expressed at least formally by the monarch in his coronation oath: to defend the realm, the church and the subject, and to offer justice to all.[12] In return, it was incumbent on the subject to provide military service in defence of the king and the realm, and to co-operate in the preservation of law and order. John Alban's essay on coastal defence illustrates these mutual obligations at work in one specific sector.[13] Protection of the ports and coast was a responsibility that perforce rested most heavily on the inhabitants of the 'maritime land' and it was at its most immediate during those decades of the fourteenth century when England was subjected to repeated French attack. The system showed itself to be capable of adaptation, experimentation and reform, particularly from the 1370s, and as such it remained in being until Tudor times. The crown's obligation to extend justice to every subject was far less effectively discharged in the fifteenth century, when political instability and, perhaps, economic uncertainty were matched by a legal system that was impeded by bewildering complexities of law and procedure. This is demonstrated by Ailsa Herbert's study of Herefordshire, whose distance from Westminster and proximity to Wales and the peculiar jurisdictions of the march were further obstacles to the effectiveness of the court of king's bench in suppressing crime and maintaining public order.[14] Equally, some of the nobility and gentry of Herefordshire and the west country (as described by Martin Cherry) were far less ready to co-operate in upholding the law than their obligations and their position as local office-holders and commissioners demanded. A feeling of being victimised by their exclusion from local positions of influence, a willingness to resort to self-help in disputes rather than endure the frustrations of lawful process, a sense of afront when the crown showed itself to be a partisan patron and judge towards the county community — these are the factors that produced a degree of violence which in Devon (and elsewhere) was 'qualitatively different' by 1455 from what had occured before. The failure of the relationship between king and subject on this level had a significant contribution to make to the spread of lawlessness in fifteenth-century England and even to the outbreak of civil war.[15]

When the sense of obligation proved too fragile to cope with practical needs, it was sometimes replaced by the bonds of patronage, though sometimes weakened still further by them. The role of patronage was not new in the later middle ages in either church or state or more private contexts. But in forging links between men, it does appear to have been more significant then: ties of tenancy, the obligations of a feudal society, and the traditional organisation of military service were less potent features than in the past, and 'good lordship' came to depend almost exclusively on mutual interest: the patron stood in need of support, service and influence; the patronised sought reward, protection and a living. This did not necessarily make for a less stable society, though it often promoted personal and sectional interests at the expense of the broader needs of the realm and the crown.[16]

As several of these essays make clear, the role of the crown and the aristocracy as reservoirs of patronage has long been appreciated; and for reasons already mentioned it has been strikingly illuminated in recent years, not least in *Patronage, Pedigree and Power*. The balance is here redressed in other directions: by Anne Crawford's judgements on the role of queens in England; by Rosemary Horrox's revelations of the lengths to which provincial towns would go to secure the goodwill of noblemen, lawyers, and others in their quest for gifts, exemptions and charters; and by Robert Dunning, who takes his stand beside ambitious or nervous clerks whose promotion in the church depended on eiscopal, aristocratic, and royal patronage just as much as on ability or birth. For the patron, the benefits were no less obvious: men and money when needed, service and support more constantly.

The dangers inherent in defective or unwise patronage are also exemplified here. When the crown proved to be an unworthy patron, a most serious threat was posed to political and social stability. Michael Jones's reconstruction of the circumstances in which Edmund Beaufort's expedition to France was launched in 1443 reveals the unwarranted and ultimately disastrous lengths to which Henry VI was prepared to go to gratify a favoured relative; and Martin Cherry's chronicle of the rivalry between the earl of Devon and Sir William Bonville testifies to the insensitive patronage of which the king and his ministers were capable. Not only had lordship to be 'good' for both sides, but it had to be circumspect and take account of wider implications. Aristocratic, gentry, urban and ecclesiastical patronage had less propensity for disputes and violence; but with the crown's effective supervision it too could be disruptive of social peace. The patronage of queens (as Anne Crawford indicates) might be a useful adjunct to that of the king himself, but aristocratic and gentry affinities too often undermined public order in town and country and, as events in Herefordshire and Devon demonstrate, offered the raw material for partisan causes to utilise. Much as Rosemary Horrox's towns might strive to avoid the consequences of their 'connections' in uncertain times, and some ecclesiastical promotions might be tolerated with resentment but nothing more, among the governing classes the risks of widespread unrest were much greater.

This volume would not have seen the light of day but for the enterprise of Alan Sutton Publishing Ltd., whilst the symposium on which it is based owed its success not only to those who took part but also to the support, including financial support, of the Principal and Registrar of the University College of Swansea. My thanks go to them all.

University College, Swansea, 1980.   R.A. Griffiths.

1. *The Nobility of Later Medieval England* (Oxford, 1973), p.2.
2. Though most studies of individual bishops of the later middle ages are of prelates who were far from typical: e.g., V.H.H. Green, *Bishop Reginald Pecock* (Cambridge, 1945); E.F. Jacob, *Henry Chichele* (1967). However, R.L. Storey, *Thomas Langley and the Bishopric of Durham, 1406-1437* (1961), and M.E. Aston, *Thomas Arundel* (Oxford, 1967), provide a balanced study of both prelate and see.
3. N. Denholm-Young, *Seignorial Administration in England* (Oxford, 1937), and K.B. McFarlane's work, as reflected posthumously in the book cited above n.1, were the inspiration for such studies as R. Somerville, *History of the Duchy of Lancaster*, I (1953); C.D. Ross, *The Estates and Finances of Richard Beauchamp, Earl of Warwick* (Dugdale soc., occasional paper XII, 1956); G.A. Holmes, *The Estates of the Higher Nobility in Fourteenth-century England* (Cambridge, 1957); J.M.W. Bean, *The Estates of the Percy Family* (Oxford, 1958); R.I. Jack, *The Grey of Ruthin Valor* (Sydney, 1965); J.T. Rosenthal, 'The Estates and Finances of Richard, Duke of York (1411–1460)', in W.M. Bowsky (ed.), *Studies in Medieval and Renaissance History*, II (Nebraska, 1965); C. Rawcliffe, *The Staffords, Earls of Stafford and Dukes of Buckingham, 1394-1521* (Cambridge, 1978); and several other studies that remain unpublished in thesis-form. For some magnate records, see C.D. Ross and T.B. Pugh, 'Materials for the study of Baronial Incomes in Fifteenth-century England', *EconHR*, 2nd. ser., VI (1953), 185-94; and one magnate's reconstructed archive, C. Rawcliffe, 'A Tudor Nobleman as archivist: the papers of Edward, third Duke of Buckingham', *Journal of the Society of Archivists*, V, no. 5 (1976), 294-300.
4. *The End of the House of Lancaster* (1960).
5. In relation to Henry IV, see A.L. Brown, 'The reign of Henry IV: the establishment of the Lancastrian regime', in S.B. Chrimes, C.D. Ross and R.A. Griffiths (eds.), *Fifteenth-century England, 1399-1509* (Manchester, 1972), pp. 14ff; and T.B. Pugh, 'The Magnates, Knights and Gentry', ibid., pp. 107-8. D.A.L. Morgan, 'The king's affinity in the polity of Yorkist England', *TRHS*, 5th ser., XXIII (1973), 1-25 (esp. pp. 20-21), is important for Edward IV.
6. For the duchy of Lancaster, see Somerville, op. cit., 'List of Officers'; and Wales (esp. under Henry VI), R.A. Griffiths, 'Patronage, Politics and the Principality of Wales, 1413-1461', in H. Hearder and H.R Loyn (eds.), *British Government and Administration: Studies presented to S.B. Chrimes* (Cardiff, 1974), pp. 77-86.
7. 'Some examples of the distribution and speed of news in England at the time of the Wars of the Roses', in R.W. Hunt, W.A. Pantin and R.W. Southern (eds.), *Studies in Medieval History presented to F.M. Powicke* (Oxford, 1948), pp. 429-54 (esp. pp. 444-54).
8. See Brown, op. cit., pp. 19-20.
9. *The Royal Demesne in English History* (1971), p.52; ch. II esp. makes important points in this regard.
10. But the regional hegemony of Edward IV's 'adopted' family of Woodvilles has recently been judged 'malign': M.A. Hicks, 'The changing role of the Wydevilles in Yorkist politics to 1483', in Ross, *Patronage, Pedigree and Power*, pp. 60–83 (esp. pp. 82–83). See the efforts of Henry VI , an only child with no immediate family after 1447, to bring greater cohesion to his wider kin: R.A. Griffiths, 'The sense of dynasty in the reign of Henry VI', ibid., pp. 18-25.
11. The value of Elizabeth of York's rightful inheritance was recognised by her husband, Henry VII, after 1485; it was 'quietly incorporated into the crown's holdings' (below p.47).
12. For the oath of 1308, see S.B. Chrimes and A.L. Brown (eds.), *Select Documents of English Constitutional History, 1307-1485* (1961), pp. 4-5.
13. See, in general, M.R. Powicke, *Military Obligation in Medieval England: a Study in Liberty and Duty* (Oxford, 1960).
14. See also M. Blatcher, *The Court of King's Bench, 1450-1550: a Study in Self-help* (1978).
15. Compare R.A. Griffiths, 'Local Rivalries and National Politics: the Percies, the Nevilles and the Duke of Exeter, 1452–55', *Speculum* XLIII (1968, 589–632; R.L. Storey, 'Lincolnshire and the Wars of the Roses', *Nottingham Medieval Studies*, XIV (1970), 64-83.
16. See K.B. McFarlane's cautionary remarks on this score, op. cit., pp.113-21.

1. Rumour, Propaganda and Popular Opinion During The Wars of The Roses

Charles Ross
University of Bristol

The history of England in the fifteenth century, especially in its troubled and divisive latter half, is marked by a vastly increased use of propaganda of all kinds, much of it more sophisticated than that which had gone before. It came not only from the government, but also from opposing factions or particular groups (for example, the Lollards), and the whole process was to be continued on an even more massive scale, including the use of censorship (not really a fifteenth-century phenomenon) by the Tudor successors of the Yorkist kings, who were, for the most part at least, as dynastically insecure as Henry IV, Henry VI, Edward IV and Richard III had been.[1]

Why did this development of propaganda take place? It is very clearly connected with the spread of literacy, with the emergence ·of 'standard English', which everyone could understand, without the help of regional dialects,[2] and, later, with the circulation of the printed word (hence censorship). But these were *pre-conditions*, not causes, at least in terms of political propaganda. It is the contention of this paper that, given this context of increasing and vernacular literacy, the use of propaganda was largely a response by governments to the circulation of seditious rumours, especially in times of political unease. Both rumour and propaganda fed upon this same phenomenon of growing literacy, with the written or printed word assuming an enhanced importance. Both reflect also a growing awareness, both by the government and its opponents, of the importance of influencing popular opinion within the realm.

Because of the nature of our sources, popular opinion is far from easy to define. If one may be permitted a small semantic distinction, 'public' opinion may be taken as reflecting the outlook, attitudes, and interests of the commons in parliament, and, to a lesser degree, those of many members of the lords also. These were the politically active classes with a voice in government: barons, knights, esquires, merchants. They were, so to speak, part of 'the Establishment' of the time, and they had the will and the money and the political position which entitled them to a decent and respectful hearing of their views by king and council, even if these were not ultimately accepted. But both rumour and propaganda were designed to appeal to a much wider audience — to the mass of the people of England. It is unfortunate that we know so little, *directly*, of what ordinary people thought and felt about the government under which they flourished or suffered. Even the many surviving political poems and ballads which have come down to us seem often to represent an appeal to popular opinion rather than its expression[3]; the well-known 'Ballad on the Gates of Canterbury' of 1460, for example, is highly sophisticated in its appeal, at least if it were to be fully understood, as V.J. Scattergood has rightly pointed out.[4] Nor can the apparently abundant surviving evidence in the class of records known as Ancient Indictments in the Public Record Office be taken wholly at face value. Admirable use of such records has been made by scholars, notably R.L. Storey and R.A. Griffiths,[5] but by their very nature they deserve to be treated with scepticism, since they were often produced by interested parties, private enemies, informers or spies working for the government. For example, did the 'Wessex peasants' of 1462 really believe that 'We commons have brought King Edward (IV) to his prosperity in the realm of England, and if he will not be ruled after us as we will have him, as able as we were to make him king, as able we be to depose him and put him down'?[6] But who produced this report? Does it necessarily command belief? It may represent nothing more than a recording of the boastful and wild remarks of groups of inebriated men gathering outside the local ale-house, although at the same time it does suggest both the credulity and volatility of the common people (points which are discussed further below). On the other hand, those who chose to rely upon the *written* word to circulate rumours or slanders faced lethal consequences, for here the evidence against them was clear and irrefutable. Thus in 1456, according to Abbot Whetehamstede, one John Holton was hanged, drawn and quartered 'for writing bills touching the person of the king', and in 1484 William Collyngbourne met a similarly gruesome end in connection with his circulating the famous lampoon directed against Richard III and his advisers ('The Catt, the Ratt, and lovel owyr dogge Rulyn all Engeland, undyr an hogge' — representing Catesby, Ratcliffe, Lovell and the White Boar of Richard), although it is to be noted that the principal charge against Collyngbourne was that of having been in treasonable correspondence with Henry Tudor in Brittany.[7]

These considerations need to be combined with two others. First, as K.B. McFarlane pointed out, the common people were far from indifferent to the political events of the day: apart from the specific examples of their violent interventions which he quoted, it is quite possible to point to other occasions when the general attitudes of the populace had a significant bearing upon events.[8] At the same time, they were volatile in their opinions:

> With little to lose and grievances that were real enough, the commons were easily incited to rebellion by magnates whom they admired . . . Their discontents were not readily assuaged by the substitution of one dynasty for another. Inevitably, they were disposed to regard whoever was in power as responsible for the evils they suffered. Some of them could usually be relied upon to join in any attempt to turn out the existing government . . .[9]

Both popular discontent and popular volatility were facts of political life, especially after 1397, as régimes came and went. Both provided feeding-grounds for rumour and propaganda alike, the one intended to inflame and excite, the other to appease and assuage.

The second point concerns the apparent credulity, sometimes gullibility, of medieval people, especially perhaps the common people, and the difficulty which a medieval government, without the resources of modern mass media, had in correcting the spread of wild rumours, or even of a politically undesirable religious cult. Two examples will suffice to illustrate this point. The annalist who wrote at Ely in the early years of Edward IV, author of the 'Brief Notes' printed by James Gairdner, was apparently a sober enough man; he based his entries on what Kingsford called 'flying reports' (but they were more probably news-letters, a small but significant subject in itself) which were of his immediate time.[10] For the northern campaign in the winter of 1462, he gives an admirable and apparently accurate list of those serving Edward IV against the Lancastrian die-hards. Soon after come details of exactly who was conducting which siege, followed by details of the price of corn and other cereals in East Anglia. He was not, it may be suggested, a romantic author. But then he turns to the invasion scares which so alarmed Englishmen in the years 1461-62, when Edward IV had received no foreign backing and was certainly under threat from a king of France who had chosen to give support to Henry VI and Margaret of Anjou:[11] it is interesting to note that the annalist seems to give authenticity to his report of the threat of invasion by pin-pointing his source ('one in the county of Worcester, taken by the Lord Southwell'). See what he appeared to believe — just rumour? but for him worth recording in an otherwise sober set of annals.[12]

> Blessed be God, divers of our adversaries be overthrown, and we understand the privity and false imaginations of the French party . . . the spy hath confessed that Henry VI, Margaret of Anjou, *the duke of Brittany, Edward duke of Burgundy*, [and others] be in Scotland with

the Scots. The duke of Exeter, the earl of Pembroke, the baron of Burford, John Ayne. These shall land at Beaumaris by the appointment of Robert Gold, captain of the duke of Burgundy. Duke Harry of Calabria, the lord Hungerford, the lord Morton, the duke of Somerset with 60,000 men of Spain: these shall land on the coast of Norfolk and Suffolk.

The 'duke' of Spain, the French Dauphin, and others were to land at Sandwich 'by appointment',

> with all the power possible they may make; the King of France with 100,000, the King of Denmark with 20,000, the King of Aragon 50,000, the King of Navarre with 20,000, the King of Sicily with 25,000, the King of Portugal with 10,000: the which be appointed to enter the realm of England.

A vast international conspiracy to overthrow the struggling house of York, with the usual medieval exaggeration of numbers, is laid before our eyes. But it is perhaps worth noting that the government itself responded to threats of foreign invasion with calculated alarmism but with similar degrees of exaggeration. In a letter of March 1462 to the London alderman, Thomas Cook, Edward IV spoke of a fearful alliance between Lancaster and England's enemies which was likely to bring upon the realm 'such war, depopulation and robbery and manslaughter as here before hath not been used among Christian people', and which might extinguish 'the people, the name, the tongue and the blood English of this our said realm'.[13] (The blatant appeal to English nationalism in this piece of royal propaganda is itself not without interest.) But it is with this degree of credulity that one has to deal in considering the power of rumour.

The inability of government to counter popular belief and sentiment is displayed in a somewhat different context in the cult of Henry VI as a saint, which has been so well charted by J.W. McKenna.[14] By any standards, Henry VI had been a wretchedly inadequate king, under whose rule the populace had suffered greatly, but by no means did this prevent his becoming a popular (if unofficial) saint, an opinion reflected in the London chronicles of c. 1497.[15] Shrines were erected to his memory not only in country churches but also in Ripon, Durham and York, where the cult was condemned by Archbishop Booth in 1479; Henry's tomb at Chertsey abbey became a centre of pilgrimage, and Richard III's translation of the body to Windsor (to lie opposite Henry's ancient enemy, Edward IV) did little to stop the cult. Miracles were already attributed to him, including skin cures which only a rightful monarch could procure, and, moreover, *rumours* circulated that on removal his corpse had been discovered in a state of perfect preservation.

This, then, is the mental and psychological climate against which the circulation of rumour and the development of propaganda must be considered.

The trouble with rumour, particularly in times of political unease and uncertainty, lay in the fact that it was not only difficult to control but that it was only too often seditious in character. Further, rumour spread like wildfire, and, moreover, became more exaggerated as time went on, for such is the nature of rumour. One good earlier example of the way in which rumour played on the fears and prejudices of the populace comes from the rather obscure Cheshire rebellion of 1393.[16] Thomas Walsingham tells us that 'certain disaffected persons' informed the people of the area that the dukes of Gloucester and Lancaster and the earl of Derby intended to withdraw the realm of France from its allegiance to the king of England, and wished to destroy the ancient liberties of the county of Chester.[17] The official version of these events adds the significant dimension that the king intended to destroy the magnates of the realm, an accusation taken sufficiently seriously for Richard II to refute it officially, stating that, on the contrary, the aristocracy were 'the diadem of his crown'.[18] Yet these unlikely stories obviously gained a good deal of popular credence, judging by their rapid spread. Walsingham goes on to tell us that the dissidents were actively concerned to widen their appeal geographically: 'Not only did they announce this *inter se privatim*, but also drawing up bills which they fixed to the doors of churches,[19] transmitting them to neighbouring counties, seeking thereby to attract help'. The truth of this statement is born out by Richard II's response. Orders to make proclamations against the dissidents were sent not only to the duke of Gloucester as justice of Cheshire, and to the duke of Lancaster in his county palatine, but also to the sheriffs of Shropshire, Staffordshire, Derbyshire, Leicestershire and Warwickshire, thereby indicating the government's view of obvious areas of discontent.[20]

A similar situation existed in 1470, although it is less well documented: all our information comes in fact from the contemporary, but official, chronicle of the Lincolnshire rebellion.[21] Again the use of churches, in this case their large Sunday congregations, is worthy of note:

> . . . on 7 March there was brought word to him (the king) that Robert Welles, calling himself *great captain of all the commons of Lincolnshire* had made do proclamations in all the churches of the shire the Sunday the 4th of March [Quadragesima, the Sunday before Shrove Tuesday in 1470], in the king's name, the earl and the duke in his own name, every man to come to Ranby Hawe, upon pain of death, to resist the king in coming into the said shire, saying that his *coming thither was to destroy the commons of the said shire, as appeareth by the copy of the same.*

Robert Welles was, after all, the son of a peer. How far was the wide-spread rumour that in 1450 Kent would be turned into a deer-forest in revenge for the death of the duke of Suffolk put about by a genuine 'captain of the commons', by his gentry supporters, or spontaneously by popular fears? It is hard to tell. It is easy to find examples of seditious rumours or alarmist reports (that is, calculated to alarm the people) promoted by disaffected magnates and gentry, but much less easy to establish to what degree they might be of popular origin, not invented and fomented by members of the upper classes. This is a subject which deserves much more research than it has received so far.

Thus far we have been considering rumours deliberately circulated by those bent on insurrection. In some ways, however, the most dangerous rumours were those which spread insidiously (rather than by open rebels), achieved wide circulation, could not be pinned down readily to any particular person or source, and yet which nevertheless tended to smear the character of the king, cast aspersions on his intentions, and, in general, eroded the credibility of his government. Again, we have an early example from the troubled later years of Richard II. In 1397 Richard found himself compelled to order the sheriffs to make general proclamations to allay the fears of those who had supported the Appellants in 1388. The recent arrests of Gloucester, Arundel and Warwick, he said, had been made for new offences, and not for the assemblies of 1388: 'it was not nor is it the king's intent that any of the prisoners' household be troubled, nor any who were in their company at the aforesaid time, *as it has come to the king's ears that there are many who believe that their arrest and imprisonment was because of those assemblies, and in fear of impeachment for that cause*'.[23] The use of proclamations by sheriffs is not unexpected, before more sophisticated methods of royal propaganda had been developed. What is more relevant in this context is that Richard II and his advisers clearly felt that they had to make some public response to the circulation of rumours which came from sources they could not identify but which were having a deeply corrosive effect on the reputation of the king, and indeed on his honesty.

Richard II may have been disliked, but at least he was a legitimate king. Seditious rumour was far more dangerous to a usurper. Two good examples come from the reign of Richard III (again a period of political uncertainty). In 1483 — so the official theory went — Richard was asked to assume the throne by a meeting of the 'Estates' (that is, the elements of parliament summoned in the name of his predecessor, Edward V, but which were in fact 'extra-parliamentary'). In 1484 Richard found it necessary to have his first and only parliament rehearse his claim and give it formal parliamentary approval. Very high claims have been made concerning the 'constitutionalism' of this parliament.[24] The solemn enrolment of the king's title, it is suggested, was a vindication of parliament's role as the high court of the realm, and should be seen as a conscious act of cooperation between king and parliament. Not so: unless we are to disbelieve totally the evidence of the only contemporary source we possess, the roll of the 1484 parliament, Richard's purpose was far more pragmatic; that is, he wished to use the authority of parliament to refute all rumours concerning the legitimacy of his rule. Consider the preamble, referring to the 'extra-parliamentary' assembly of 1483: here it says[25]

> Yit, neverthelesse, forasmuche as it is considred, that the most parte of the people of this Lande is not suffisantly lerned in the abovesaid Lawes and Custumes, whereby the truth and right in this behalf of lyklyhode may be hyd, and nat clerly known to all the people, and thereupon put in doubt and question.

Therefore, Parliament, whose authority 'maketh, before all thyngs, most feith and certaynte', is to give its blessing to the king's title,
> and quieting mens myndes, removeth the occasion of all doubts and seditious langage.

Richard's purpose is wholly clear. He wished to use the authority of parliament, and the publicity of a parliamentary act, to refute the general disbelief in the validity of his title. It was at once an appeal to popular opinion ('people of this Lande . . . not suffisantly lerned . . .') and an attempt to quash 'doubts and seditious langage'. Any 'constitutional' theories based upon this act sit sadly awry with its essentially practical purpose — some might say cynical purpose, since neither he nor the people at large believed in his claim to the throne. And yet, in this context, he wished to influence general opinion by all means at his disposal.

An even more interesting example of the dangers of seditious rumour comes from the following year, 1485. Queen Anne (Nevill) died on 16 March 1485. Immediately there was a crop of rumours that Richard III had done away with his wife in order to marry his niece. The Croyland chronicler, very hostile to Richard at this point, tells us that Catesby and Ratcliffe strongly advised the king that he must at once deny his intended purpose before the mayor and commons of the city of London.[26] Otherwise, they claimed, 'all the people of the north, in whom he placed the greatest reliance, would rise in rebellion . . . and impute to him the death of the queen, the daughter and one of the heirs of the Earl of Warwick, through whom he had first gained his present position . . . in order that he might gratify an incestuous passion . .[27]'. Richard took their advice and made a wholly solemn declaration that he did not intend to marry his niece. But the wildfire of rumour overtook him; the rumour spread and, indeed, reached the north, as Richard's letter, dated 5 April

1485, to the mayor and his brethren of the city of York, clearly demonstrates.[28] This letter provides a particularly clear illustration of the dangers of seditious rumour, the means by which it circulated, the anxiety which it caused in government, and the methods which the government used to try and pin it down and prevent its further dissemination:

> diverse sedicious and evil disposed personnes both in our Citie of London and elleswher . . . enforce themself daily to sowe sede of noise and disclaundre ageynst our persone . . . to abuse the multitude of our subgetts and *averte ther mynds from us* . . . some by setting up of *billes*, some by messages and sending furth of false and abhominable langage and lyes, some by bold and presumptuos opne speche and communicion oon with other, *wher thurgh the innocent people whiche wold live in rest and peas, and truly under our obbeissance as they oght to doo*, bene gretely abused.

The mayor and the authorities of York were firmly charged that if they encountered anyone speaking against the king or his lords, 'or telling of tales and tidings' wherby the people might be stirrd to commocions and unlawful assembles', then they should arrest anyone they suspected of having so spoken.

> and so preceding from oon to thothre unto the tyme the furnisher, auctor and maker of the said sedicious speche and langage be taken and punyshed according to his deserts.

Further, it was the duty of all citizens to remove any seditious bill and

> take it downe and without *reding* or shewing the same to any othre persone bring it furthwith unto us or some of the lords or othre of our Counsaill.

If the city authorities ignored this firm directive, they faced the king's 'grevous indignacion', and they must answer to the king at their extreme peril.

One could scarcely wish for a clearer indication of the deep anxiety which the circulation of seditious rumour caused to an insecure government, and the emphasis upon 'billes' and the prohibition of 'reding' of the same underlines the growing power of the written word.

The obvious counter to this development in the dangers of seditious rumour was propaganda, using similar methods. Although propaganda was not unknown in earlier times, it has been clearly shown by Dr. Gransden that it was never intended to appeal to more than a very limited circle of people, and, being in the hands of foreign writers, rather than in the mainstream of medieval English historiography, represented for example, by Matthew Paris, it had little success.[29] We have to wait until the reign of Richrd II for conscious attempts to mould 'public opinion' by the use of official propaganda, as, for example, in the parliament of 1388.[30] It has been claimed by J.W. McKenna[31] that 'Fifteenth-century England was distinguished for a series of royal governments which developed increasingly sophisticated methods of reinforcing their increasingly tenuous claims to the throne'. This is at once to restrict the scope of propaganda unduly, and to avoid any distinction between the Lancastrian and Yorkist periods. The Lancastrian kings had certainly been aware of the value of propaganda, but, except in respect of their foreign policy, they had proved singularly inept. It was left to another usurping dynasty, the Yorkists, displacing a dynasty which had, after all, occupied the throne for sixty years, to appreciate more fully the need for displaying the virtues of the White Rose, which they did with effect and increasing sophistication.

The use of propaganda by the Yorkist kings (with the exception of one or two constant themes) tends to coincide rather closely with periods of political crisis (1460-61, 1469-71, and 1483-85). The dynasty itself came to power in the wake of a veritable flood of propaganda, used in the preparations for the Yorkist invasion of 1460. This was maintained up to and beyond the victory of Edward IV at Towton in April 1461. The campaign of 1460-61 included all the then known propaganda devices: political songs and poems, ballads and rhymes, broadsheets pinned up in public places advertising the many virtues of the Yorkist leaders and the righteousness of their cause, the harnessing of the papal legate to invest them with clerical blessing, addresses to convocation, political sermons at St. Paul's Cross, the use of every possible ceremonial precedent in the ceremonies of accession and coronation to emphasize their proper title to the throne, and, finally, since they claimed the throne on a basis of legitimacy, the production of a number of genealogical rolls taking their supposed descent right back through the earlier kings of England and the Roman emperors to the kings of Israel, at least as far back as Jehosophat. For Welsh consumption, there was much play with the descent of the Yorkists through the Mortimers from the ancient kings of Wales, notably Cadwallader.[32]

The second phase is that of Warwick's rebellion, Edward's flight abroad, Henry VI's restoration, and Edward's eventual recovery of the throne. In connection with his rebellion of 1469, Warwick made skilful use of the political manifesto, which contains all the snide nuances of this genre. He attacked 'the disceyvabille covetous rule and gydynge of certain cecudious persones [Rivers, his wife, the duchess of Bedford, Herbert, Humphrey Stafford]. . . and other of theyre myschevous rule opinion and assent', who have impoverished the realm, disturbed the administration of the laws, and intended only their own promotion and enrichment. Then follows a far more dangerous and most highly seditious commentary on the activities of Edward II, Richard II and Henry VI, who estranged the great lords of their blood from their council, and were not advised by them, 'takyng abowte them other not of thaire blood, and enclynyng only to their counsell, rule and advice, the whiche persones take not respect ne consideracion to the wele of the said princes, ne to the commonwele of this lond, but only to theire singuler lucour . . .'.[33] The implied threat was clear enough.

The royal response to all this provided a significant innovation in terms of official propaganda: the use of official chronicles. This means of communication was already established on the continent (but,[34] unfortunately for the historian, not in England) and the experiment was not to be repeated. Three short chronicles tell the story of these events not only in English, but also in French translation (accomplished in a matter of weeks) intended for circulation on the continent, especially in the duchy of Burgundy.[35] These chronicles, especially the last (the 'Arrivall'), were skilfully written. The propaganda element in them is subtly rather than obviously stated. Take, for instance, the evocative story of Edward IV's attendance at a Palm Sunday service in the parish church at Daventry, where he,[36]

> with greate devocion, hard all divine service upon the morne . . . wher God, and Seint Anne, shewyd a fayre miracle; a goode pronostique of good adventure that aftar shuld befall unto the Kynge by the hand of God, and the mediation of that holy matron Seynt Anne.

The doors of an alabaster image of St. Anne, which were 'shett, closed, and clasped', according to the rules of the church in England, then miraculously opened with 'a great crak', revealing the image of the saint. 'The Kynge, this seinge, thankyd and honoryd God, and Seint Anne, takynge it for a good signe, and token of good and prosperous aventure that God wold send hym . . .' It would be hard to better this as a play upon both the religiosity and the credulity of the medieval populace, with the added element of emphasising the personal piety of King Edward IV. The main problem for the author of the 'Arrivall' lay in explaining the death of Henry VI on the same night as Edward IV arrived, victoriously, in London: though cleverly phrased, it is permissible to wonder whether the chronicler's claim that Henry, 'late called Kyng', died of 'pure displeasure, and melencoly', could have been widely believed.[37] But, as a projection of a royal image, the chronicler's closing paragraphs (too long to quote here in detail) were phrased in masterly fashion. One sentence may give the flavour: piety, justice, benevolence and authority all appear. The King[38]

> with the helpe of Almighty God, whiche from his begynning hath not fayled him, in short tyme he shall appeas his subgetes thrwghe all his royalme; that peace and tranquillitie shall growe and multiplye in the same . . . to the honour and lovynge of Almyghty God . . . and to

the great ioye and consolation of his frinds, alies and well-willers, and to all his people, and to the great confusion of all his enemys, and evyll willars.

Here we are concerned with a different aspect of propaganda, the projection (to use a modern term) of a favourable image of king and government. In this context perhaps the most interesting development of the media in Edward's reign lies in the increasing use of proclamations. The notable volumes of Hughes and Larkin give the impression that these sprang fully-formed from the bosom of Henry VII.[39] In fact, they were quite common, and becoming more common, under Edward IV. The germ lies in the intentions proclaimed publicly by King Edward in the first parliament of his reign on such matters as the repression of illegal retaining and the maintenance of misdoers: there are repeated references that the king wishes *all* his subjects to know of his wishes on such matters, and all the members present were commanded to report these to everyone when they returned to their own places.[40]

From this it was a short step to issuing written proclamations directed to the sheriffs and the city authorities commanding them to make them known to the *people at large* (not just lords, knights, or the 'politically responsible classes'). These are of two kinds: first, those which were essentially administrative, concerning the enforcement of the curfew, the protection of aliens, against mendicancy, the forbidding of the carrying of arms, against smuggling, and the like. More interesting, in this present context, are the political proclamations, issued in times of rebellion or in face of challenges to the throne. Here the several proclamations put forth by Edward IV in 1470 during the rebellion of Warwick and Clarence are of interest.[41] Edward's proclamations may state an official view of events, but they remain essentially factual in tone. They speak of the rebellion in Lincolnshire, of how there was evidence that Warwick and Clarence were implicated, of how he (the king) had given them every opportunity to explain themselves; but since they had not done so, he had proclaimed them rebels, but he assures his subjects that he meant to abide by his recent general pardon *contrary to seditious rumours.*

Edward IV's proclamations, therefore, made no attempt to smear or blacken the character of his enemies, except by implication from their treason. With Richard III one arrives at a different dimension. Not surprisingly, given the circumstances of his accession, the fact that his claim to the throne was generally disbelieved and the widespread belief that he had been guilty of heinous deeds, including the murder of his nephews, Richard made more widespread use of proclamations than his brother had done. It has been suggested recently that Richard 'went to his coronation with lies on his lips and blood on his hands'.[42] Hence the need for a more sustained attempt both to project an image of Richard as a model king (and a moral one), and at the same time to smear the character of his opponents. Richard III was the first king to use character assassination as a means not merely of moulding popular opinion, but also of manipulating it by misrepresentation. Here we approach the concept of propaganda in its modern sense.

The direct ancestor of Richard's propaganda was probably Warwick's manifesto of 1469 (and Warwick was his mentor in more ways than one).[42] Here we have the attack on the 'court circle' which had displaced Warwick from power:

> . . . the disceyvabille couetous rule and gydynge of certeyne ceducious persones [Rivers, his wife, the Earl of Pembroke, Humphrey Stafford, earl of Devon, Scales, Audley, Sir John Woodville] . . . and other of theyre mischevous rule opinion and assent, wheche have caused oure seid sovereyn Lord and his seid realme to falle in grete poverte of myserie, disturbynge the mynystracion of the lawes, only extending to thaire owen promocion and enrichment . . .

Then follows, in Warwick's manifesto, the menacing comparisons between Edward IV and his predecessors:

> In three the next articles . . . are comprisid and specified the occasions and verrray causes of the grete inconviencis and mischeves that fall in this lond in the dayes of [Edward II, Richard II, and Henry VI] . . . to the distruccion of them, And to the gret hurt and empoverysshing of this lond.

Richard III takes off in similar vein, in the preamble to his parliament roll of 1484:[43] for the most obvious reasons he omits all reference to the deposition of kings, but he adds his own characteristic themes, references to the approval of the Almighty, a disapproval of alleged immorality on the part of his opponents, and an outright appeal to the interests of the common people — all features which recur in his later propaganda. A few sentences may suffice to give the flavour and the none-too-subtle innuendo. Under previous kings, it is stated, while the king relied upon the counsel

> of certaine Lords Spirituelx and Temporelx, and othre persones of approved sadnesse, prudence, policie and experience, *dreding God*, and having tendre zele and affection to the common and politique wele of the Lond . . .

all was well:

> *oure Lord God was dred, luffed and honoured;* than within the Land was peas and tranquillite . . . the Land was greatly enriched, soo that as

wele the Merchants and Artificers, *as other poure people*, laboryng for theyr livyng in diverse occupations, had competent gayne . . . without miserable and intollerable povertie.

But things changed, as the king fell into evil hands:

such as had the rule and governaunce of this Land, deliting in adulation and flattery, and lede by *sensuality and concupiscence*, [the king] folowed the counsaill of persones insolent, vicious, and of inordinate avarice . . .

It was a particular consequence of Edward IV's alleged marriage to Elizabeth Grey that things went really wrong (and here once again the moralistic tone):[44]

. the ordre of all poletique Rule was perverted, the Lawes of God . . . and also the Lawes of Nature, and of Englond . . . wherein every Englishman is inheritor . . . broken . . . Murdres, Extorsions and Oppressions, namely of *poore and impotent people,* so that no Man was sure of his Lif . . . ne of his Wif, Doughter ne Servaunt, every *good Maiden and Woman standing in drede to be ravished and defouled.*

This puritanical note, and the evident concern with the king's popular image, continues remorselessly through Richard's propaganda. Indeed, one might be forgiven for thinking that his proclamation of 23 October 1483 was not indeed a *Proclamacio Pro Morum Reformacione* (as it is headed) rather than a denunciation of the treason of the rebels of 1483.[45] The king mentions his general pardon and his royal progresses; there is here a subdued note of dismay, since no one needed popular approval more than Richard III:

and eftsoon his Grace, in his own person, as is well known, hath addressed himself to divers parts of his realm for the indifferent administration of justice to every person, having full confidence and trust that all oppressors and extorcioners of his subjects, horrible adulterers and bawds, provoking the high indignacion of God, should have been reconciled to the way of truth and virtue . . .

But not so, for

Thomas Dorset, late marquess Dorset, which not fearing God nor the peril of his soul, hath many and sundry maids, wives and widows damnably and without shame deflowered, devoured and defouled, holding the unshameful and mischievous woman called Shore's wife in adultery . . .

Dorset, the proclamation goes on, had raised rebellion with various named persons, including the duke of Buckingham, but this hardly seems to have been his main offence. Intending the destruction of the royal person, and the breaching of his peace, he was also concerned 'in letting of virtue, and the damnable maintenance of vices and sin'. The king continues to state his tender and loving disposition 'for the common weal of his realm, and the putting down and rebuking of vices', but he goes on to say that *no yeoman nor commoner* (here is the appeal to popular opinion: there is no reference to lords, knights and esquires, who were supposed to be politically responsible anyway) be

> abused or blinded by these traitors, adulterers and bawds [and that no man shall] be hurt or suffer in any way if he withdraws from their false company . . .

Richard's next major propaganda effort lay in the two proclamations he directed against Henry Tudor and his supporters, the one issued on 7 December 1484, the other, with only minor changes, on 23 June 1485.[46] In between, however, although the date is not certain, he sent out what amounted to an open letter to the bishops, headed in the manuscript *Littera Bona,* about the repression of immorality:[47]

> . . . amongst othir our seculer besynesses and cures, our principal entent and fervent desire is to see vertue and clenesse of lyving to be advanced encreased and multiplied and vices . . . provoking the high indignacion of God to be repressed and adnulled . . . We therefore woll and desire you and on Goddes behalf inwardly exhort and require you that according to the charge of your profession . . ye wol see . . alle suche persones as set aparte vertue . . . be reformed repressed and punysshed condignely . . .

Coming from a king who publicly acknowledged two bastards (unlike his brother)[48], this proclamation has a certain element of cynicism. The theme recurs, however, in the proclamations against Henry Tudor mentioned above, together with the alleged concern with 'the commons'. In 1484 Richard attacked Jasper Tudor, John de Vere and many others who were known for 'open murders, *adulterers*, and extorcioners' for their assorted treasons. Taking themselves to France, into the obedience of the king's enemy, Charles of France, they had sought to 'abuse and blind the commons of this said realm' by choosing as their captain 'Henry Tydder', whose faults were various, conceived, amongst other things, in double adultery (Owen Tudor and Katharine Swynford), 'as every man knoweth'. His intent was evil, to say the least: to achieve French aid they had resigned (and here follows the appeal to English nationalism) all right to the throne of France and to the possession of Calais, Guisnes and Hammes. Moreover, they were intent on subverting the laws of the realm, and doing the most cruel murders, slaughters and 'disherisons' that were ever seen in any Christian realm. All 'good and true Englishmen' or 'true and natural Englishmen' should, therefore, rally to the support of a 'well-willed, diligent and courageous prince' who would put his royal person to 'all labour and peine necessary' for the comfort and well-being of his subjects.

How successful was all this Yorkist propaganda? It is clearly impossible to consider, within the confines of a short article, all aspects of the phenomenon, and the emphasis given above to the use of proclamations may introduce an element of distortion, although this was to be the growth-area under the Tudor kings and queens. For Edward IV it may had had some success, especially at the beginning of his reign. For Richard, despite all his efforts, it appears to have been a failure, since he never seens to have won the hearts of his people, given what appears to have been their entrenched belief that he had murdered his innocent nephews. But the interest of the exercise lies less in immediate success or failure than in the evidence it provides as to the growing awareness of the ruler's need to influence popular opinion, as distinct from 'public opinion' (as defined above). The lesson was not to be lost upon the Yorkists' Tudor successors.

I am extremely grateful to the respective authors for allowing me to draw upon unpublished papers by Professor V.J. Scattergood ('Propagandist Verse during the Wars of the Roses') and Dr. R.A. Griffiths ('Public Opinion and Propaganda during the Wars of the Roses' and 'English Politics and the Uses of Literacy before Caxton'). Whilst I have benefited greatly from their reflections, they must not be held responsible for any arguments advanced or conclusions stated in the paper which follows.

NOTES

1. See, for example, Mortimer Levine, *Tudor Dynastic Problems, 1460-1571* (1973), and, for one aspect of Tudor proaganda at work, P.L. Hughes and J.F. Larkin (eds.), *Tudor Royal Proclamations* (3 vols., New Haven, 1964-69).
2. J.H. Fisher, 'Chancery and the Emergence of Standard Written English in the Fifteenth Century', *Speculum*, LII (1977), 870-99, although some of the arguments contained in this article are difficult for an historian to accept (cf. the signet letters of Richard III).
3. V.J. Scattergood, *Politics and Poetry in the Fifteenth Century* (1971), for the subject in general, and esp. pp. 182ff.
4. Op. cit., p. 183: This poem is fairly long, by contrast with the usual 'bill' (ten eight-line stanzas and a six-line coda): 'It is also far from simple, using frequent biblical quotations in Latin, together with other Latin phrases, and having in general a highly aureate English vocabulary . . . How much effect this poem had is impossible to determine, but it was apparently well enough known . . to be used in later partisan verses.' The ballad is printed in J.S. Davies (ed.), *An English Chronicle, 1377-1461* (Camden Soc., 1856), pp. 91-94 (and elsewhere, e.g., R.H. Robbins, *Historical Poems of the XIVth and XVth Centuries* [New York, 1959], pp. 207-10).
5. Storey, *The End of the House of Lancaster* (1966); Griffiths, 'Local Rivalries and National politics: the Percies, the Nevilles, and the Duke of Exeter, 1452-1455', *Speculum*, XLIII (1968), 589-632.
6. Quoted by Storey, op. cit., p. 197.
7. *Registrum Abbatiae Johannis Whethamstede*, ed. H.T. Riley (RS, A.H. Thomas (1938), p. 236.
8. 'The Wars of the Roses' (Raleigh Lecture), *Proceedings of the British Academy*, L (1964), 112-13. McFarlane cities (i) the lynching of Lord Scales by the Thames watermen, in 1460; (ii) the attack upon Somerset by the men of Northampton, 1464; (iii) the death of the earl of Salisbury in 1461 because of the hostility of the local populace, in support of a case for their violent interventions. But one could easily add to this list (a) the widespread popular support given to the rebellion of 1469 (C. Ross, *Edward IV* [1974], pp.127-88; (b) the effects of lack of any general popular support for Edward IV in the autumn of 1470, which forced him into exile (ibid., pp. 15354), and (c) the difficulties of controlling opinion in London in 1483 (*The Usurpation of Richard III* [by Mancini], ed. C.A.J. Armstrong [2nd edn., 1969], esp. pp. 79, 99). Mancini states his view that it was the force of popular opinion which caused Elizabeth Woodville to seek sanctuary in the abbey of Westminster, and, later, dictated Richard's summoning of a great force from the north of England to overawe London.
9. McFarlane, op. cit., p. 113.
10. *Three Fifteenth-Century Chronicles*, ed. J. Gairdner (Camden Soc., 1890), pp. 157-58. The 'flying reports' are based upon statements such as, for 1464, 'Thes tythinges hath my lord of Lyncolne, and the same be come to Stamford' (concerning the battle of Hedgeley Moor).
11. Ross, *Edward IV*, pp. 43-44.
12. *Three Fifteenth-Century Chronicles*, p. 158.
13. *Original Letters Illustrative of English History*, ed. H. Ellis (11 vols., 1824-46), I, 126.
14. J.W. McKenna, 'Piety and Propaganda: The Cult of Henry VI', in *Chaucer and Middle English Studies In Honour of R.H. Robbins*, ed. B. Rowland (1974), pp. 72-88.
15. E.g., *The Great Chronicle of London*, ed. A.H. Thomas and I.D. Thornley (1938), p. 220: 'Soo he was thens conveyed unto the watyrs syde, and From thens unto Chertsey and there buryed, For whom shortly afftyr God shewid sundry myraclys . . .'
16. See, in general, J.G. Bellamy, 'The Northern Rebellions in the Later Years of Richard II', *BJRL*, XLVII (1964-65), 254-74.
17. *Annales Ricardi Secundi* (RS, 1866), pp. 159-62.

18. *CPR, 1391-46*, pp. 140-41; T. Rymer, *Foedera*, VII, 746.
19. The reference to bills (presumably in English) is an interesting reminder that recourse to the written word as a means of influencing opinion was by no means confined to the Lollards.
20. *CPR, 1391-96*, p. 141.
21. *Chronicle of the Rebellion in Lincolnshire, 1470*, ed. J.G. Nichols (Camden Soc., 1847).
22. Ibid., p. 5.
23. *CCR, 1396-99*, p. 208.
24. B. Wilkinson, *Constitutional History of England in the Fifteenth Century, 1399-1485* (1964), p. 163 ('Richard felt obliged to give a most striking expression to the authority of the Estates . . . In a sense, it is he even more than Henry IV who deserves to be called the most "parliamentary" monarch of the fifteenth century'); W.H. Dunham, Jr. and Charles T. Wood, 'The Right to Rule in England: Depositions and the Kingdom's Authority, 1327-1485', *American Historical Review* (1976), 738-61, esp. pp. 754-59; but cf. the criticisms of J.W. McKenna, 'The myth of parliamentary sovereignty in late-medieval England', *EHR*, XCIV (1979), 482-506.
25. *RP*, VI, 240-41.
26. Croyland Chronicle, in *Historiae Croylandensis Continuatio* in *Rerum Anglicarum Scriptores Veterum*, ed. W. Fulman (Oxford, 1684), p. 572.
27. Quotation from the translation of Fulman's text by H.T. Riley (ed.), *Ingulph's Chronicle* (1893), p. 499.
28. *York Civic Records,* vol. I, ed. A. Raine (Yorkshire Archaeological Soc., Record Ser., XCVIII, 1939), pp. 115-16.
29. Gransden, 'Propaganda in Medieval English Historiography', *Journal of Medieval History*, I (1975), 363-81.
30. T.F. Tout, 'The English Parliament and Public Opinion', in *Collected Papers* (3 vols., Manchester, 1932), II, 173-90, and the comments of Anthony Steel, *Richard II* (Cambridge, 1941), pp. 145-46.
31. McKenna, 'Piety and Propaganda . . The Cult of Henry VI', p. 72.
32. See, in particular, V.J. Scattergood, *Politics and Poetry in the Fifteenth Century* (1971), esp. pp. 173ff., and A. Allan, 'Yorkist Propaganda: Pedigree, prophecy and the "British History" in the reign of Edward IV', in *Patronage, Pedigree and Power in Later Medieval England* (Gloucester, 1979), ed. C. Ross, pp. 171-92; and, more generally, Ross, *Edward IV*, pp. 24-25, and C.L. Kingsford, *English Historical Literature in the Fifteenth Century* (Oxford, 1913), esp. pp. 193ff. The official judgement of Pius II on Henry VI of England probably owed much to this propaganda (and the suborning of the papal legate): 'a man more timorous than a woman . . . who left everything in his wife's hands . . .' (C. Head, 'Pope Pius II and the Wars of the Roses', *Archivum Historiae Pontificiae,* VIII [1970], 139-78).
33. The manifesto is printed as an appendix to John Warkworth's *Chronicle*, ed. J.O. Halliwell (Camden Soc., 1839), pp. 46-51.
34. D. Hay, 'History and Historians in England and France during the fifteenth century', *BIHR*, XXXV (1962), 111-27.
35. See, particularly, J.A.F. Thomson, ' "The Arrival of Edward IV" — The Development of the Text', *Speculum*, XLVI (1971), 84-93.
36. *Historie of the Arrivall of Edward IV in England*, ed. J. Bruce (Camden Soc., 1838), pp. 13-14.
37. Loc. cit., p. 37.
38. Loc. cit., pp. 38-39.
39. P.L. Hughes and J.F. Larkin (eds.), *Tudor Royal Proclamations* (3 vols., 1964-69).
40. *RP*, V, 487-88.
41. E.g., *CCR, 1468-76*, pp. 137-38; Warkworth, *Chronicle*, appendix, pp. 52ff.
42. Dunham and Wood, loc. cit., p. 756.
43. Warkworth, *Chronicle*, pp. 46ff.

44. *RP,* VI, 240.
45. Ibid.
46. This version from *Paston Letters,* ed. J. Gairdner, VI, 81-84.
47. BL, Harleian MS. 433, f. 28lb.
48. His illegimate son, John, was to be made captain of Calais in 1485, and the daughter, Katharine, was married off to the impecunious William Herbert, second earl of Pembroke. Edward seems never to have acknowledged any of his bastards, although one, Arthur, was afterwards created Viscount Lisle by his nephew, Henry VIII, in 1523, forty years after his father's death (*CP,* VIII, 63-64).

2. The King's Burden? — the Consequences of Royal Marriage in Fifteenth-century England

Anne Crawford
Bristol Record Office

This paper is a work of synthesis, an attempt to look at the fifteenth-century queens as a group. It is a task not so far undertaken, since queens have usually been considered as individuals in the context of their husbands' reigns.

The choice of a suitable wife was the most important single decision ever made by a medieval king. Upon her ability to produce a male heir rested the continuation of the royal line. To bear a son in time for him to come of age before his father died was scarcely a less central duty. The six queens in question are Joan of Navarre, Catherine of Valois, Margaret of Anjou, Elizabeth Woodville, Anne Neville and Elizabeth of York. Anne Neville will be referred to only in passing, since she was not chosen as a bride for a king but for a king's brother, and was, moreover, queen only for two years. The last three of these queens were English, a complete break with Plantagenet tradition. Until Edward IV's marriage, no English king since the Conquest had chosen a bride from among his own subjects. Almost all the queens for four centuries had been French; with the exception of Mathilda of Scotland, Eleanor of Castile, Philippa of Hainault and Anne of Bohemia, they had come from France's royal family or one of its great feudal houses. The diplomatic aspect of choosing a royal bride is obvious. The marriage was usually made by the couple's fathers to cement an alliance or seal a peace treaty. Few, if any, of the bridal couples had set eyes on each other before the marriage and in a number of cases even the wedding itself was by proxy.

Upon her marriage the queen had to be suitably dowered. The sum involved was usually agreed upon in the negotiations with her father and it was intended to give her financial independence until her death. The dower, or much of it, was customarily secured upon royal lands and meant a substantial loss in revenue and source of patronage for her spouse. It also made the queen one of the principal landowners in the country. Although her officials were ultimately responsible to the king and she was unlikely to act against his interests, the queen behaved like any other land-owner and her influence was felt up and down the country. Indeed, in the previous century, Queen Isabella, at the height of her power, held land in virtually every shire in England, something that could not be said of even the mightiest subject.[1]

Upon her marriage, a foreign princess usually brought a small train of fellow-countrymen to England. Since these were almost invariably French, they were regarded with suspicion by her new subjects, and on the slightest excuse they were denounced as spies and their repatriation demanded of the king. The new queen's ladies were selected from baronial or gentry families and she had, perforce, to choose her friends from among them. Her household was officered by men who had previously served in the king's household, and many of them later returned to his service. In effect, the personnel of the two households was interchangeable. In many cases the queen's waiting women were the wives of minor household officials. The running of the household was intended to be financed from her dower as an independent unit. The queen's private expenditure on her clothes, jewels, gifts and alms was funded by a payment made to her from the exchequer for her chamber expenses, quite separately from her dower. As the years went by, additional payments were made in the same way for the support of any royal children.

Once married, a queen's duties were clear. First, she had to secure the succession; second, she had to preside in a fitting manner at her husband's court; third, she had, like any other wife, to make her husband as happy and contented in his domestic life as lay within her power. If she were a foreign princess, bred for queenship, she knew she had to become English, to suppress her own national inclinations and never interfere in the internal affairs of her new country. For some queens this proved possible; for others, either their own character or that of their husbands forced them into very different roles. These are the topics to be discussed in relation to the queens: the political background determining the choice of queen, her dower and financial position, her household and family, and her influence (if any) on the king.

It so happens that none of the six fifteenth-century kings had his queen selected for him by his father. This in itself is unusual. Most royal princes were at least betrothed, if not actually wed, before they came of age. Henry of Derby was married to Mary de Bohun when they were fourteen and eleven respectively, and John of Gaunt purchased the marriage for his son from the king for 5,000 marks. The couple had four sons and two daughters before Mary died in childbirth at the age of twenty-four.[2] When Henry usurped the throne in 1399, he faced many problems, but securing the succession was not one of them. It is worth bearing in mind, however, that those four sons produced only one legitimate child between them, and therefore the succession was not truly safe but only apppeared so. Nevertheless, Henry's need for a queen was not primarily for procreation, but to provide him with a consort to comfort him in the lonely task of kingship.

There seems to be a strong presumption, but no positive evidence, that at some point before he became king, Henry had met Joan of Navarre and that some personal preference was involved in his choice of her as his second wife. Joan was born about 1373, the daughter of Charles II, king of Navarre, and in 1386 she became the third wife of the elderly Duke John IV of Brittany and mother of his children. Both the duke's previous two wives had been English and childless.[3] On his death in 1399, Joan became regent for her young son, John V, then aged ten. Henry was certainly in constant touch with Brittany by letter from the beginning of his reign and in 1401 Joan secured a papal bull from Benedict XIII at Avignon giving her permission to marry whom she chose. Henry, of course, recognised the rival pope. More importantly, Joan secured the tacit consent of both the king of France and the duke of Burgundy to her remarriage. The preliminary negotiations were conducted in some secrecy in England and Henry's marriage came as a surprise to most of his people. For Joan, the marriage to a king in the prime of life might appear a social triumph for a widow, but she had to pay a high price for it. Under pressure from the Bretons, she had to surrender her regency and leave all four of her sons behind, though she was permitted to bring her two small daughters to England with her. Duke John had left her a large sum of money as her own absolute property and this she brought to Henry; but she had to appoint a governor for her Breton dower lands, the county of Nantes, and thus lost control over it, though she continued to receive the income. Although his bride hardly came to him penniless, any hopes Henry might have had of controlling Brittany in her right or even of gaining a strong ally were thwarted by the Bretons, for when Joan surrendered her regency and her sons, they fell into the hands of her maternal uncle, the duke of Burgundy.[4]

Henry and Joan were married by proxy in April 1402 and in person at Winchester on 7 February 1403. The king's gift to the new queen was a collar worth 500 marks and the wedding expenses totalled £433 6s. 8d. When they reached London, Joan was crowned almost immediately, with an appropriate coronation banquet. The total cost of the marriage and coronation was in the region of £1,500. Although there were no children of the match, Henry, according to J.L. Kirby, proved a 'faithful husband, always generous', and the queen's relations with her step-children seem to have been good.[5]

Having found himself a wife, Henry had now to think seriously about one for the prince of Wales. Young Henry had at one time been contracted to Joan's daughter, Mary of Brittany, but the match had been abandoned for diplomatic reasons. During the peace negotiations with France in

1408-9, a marriage was proposed between the prince, already twenty-one, and Charles VI's youngest daughter, Catherine, who was eight, but nothing came of it at that time.[6] Catherine's eldest sister, Isabel, had been a major embarrassment to Henry IV on his accession, for she was the eleven-year-old widow of Richard II. A plan to marry her to the prince was abandoned and in 1401, despite disputes over her dower, she was sent home to France. In many ways the match proposed with Prince Henry would have solved everything, but there is little doubt that neither Queen Isabel herself nor her father would have countenanced a union with the usurping dynasty. Since the cost of maintaining her household was nearly £3,000 during the first year of Henry's reign, he was eager to staunch this drain on royal resources. Nevertheless, for the honour of his house, he was obliged to send her back in a fitting manner and that cost him a further £4,000.[7]

When Henry IV died in 1413, none of his sons was married, though their sister Blanche (by then dead) had been wed to the king of the Romans and Philippa was queen of Denmark. This was an important lapse on Henry's part, though its causes were probably complex; his own ill-health, his poor relations with his heir and the fact that his usurping dynasty was seen to be insecure may all have played their part. Be that as it may, when Henry V succeeded to the throne he was twenty-six and unwed. In the following year further peace negotiations with France revived the proposed match with Catherine, who was regarded as a personable twelve-year-old. This did not prevent Henry from negotiating with the duke of Burgundy for a possible marriage with his youngest daughter, also called Catherine. Henry's negotiations with France, interrupted by war, lasted for six years. By the treaty of Troyes he won Catherine of Valois and the kingdom of France on the death of her father. In view of this, she brought no cash dowry, though the French agreed to pay her 20,000 crowns per annum in the event of her widowhood. The couple were married in Troyes Cathedral in May 1420. In the following February, Henry made what was to be his last visit to England, taking his queen with him. Henry having gone on ahead, Catherine made her triumphal entry to London alone. She spent the night at the Tower and was crowned by Archbishop Chichele the next day. When Henry returned to France, Catherine stayed in England, where she gave birth to her son on 6 December 1421. Early in 1422 Catherine crossed to France, leaving her son behind in England. She was staying with her parents when Henry was taken ill and the king did not see fit to send for her. The perils of Henry's late marriage were now all too apparent. His queen had done all that could have been expected of her, but on her husband's death, their son was barely nine months old. This is not the place to discuss the problems of a minority save one, namely, the future of a queen widowed at twenty-one.[8]

Since the Conquest, only four queens had been widowed while young. Berengaria of Navarre never in fact came to England and on Richard I's death retired to Maine. Isabella of Angoulême returned to France to marry the son of the man from whom John had snatched her. Margaret of France, Edward I's second wife, with three small children, was content to live out her widowhood in comfort as queen-dowager. Only Isabel, a child and the widow of a deposed king, was returned to her parents. Catherine of Valois was not as fortunate as her sister. There was little point in returning to France, of which her son was titular king and her brother, Charles VII, unrecognised by the English. In the first few years of Henry VI's reign, his mother appeared with him on formal occasions and was accorded all the dignity due to a queen-mother. She appears never to have attempted to use her position in any political way, but the question of her remarriage raised all sorts of problems. Chief among them was the likelihood that if she took an Englishman as her second husband, the king's new step-father would be in a strong position to influence an impressionable boy. There is a suggestion in one chronicle that she was contemplating marriage with Edmund Beaufort, her late husband's cousin. In the internal politics of the day, Cardinal Beaufort might have regarded the idea with favour, but it was not pleasing to Duke Humphrey of Gloucester or to other members of the council. In fact, it gave rise to a parliamentary statute stating that he who married a queen-dowager without the king's permission would forfeit his lands and possessions during his lifetime, and also that the king's permission might only be given for such a match after he reached years of discretion. But Catherine was not prepared to wait fifteen years until her son was of age nor, as a contemporary put it, was she 'able fully to curb her carnal passions'; the result was not a marriage to Beaufort, but a secret marriage with an obscure Welsh squire named Owen Tudor in about 1428-29. There were four children of the match, three sons and a daughter. Although it was not generally known in the country, the council certainly knew of the marriage but took no steps until the queen's death in 1437. Owen was then arrested and his goods (worth £137) seized; he was imprisoned for a time, but later secured a pardon from his stepson and entered his household. His sons, Edmund and Jasper, were created earls of Richmond and Pembroke respectively by their half-brother in 1452; the third son became a monk.[9]

Henry VI's own marriage took place in 1444, when he was twenty-two. Given the political involvement with France, there was little likelihood that his bride would be anything other than French. More than one prospective bride was considered, but Henry's ministers were anxious to gain a peace — or at least a truce — in France and when Charles VII proposed his wife's niece, Margaret of Anjou, she was found acceptable. Margaret was fifteen and reputedly beautiful. She was the daughter of

Réné, duke of Anjou and titular king of Sicily, Naples, Hungary and Jerusalem, and his wife, Isabelle, heiress of Charles, duke of Lorraine. Margaret had been raised as a princess, her grandmother and parents were called king and queens, but Réné was rich only in titles; he had no land except Anjou, which he could not settle on her, and he had little money to compensate in the form of a rich dowry. Eventually he endowered her with the islands of Majorca and Minorca, which he claimed through his mother, Yolande of Aragon, but over which he had not the slightest control. The English gained a two-year truce and their king a portionless bride. This was overlooked amid the general atmosphere of optimism that a permanent peace would follow. The clergy of Anjou made Réné a grant of 1½ tenths and his Estates an aid of 33,000 crowns to pay for the expenses of the actual wedding. The cost of the new queen's journey to England was naturally borne by her husband. Between 17 July 1444, when an English party led by the duke of Suffolk left England to fetch her, and 16 October 1445, six months after her wedding at Tichfield Abbey, a total expenditure of £5,573 17s. 5d. was paid out on the queen's behalf on household expenses, the wages of sailors and attendants, the cost of horses and even the upkeep of a lion. This did not include the refurbishing of royal palaces which had effectively seen no queen for twenty years; this cost another £1,000 which the impoverished king did not have. Fortunately, the idea of a royal marriage was popular enough for Henry to ask for the money in gifts and to receive it.[10] On 30 May 1445, a month after her wedding, Margaret was crowned.

When Edward IV ascended the throne in 1461, he was nineteen years old and a bachelor. Like Henry IV, his fellow usurper, he was a dubious quantity on the international marriage market, but again like Henry, he could afford to wait a little. He might not have sons, but he had two surviving brothers. In the following years, several royal ladies were considered as possible brides, but in 1464 Edward surprised everyone by announcing that he had just married the widowed Elizabeth, Lady Grey.[11] This is the first match of an English king with one of his own subjects since the Conquest.* It was also a political blunder of the first magnitude. Not only did it deprive England of a diplomatic advantage, but it introduced the queen's family to royal politics, something that had only rarely occurred before, most notably in the reign of Henry III with the arrival of the relatives of his wife, Eleanor of Provence. Elizabeth's family was already on the spot. It was also extremely large, not very rich and highly ambitious. The only pretentions the family had to anything more than gentility came through her mother, Jacquetta of Luxembourg,

---

* The marriage of Edward, the Black Prince to his cousin, Joan of Kent, which was expected to make her queen, must not, however, be overlooked.

widow of John, duke of Bedford. Like her sister-in-law, Queen Catherine, Jacquetta took a social inferior, Richard Woodville, as her second husband; he was created Lord Rivers in 1448. On the marriage of Margaret of Anjou, it is hardly surprising that Jacquetta, a royal Frenchwoman and, as the widow of the king's eldest uncle, the second lady at court, found favour with the new queen and was able to provide her elder daughters with places at court. At about fifteen, Elizabeth Woodville was married to Sir John Grey, son and heir of Lord Ferrers of Groby, who was killed nine years later at the second battle of St. Albans in 1461, leaving her with two small sons. Elizabeth was five years older than Edward IV, but at least she had proved capable of a queen's first duty, the production of sons. When and where Edward met her and why he decided to marry her have been the subject of much speculation, all of it fruitless. Marry her he did, breaking all precedents, on 1 May 1464 in a secret ceremony at her father's home of Grafton. It was not until September that she was introduced publicly at court and her coronation took place in May 1465. Although this was a longer delay than was customary, it does not appear to have aroused comment, and indeed served the purpose of allowing the surprised nation time to accept Edward's *fait accompli*. When Elizabeth was crowned, Edward certainly spared no expense to honour her and make it a truly splendid occasion.[12]

The marriage of Richard III's queen, Anne Neville, lies somewhat outside the scope of this paper. Richard married her in about 1472 when he was duke of Gloucester and she the younger daughter and co-heiress of Richard, earl of Warwick. It was, in fifteenth-century aristocratic terms, a conventional marriage. The match of a king's younger son or brother and an English heiress had good precedents, since it provided for him without depleting royal resources. John of Gaunt's marriage to Blanche of Lancaster, his brother Thomas's to Eleanor Bohun, and that of Edmund of Woodstock, son of Edward I's second marriage, to Margaret, heiress of Lord Wake, shows how well-established the convention was. In the early 1470s the Gloucester — Neville match caused a major feud between Gloucester and his brother, but this was due to the political situation and their own characters rather than to any inherent unsuitability in the match. By the time Richard and Anne were jointly crowned, they had been married eleven years and had one frail son, Edward, who died a year later as prince of Wales, an example of the hazards of marrying an heiress. In many ways Anne Neville's real interest lies not in her marriage to Gloucester when she was a widow, but in her first marriage to Henry VI's only son, Edward, at the end of 1470. Arranged by Louis XI as a means of reconciling Warwick and an extremely reluctant but hard-pressed Margaret of Anjou with a view to achieving a Lancastrian restoration, it lasted only briefly and within a year Anne was deprived of both husband

and father.[13] Despite the precedent set by Edward IV in marrying an English commoner, Margaret almost certainly regarded her son's match with the daughter of an English earl as disparagement and clearly hated the union with her arch-enemy's daughter.

Henry VII also married an Englishwoman, but Elizabeth of York was the heir to her father, Edward IV, and regarded by most Englishmen as bearing an infinitely better claim to the throne than Henry himself. For Henry the match was dynastically essential, but dangerous. It had been arranged by their respective mothers — formidable women both — as the price of support for Henry's invasion by Edward IV's former servants, on the assumption that both Elizabeth's brothers were dead. On Christmas Day 1483, Henry swore a solemn oath to marry her as soon as he became king. He did not keep this oath. On his accession, Elizabeth, then aged nineteen, was brought from custody and restored to her mother's care. The commons in his first parliament begged Henry to marry her and he was happy to accede, but he had two obvious problems and one rather more subtle one. Elizabeth had been declared a bastard by parliament and as such could not become queen; in addition, she and Henry were related in the fourth degree through their common ancestor, Edward III. Richard III's act of title was nullified without any specific reference to its contents and the papal dispensation for the marriage arrived after it had eventually taken place in January 1486. The wedding could clearly therefore have been celebrated much earlier, immediately after parliament had been called in the autumn of 1485, but for Henry's more fundamental reason for delay. He did not wish it to appear that he owed his throne to his wife's title. The longer he reigned before he married her, the more secure he felt. It was almost certainly for this reason that he did not have her crowned until November 1487, an insulting and unprecedented delay of nearly two years, during which time Elizabeth produced their first son, Arthur, and Henry defeated his major Yorkist threat at Stoke.[14] Only then did he feel secure enough to honour his wife. In virtually all other cases a queen's coronation followed immediately upon her marriage, and even in the case of Elizabeth Woodville, the delay was far less than a year after her first appearance as queen.

The arrival of a new queen might bring pleasure to the country and delight to the king but it brought nothing but worry to the exchequer. In the words of B.P. Wolffe, 'The primary recurrent charge upon the crown estate was the dower of queens'.[15] The crown estate existed to provide endowments for all members of the royal family; the king did not retain permanently in his own hands anything save a few royal residences.*

---

*   The exception to this is, of course, the duchy of Lancaster.

Although the queen's dower was the heaviest single recurrent charge, it was only for life, while male members were usually endowed in tail male with reversion to the king and his heirs. On the death of each queen, her successor usually received the bulk of her possessions. Thus, when Margaret of France died in 1318, her niece Isabella, wife of Edward II, was granted most of her lands. On the redistribution of Isabella's lands in 1330, her daughter-in-law, Philippa of Hainault, was the chief beneficiary and she received more on Isabella's death in 1359. Philippa's dower lands were largely re-assembled for Anne of Bohemia. From the time of Eleanor of Castile, first wife of Edward I, to that of young Isabel of France, second wife of Richard II, the dower of a queen of England was customarily fixed at £4,500 per annum at the time of her marriage. It was sometimes increased to support a growing family of young children or to ease the queen's financial embarrassment. Most queens found it inadequate. This was partly due to the problems confronting any large landowner, the gap between what should in theory have been received and what was realised in practice, and partly due to the heavy demands made on the queen's purse. No doubt some of these ladies were more extravagant than others: Eleanor of Castile gained an unbecoming reputation for being grasping, while poor Philippa of Hainault got into such difficulties that in 1363 Edward III took over financial responsibility for his wife's household.[16]

Suitable lands for dower were obviously not to hand each time a king married, particularly if a queen-dowager were still alive. In the first few years of her marriage, therefore, a queen's income usually came from those few dower lands free to be granted to her, made up to the required annual sum by exchequer grants. To illustrate this problem of the provision of dower lands in detail, let us take just one of the queens, Joan of Navarre. One month after her marriage, in March 1403, the queen was granted an income of 10,000 marks per annum, to be paid from the exchequer until Henry granted her lands to the same value.[17] This in itself was a break with tradition. The accepted dower for nearly two centuries had been £4,500, and it was thus suddenly increased by about £2,000 per annum. It was a generous gesture, but one that Henry could ill-afford, and Joan's dower became a burden upon the country for the rest of Henry's reign and much of his son's. Henry's reasons for such generosity remain obscure. Unlike most previous queens, whose fathers paid a lump sum or sums in dowry which went to the exchequer, Joan received regular remittances from her Breton dower, the county of Nantes, for which she was not accountable to her husband. On his accession, Henry IV was, in Wolffe's words, 'the greatest landowner since the Conquest'. In addition to the crown lands of his predecessors, he held the great duchy of Lancaster and, for his lifetime, his first wife's share of the Bohun inheritance in trust for their son. He had no brothers to endow, and of his sons, only Henry had received anything substantial by 1403.[18] Yet by the time of his marriage to Joan, Henry was certainly not in a position to grant her a large quantity of dower lands. His financial problems are not a matter for discussion here, but they did affect Joan's dower. In 1403 she was granted in part satisfaction of her dower the following lands and cash income: the farms of Ipswich, Bedford, Gloucester, Malmesbury, Derby, Kingscliff and King's Thorpe; the castles and towns of Bristol, Nottingham, and Leeds, co. Kent; the hundred of Bosmere and Clayton; the customs of the ports between Blakeney and Tilbury; the town of Mansfield; the manors of Linby, Gretton, Brigstock, Geddington, Hampstead Marshall, Wyrardesbury, Langley Marreys, Woodstock, Marston Maisy, Ludgershall, and Stratton; the lordship of Gillingham; the castle and forest of Rockingham; the forest of Wychwood; the farms of Darlington and Ragnall; the hundred of Fawsley; the assart between the bridges of Oxford and Staunford; mills and land at Retford and Shipton; and the farm of the abbot of St. Albans for the avoidance of his abbey. They were worth a total of approximately £1,345 per annum.[19]

On 27 June 1403, on the death of his step-mother, Katherine Swynford, duchess of Lancaster, Henry gave Joan an annuity of £1,000, charged on the duchy and previously enjoyed by Katherine. It was made up from three sources, namely, 500 marks on lands in Staffordshire and Derbyshire, 700 marks on lands in Lincolnshire and 300 marks on land in Huntingdonshire. She was also given the castle, manor and town of Hertford for life. In September of the same year she was granted the manor of Havering-atte-Bower, £100 per annum from the sheriffs of London for life, together with the manor and castle of Wressell and the 'towns' of Loftsom, Brayton, Arras, Foston, and Claxby with Sloothby, forfeited by Thomas Percy, earl of Worcester, to hold from the time of his forfeiture. In October 1403 she was granted custody of two-thirds of all the lands and liberties of Edmund, late earl of Stafford, during the minority of his heir, in part satisfaction of her dower, together with the wardships of Richard Scrope, Fulk Montho and Thomas Lovell.[20]

Already by June 1404 the dower was £3,000 in arrears, and Henry was in deep trouble with the commons over finance. The result was an act of resumption of all the land Henry and his predecessors had held since 1366 in absolute possession. The royal lands thus retained were to be put under the control of the exchequer so that they could be leased out at their real value. The first charge on the revenues thus obtained was to be the expenses of the royal household, chamber and wardrobe, together with due provision for the queen's dower. Despite the king's poverty and the threat of an invasion, £3,000 from the tenth granted by the clergy in convocation went to the queen in part-payment of her arrears, and so did a sum of £1,000 from the customs of Boston. In April 1405 Henry hit on an expedient for providing his wife with money when he granted her custody of all the possessions of the alien priory of Otterton in Devon, which had come into his hands by reason of the war with France and which were worth 300 marks per annum. A similar annual sum was secured to her from the Isle of Wight and the castle of Carisbrooke. These had been granted by Richard II to the duke of York and were confiscated when he confessed to plotting in 1405.[21] Over the next few years the process continued, a little bit here, a little bit there: the wardship of Richard Despenser worth 400 marks per annum in 1405; a grant of £200 per annum from the first customs on goods at Great Yarmouth (except on wool, woolfells and hides) and from there to Blakeney on one side and Tilbury on the other in lieu of her earlier grant of customs; the manor of Kirby Malzeard while it remained in the king's hands. In January 1405 she was granted whatever money might accrue from the sale of French prisoners taken at Dartmouth and held in custody by Sir John Cornwall. Apart from all this, Joan also received cash grants amounting to nearly £3,000 in the first quarter of 1405. In May 1408 came a considerably more substantial grant for life of certain possessions, lately Queen Anne's. These were the castle of Devizes and rents from the borough and parks there; the manors of Rowde and Cosham; further sums from the farms of Ipswich and Derby and from the farms of Shrewsbury, Southampton, Great Yarmouth and Scarborough; the manors of Odiham, Weedon Pinkney, Moresende, Weston Turville, Hogston, Beachampton, Kimble, Falsgrave, and various other rents. It was a total of approximately £625. Leeds castle had also been part of Queen Anne's dower, and it and Odiham, Bristol, Devizes and Havering-atte-Bower, to name but a few, had all formed part of earlier dowers.[22]

In the winter of 1408-9 came a crisis in the king's health, and Henry prudently made his will. In it he charged the queen's dower against the revenues of the duchy of Lancaster. A privy seal writ sent to the chancellor about the dower had a long note in Henry's own hand (quoted by J.L. Kirby) and this had the effect of granting the queen in July 1409 various rents and farms, many of them from alien priories, together with about £1,000 per annum from the customs of London, Southampton, Boston and Bristol in full satisfaction of her dower. It had therefore taken six years from the time of her marriage for Queen Joan to receive some form of endowment for her dower. The endowment was by no means all secured in the most satisfactory way, on land, fee-farms and customs. Henry had been forced to rely on temporary expedients and the problem of Joan's dower was a legacy to his son. In January 1414, Henry V granted to the queen, in part-satisfaction of her dower, sums from a number of sources, mainly again the alien priories, totalling nearly 4,000 marks per annum, with any deficiency made up by the exchequer, because various heirs had come of age and several forfeitures had been restored. A year later, Henry took possessions of all the alien priories and had to compensate the queen with a grant of 1,000 marks per annum from the issues of the hanaper.[23]

It is worth remembering that for most of Henry V's reign, Joan was the only queen and consequently appeared as such on most formal occasions until, that is, the events of 1419. These are relevant to the question of dower. Joan appears to have had a very amicable relationship with her step-children, and after her husband's death Henry V seems to have treated her with the honour and respect he might have paid his own mother, which indeed was the name he gave to her. Grants were made, not to the queen, but to 'the king's mother, the queen'. In 1419, not only was England at war, with all the financial strain that that implies, but Henry V was likely himself to wed in the near future, adding the burden of a second dower to the crown's resources. When Henry left England in 1417 his relationship with Joan was so good that the truce with Brittany he concluded shortly afterwards was due (he maintained) to her appeals. Yet on 27 September 1419, on the order of her step-son, Bedford, and the council, Joan was arrested at her manor of Havering and all her possessions were sequestered. The reason stated in parliament was that her confessor, John Randolph, a Franciscan friar, accused her of 'compassing the death and destruction of our lord the king'. The accusation of witchcraft obviously required some response from the council, though it is doubtful if the charge was taken seriously by people in court circles, because Joan had nothing to gain by Henry's death (a similar charge later against Eleanor Cobham, duchess of Gloucester, was very different because her husband was heir presumptive). Joan was never formally charged and after an initial imprisonment at Pevensey, she lived in style and comfort at her own castle of Leeds until Henry's conscience on his death-bed secured her release. For three years, therefore, the crown had an additional income of nearly 10,000 marks per annum from her sequestered possessions. Joan had difficulty in regaining her dower in 1422 because so much of it had been granted away, but she did receive other lands in compensation. She lived on until 1437 and was treated with affection and generosity by Henry VI.[24]

Catherine of Valois's dower was set at the same level as Joan's, 40,000 crowns or 10,000 marks. Learning the lesson of the trouble raised by his step-mother's dower, Henry endowed Catherine, at least in part, from the duchy of Lancaster. What she was given was basically the Bohun inheritance of his own mother, together with the honours of Leicester, Knaresborough, Hertford and Melbourne. Somerville says that for the next fifteen years or so there is no record of how this part of the duchy was administered.[25] Catherine had to respect existing annuities, fees and offices, but when they fell vacant she was free to make her own appointments. Wisely she chose for the most part duchy officials to fill her chief posts. Her chancellor, John Wodehouse, was also chancellor to the duchy, and her steward, John Leventhorpe, was the duchy's receiver-general. One surviving valor, for 1432, which covers all her lands, gives a total gross income of £5,098 16s. 7d. After the usual charges had been met, the queen's net income was £4,360 9s. 7d. or 6,540 marks. This was far sort of the stipulated 10,000 marks, but close to the old, accepted level of the fourteenth century. As a widow, the queen also received income from land in France, presumably the 20,000 crowns per annum guaranteed her in lieu of dowry by the treaty of Troyes.[26] Unlike most queens, Catherine never held lands which had previously formed royal dowers, for these were still in the hands of the dowager-queen and Joan in fact outlived Catherine by a few months.

When Henry VI married in 1445 there had been no queen in England for eight years, though there were three royal duchesses, the widowed duchesses of Bedford and Clarence and the imprisoned duchess of Gloucester, whose husband was still alive.[27] Margaret of Anjou's dower was likewise set at 10,000 marks, considerably in excess of what the war-impoverished crown could afford. Parliament settled the dower as £2,000 in lands and the rest in cash. Yet in the 1440s it has been estimated that only a total of about £10,000 was reaching the exchequer in cash each year. Already prodigious sums (about £3,000) had been spent on bringing her to England, clothing and crowning her and refurbishing the royal palaces. Her lands included the duchy honours of Tutbury, Leicester and Kenilworth and lands in Essex, Hertfordshire, Middlesex, Surrey, and London, and the 'ancient south parts' of the duchy, comprising lands in Hampshire, Wiltshire, Somerset, Dorset, Devon, Cornwall, Oxfordshire, Herefordshire and Worcestershire. These were estimated to be worth £2,000 and her grant also included knights' fees, advowsons and all the liberties enjoyed by the king therein. In addition, she was granted a cash annuity from the duchy of £1,000 and on the death of Duke Humphrey in 1447, a further annuity of 500 marks. The rest of her income comprised approximately £1,000 from the customs of Southampton, a similar sum from the revenues of the duchy of Cornwall and approximately £1,500 in the form of an exchequer grant. Margaret was also gradually granted a number of traditional dower manors such as Shene, Queenhithe, Havering-atte-Bower, Haverfordwest, Rockingham, Gillingham, Odiham, Hadley and others, but no attempt is made here to give full details of her dower lands.[28]

Elizabeth Woodville's dower was much more modest than that of her Lancastrian predecessors. The change of dynasty ended the hopelessly over-generous precedent of 10,000 marks and reverted to the earlier en-

dowment of about £4,500. Although the crown became solvent, Edward
IV was a good deal more financially careful than earlier fifteenth-century
kings, and Elizabeth, of course, was in no position to be other than
grateful for what she was given. Nor can it really be argued that the
balance went to her family, since the Woodvilles in fact received very
modest gains in terms of lands and cash, though in other ways the queen
was able to see that they were very well provided for. In December her
jointure was set at 4,000 marks and in March 1465 a grant of both crown
and duchy lands was made to her. Edward had learned the lesson that
income from anything other than land was difficult to collect and often in
arrears, and so, unlike her predecessor, Elizabeth's income derived almost
solely from land and not from customs, fee-farms or exchequer grants. It
is possible that it was Elizabeth who had learned the lesson while in
Margaret's financially embarrassed household and pointed it out to
Edward. Her endowment from crown lands not unnaturally included
many of the traditional queen's manors, but by the end of Edward's reign,
she was also receiving the income from most of the duchy lands south of
the Trent.[29]

On the usurpation of Richard III, his parliament declared Edward IV's
marriage invalid, and at a stroke Elizabeth's position as queen–dowager
was demolished. A few months later, as Dame Elizabeth Grey, she came
out of sanctuary and accepted an annuity of 700 marks. One of the first
acts of Henry VII's parliament was to repeal the act illegitimating her
children and restore her to her former title and dignity. It did *not* vest in
Elizabeth Woodville any of her former dower lands, thus leaving Henry
free to decide what she might have. Since he had to make provision for his
own wife, his mother and his wife's grandmother, Cecily of York (since
the York lands had reverted to the crown), as well as his mother-in-law, it
was unlikely that she would regain anything like her old dower. Nevertheless, Henry was not ungenerous. In March 1486, after his own
wedding, he granted Elizabeth Woodville the lordships and manors of
Waltham Magna, Badow, Mashbury, Dunmowes, Leghes and Farnham,
co. Essex, all duchy lands, in part compensation for her dower, and on
the following day, in full satisfaction of it, £102 per annum from the fee
farm of Bristol and smaller sums from a number of other sources, together
with twenty-three manors, including many of the traditional ones she had
formerly held.[30] Just over a year later, in May 1487, Henry ordered his
treasurer to ensure that all issues from lands late of the queen dowager that
by the advice of his council were 'seased into our hands', should be paid to
his queen. In exchange, her mother was granted an annuity of 400 marks
(300 marks less than Richard III had granted her). It is often said that
Elizabeth Woodville was stripped of her lands and confined to
Bermondsey Abbey for complicity in the Lincoln rebellion. Not only does

this make no political sense, but Henry continued to show her marked favour. She stood godmother at Arthur's christening, was proposed as a wife for James III of Scotland and continued to receive gifts from the king made to 'our right dere mother, Queen Elizabeth'. It would seem, therefore, that Elizabeth's retirement to Bermondsey on grounds of ill-health should be taken at face-value. In 1490, her pension was increased to £400 and she died two years later.[31]

Because of the unusual circumstances surrounding her marriage, no specific sum was fixed for the dower of Elizabeth of York. She was, in fact, like her aunt, Anne Neville, a co-heiress. The Mortimer-Clare inheritance which had passed to York did not technically form part of the crown lands and should by right have gone to her and her sisters if she had married anyone other than the king. Part of Elizabeth's dower lands were indeed former Mortimer-Clare possessions, quietly incorporated into the crown's holdings. Her grandmother, Cecily of York, was also dowered from them and in 1492 Elizabeth was granted the reversion of Cecily's lands. Previously, in 1487, all her mother's estates had been transferred to her, and it seems reasonable to suppose that ultimately her dower was approximately that held by her mother as queen. Unlike both Margaret of Anjou and Elizabeth Woodville, Elizabeth of York has left no surviving household accounts on which to base an estimate of her income from dower. Between Elizabeth Woodville and her daughter, Anne Neville tends to be overlooked, but despite the short time she was queen, she holds a significant position. She was the only English queen of the later middle ages to be granted no dower. She inherited the lordships of Glamorgan and Abergavenny in 1474 when her mother Anne, the Beauchamp heiress, was deprived of her lands as though she were legally dead; and these lordships appear to have been the source of her income as queen, since Richard apparently made no additional provision for her when he became king.[32]

Having studied in some detail what provision was made for each queen, it is time to look briefly at how their households were organised and their income spent. The queen was the centre of her court and the occupier of a great landed estate. Obviously, the king had some control over her affairs since her chief financial officer, her treasurer, was answerable to the exchequer; but a wide range of her business was subject only to the internal supervision of herself and her council. The work of the council, like that of any landowner's council, was to advise, administer estates and handle all legal business. Its nucleus was the chief officers of the household, most of them men who had gained their experience in the king's household. In the fifteenth century, many of the queens' senior administrators were duchy of Lancaster officials, but there were also important outsiders on the council, in Margaret's case, men as influential as Somerset and Lord Scales. The council usually met every day in the chamber assigned to the queen at Westminster for the purpose; there her books and deeds were stored. How dominant the queen was in the affairs of her council depended entirely on her own personality. For instance, even routine decisions were not reached by Elizabeth Woodville's council without reference to the queen, and the same was surely true of Margaret.[33]

Financial support for her household was the chief charge upon the income from the queen's dower lands. The household had two categories. First, there were the clerks and civil servants who administered her affairs. In the fourteenth century the queen's chief officer had been the treasurer, but by the fifteenth the chancellor had taken his place. The largest administrative staff was that serving Margaret. Her two successive chancellors, the half-brothers William and Lawrence Booth (who reached the sees of York and Durham respectively, aided by her pressing recommendations), had a clerk of the registers to assist them, a clerk of receipt for the receiver-general, a clerk of the jewels to record her purchases and gifts for the treasurer of her chamber, a clerk of the signet to write her personal letters, a secretary for her council and a clerk of audit responsible for engrossing the accounts of various bailiffs and receivers. The queen's attorney-general, Robert Tanfield, had five attornies to assist him in prosecuting and defending all pleas and actions on her behalf. These men were based in London, though some would also have travelled with the queen's household. The stewards and bailiffs of her estates, who were ultimately responsible to the receiver-general, William Cotton, were mainly duchy of Lancaster men. The second household group is composed of those who served the queen personally: her champerlain, her ladies, her knights carvers and esquires, her valets, chaplains and master of horse. The menials who cooked, cleaned and groomed were part of the king's household. When the king and queen were apart (which was on average about six months every year), the queen paid for her own menials, but when dwelling with the king it was customary for her to pay a set sum daily towards the cost of supporting her court. This was £7 per day and it certainly seems to have been paid.[34]

One of the best sources of information about the queen's household comes from the series of ordinances for the reform of the royal household. These are most common for the central period of the century, during the time of Margaret of Anjou and Elizabeth Woodville. Since these are the only two queens to leave household accounts, a study of the household is of necessity dominated by evidence relating to them. It has been shown that Henry VI's marriage was one of the factors undermining the finances of the royal household, which until 1445 had been reasonably solvent;

from then on they deteriorated steadily.[35] An ordinance for the regulation of the household was issued in 1445, at the beginning of Margaret's married life. Its objects were similar to those of other ordinances of both earlier and later periods: the prevention of waste and peculation, financial supervision and the listing of permitted attendants and their allowances. It is with the last of these that we are concerned here. According to its terms, the queen was allowed a total of sixty-six people in personal attendance. The list is headed by a countess, with three women and four male servants of her own, a baroness with three women and two men, and two ladies each with a damsel and a valet. Six damsels, two chamberers and two launderers complete the list of the queen's ladies. Let it not be forgotten that at one point, one of these damsels was the future queen, Elizabeth Woodville. The queen's chamberlain, Sir John Wenlock, was permitted a squire and a valet; the queen had one chaplain, one secular chaplain, and a clerk of the closet. The rest of her household comprised one secretary, three carvers and cupbearers, two ushers, two sewers (attendants at meals), four squires, a master of the horse, two henchmen, one usher-valet, eight valets, four garçons and a page.[36] If this ordinance were ever effective, it was not so for long. The next, issued in 1454, ordered the reduction of the king's household to 424 officials and servants and the queen's to 120, that is, a *reduction* to a figure *double* that permitted nine years previously. Yet in her household account for the year 1452-53, Margaret paid wages to 151 persons, ranging from John, Viscount Beaumont, her chief steward of lands, who was paid £66 13s. 4d., to men paid in the region of 40s. Although Professor Myers does not make the point, this figure of 151 includes about twenty men who were clerks and administrators rather than personal attendants. Her chief attendant, her chamberlain, received £40, as did her senior lady. It is quite clear that Margaret either would not or could not keep her household down to anywhere near the desired level. As a result, for the year 1452-53, her total household expenditure was over £7,500.[37]

Edward IV, in the course of making his household both solvent and magnificent, caused the *Liber Niger* to be drawn up in about 1472. In it, the household considered suitable for his queen was numbered at one hundred persons, that is, larger than the 1445 ordinance had stipulated but smaller than that ordered in 1454. Unlike her former mistress, Elizabeth Woodville was well able to live within her income. In her surviving household account, for the year 1466-67, her expenses are not totalled but are calculated to be approximately £4,600.[38] In the following decade, with a family of children and longer absences from her husband, her expenses would have increased, but there is little reason to believe that she did not remain solvent. She achieved this by keeping a household smaller than that of any of her predecessors for a hundred years, and much smaller than

Margaret's. Elizabeth, for instance, managed with seven ladies-in-waiting whereas Margaret needed ten; Elizabeth made do with two attornies-at-law, Margaret with five. Elizabeth could and did spend lavishly upon occasion, on furs, cloth and jewels, but in general she was far less extravagant. In many cases where the largest sums of expenditure in the accounts of the two queens are compared, Margaret's spending was the greater, often almost double — on her stables, her clothing and her general privy purse expenditure. It was this last that Margaret used for political purposes by means of gifts and rewards, to win friends and influence people, something that Elizabeth never attempted. In the early years of her marriage, Margaret's gifts at New Year were many and valuable, made to everyone she wished to reward or encourage, and even in later, more embarrassed years she could still make gifts of gold, silver or jewels to 98 persons in 1452. It is interesting to note that even in Elizabeth's time, Margaret's household account was apparently the only surviving one and was frequently used as a precedent, if only to ensure that Elizabeth's officials received smaller allowances than Margaret's had done. A number of Elizabeth's family held positions in her household, but always in established posts and never for higher than usual salaries. Her brother John was master of horse, her sister Anne, Lady Bourgchier, who was married to Essex's heir, was one of her ladies, and Essex's brother, Lord Berners, was her chamberlain, while his son, Sir Humphrey Bourgchier, was one of her stewards. Among her other ladies were her sister-in-law, Lady Scales, and Lady Alice Fogge, wife of her cousin, Sir John Fogge. It was a useful way of ensuring extra income for her family without giving offence to any or expense to the king.[39]

Another interesting comparison between the two queens arises from the question of queen's gold. This was a traditional prerogative of an additional ten per cent paid to the queen of any voluntary fine, such as for a licence or pardon. It had always been difficult to collect and generally unpopular, but it did form a useful addition to a queen's income. It obviously varied from year to year, but, for example, between 1286 and 1289 Eleanor of Castile collected £4,875, slightly more than she got from her dower lands. In 1337, Queen Philippa received £153 during two legal terms. There can be no doubt that all preceding queens had claimed their right to queen's gold, with varying degrees of success. Elizabeth Woodville presented fewer claims than Margaret, but had a greater success in collection. Even so, in 1466–67 she gained only £37 from this source. It is in this context that the celebrated issue of Sir Thomas Cook should be viewed. Elizabeth cannot be regarded as grasping merely because she claimed her right to queen's gold; she was only following a practice legitimately pursued by her predecessors. But in Cook's case, it simply added one more element to the anti-Woodville feeling generated by the whole disgraceful affair, because Cook's punitive fine of 8,000 marks was imposed on him by the court as a punishment for misprision of treason. As a non-voluntary fine, the queen had absolutely no right to claim queen's gold from it.[40]

Although no similar household accounts survive for Elizabeth of York, her privy purse expense account for the final year of her life is extant. It is obviously of less significance than a more general account, but it does afford a vivid glimpse of the day-to-day life of the queen. In itself this is not an insignificant advantage, for Elizabeth must surely rate as one of the most domestic of queens. Her privy purse expenses are much as might be expected, such as rewards for people bringing her gifts, servants' wages, repairs to her barge and litters, purchase of household articles, cloth for her own and her ladies' use, jewellery, furs, her religious offerings, and payments to her physicians and apothecaries. Although her own habits were simple and economical, her revenue had several unusual charges upon it and sometimes simply did not meet her demands. The queen and her sisters were the daughters of a king and ultimate heiresses of the Mortimers, but to all intents and purposes they were dowerless. The matches made for her sisters were not actually disparaging though far from advantageous, but even the gentle Elizabeth's pride forbade that they should be totally dependent on the goodwill of their husbands. Therefore, to Cecily, Anne and Katherine she paid an annual allowance of £50, with a further £120 each to their husbands for their support. On top of that she wholly supported her Courtenay nephews and niece, though why is not clear. They were in the care of Margaret, Lady Cotton and the queen paid for all their clothing and necessities. The king seems content to have allowed her to do so, and when she had to borrow money, he sometimes came to her aid, though she had to pledge her plate as security.[41]

One of the most striking features revealed by Elizabeth's account is the queen's constant travelling. In the last year of her life, despite her pregnancy, she made a progress to Wales and moved continuously up and down the Thames valley between Greenwich and Windsor, stopping at Baynard's Castle (her own inheritance from Mortimer), Westminster, Richmond and Hampton Court. Only as a widow, it seems, was a queen afforded the luxury of settling in one favourite manor and residing there in peace. Catherine of Valois, although she spent quite a lot of time at Windsor with her son, had two preferred residences among her dower lands, at Waltham and Hertford. For Queen Joan as a widow, Havering-atte-Bower was a favourite; it was here that she was arrested. Her only surviving accounts cover the three years of her captivity, so can hardly be described as typical, but for most of the time she was at Leeds Castle where, with an allowance of £19 per week for herself and her household, she lived in considerable style and enough comfort to entertain visitors such as Archbishop Chichele, Cardinal Beaufort and Lord Camoys. She was permitted to purchase cloth, jewellery, silver tableware, wine and other luxuries and probably passed her days in very similar fashion after her release and return to Havering.[42]

Whole papers could be written — indeed have been written — on the political influence of queens, particularly the two queens central to this article, Margaret and Elizabeth Woodville. The subject, therefore, will be touched on only briefly. First, it is worthwhile to ask what is meant by influence. Any fifteenth-century man would probably have regarded certain types of influence exercised by a queen on her husband as quite proper and indeed desirable. These would include the exercise of charity and acts of mercy, of which the classic case is Philippa of Hainault on her knees, begging for the lives of the burghers of Calais. Into this category, in a minor way, would fall Queen Joan's intercession in 1404 which resulted in the restoration of the countess of Oxford's property after she had sued for pardon. A queen was also regarded as legitimately having some interest in affairs relating to her native land, but here she was on much more dangerous ground. There is a world of difference between a short truce being arranged with France in 1407 at Queen Joan's special request, and the personal initiative shown by Margaret of Anjou soon after her marriage in her correspondence with Charles VII concerning the surrender of Maine, where English interests were directly at stake. A similar parallel exists between Joan using her influence with the king to secure preferment for scholars at Oxford and Cambridge and Margaret pressing Pope Calixtus III to accept her own recommendation of Lawrence Booth, her chancellor, to the bishopric of Durham instead of her husband's nomination of John Arundell. A queen's influence could be felt in many ways not recorded on paper. Miss Condon has said that Elizabeth of York had no influence on Henry VII, while that of his mother was paramount. By this she presumably means that unlike her own mother, Elizabeth made no attempt to interfere in political matters. There is no indication that her gentle, pious nature inclined her to do so, but this is not to say that in a happy marriage (and surely Professor Chrimes is right that theirs was a good deal happier than is generally supposed) a wife does not influence her husband in a score of ways not apparent to an outsider. There appear to be no recorded instances of either Catherine or Anne making any impact on their husband's decision-making.[43]

None of these queens, with the exception of Joan of Navarre, in whose case it did not matter, proved to be that greatest burden of all to a king, a barren wife. Whether the queen's character made her an asset or a burden for her husband at court and in the country at large was a gamble that a king, who barely knew his bride, was forced to take. Only a queen's character could make her loved by her people as Elizabeth of York was loved (and this was an inestimable boon to her husband), but there were two or three golden rules which, if followed by a new queen, would prevent her from becoming unpopular and thus doing considerable harm to her husband. The first was to produce a son as quickly as possible; the second was to be fair and just in all dealings as a landowner and to remain solvent; and the third was never, never interfere in English politics. Both Margaret of Anjou and Elizabeth Woodville broke all three of these rules and were consequently highly unpopular. Neither queen can be personally blamed for the late arrival of their son, but Margaret's failure to produce a son for eight years presented the house of Lancaster with a major dynastic problem, while the eventual birth of Prince Edward after his father collapsed only compounded the problem.[44] If Edward of York had been of age in 1483 when his father died the political situation would have been crucially different. Margaret's extravagance and insolvency hardly helped the chronic state of Lancastrian finances. Elizabeth, in the management of her own finances, was never a burden to her husband, but her greed on behalf of members of her family led her to persuade her husband into manoeuvres that were dubious morally as well as legally. Both queens were highly active in the political sphere, though here the comparison ends. The character of Henry VI left Margaret to play a role she had already seen her mother and grandmother fill — as defender of her husband's and child's inheritance. Elizabeth did not initiate political action; her power lay in her influence over a husband strong enough to have resisted her if he wished to do so. As an object lesson in how not to behave as queen consort, the French princess and the English gentlewoman could hardly be bettered. In their personal lives, each paid a bitter price for their behaviour. In contrast, Elizabeth of York was probably everything a fifteenth-century Englishman could have hoped for in his queen — beautiful, fertile, pious and good, with apparently no thoughts beyond her God, her husband and her children, and above all, not a foreigner but an English princess.

It is clear that the provision of dower for a queen was the single heaviest recurrent charge on the crown estate. That it was regarded as a substantial burden is clear from the disinclination of Bedford and the council to deal justly with Joan of Navarre after her lands had been sequestered, and Henry VII's decision not to regrant Elizabeth Woodville's dower *in toto* after she had been restored to her dignities. Margaret of Anjou was forced, quite unjustly, to surrender all rights to dower in England when Louis XI agreed to ransom her from Edward IV in 1475 for 50,000 crowns. Thus, in the fifteenth century at least, dower, which was designed to protect a queen financially for the rest of her life, failed to provide this security for three of these six queens for at least part of their widowhood. Financially, the queen would always be a burden to her husband. In every other way, whether she helped or hindered the king in his relations with his people depended entirely on her character and personality.

NOTES

1. H. Johnstone, 'The Queen's Household', in *The English Government at Work, 1327-1336,* ed. J.P. Willard and W.A. Morris (Cambridge, Mass., 1940), p. 254. B.P. Wolffe believes that his endowment of virtually the whole of the permanent royal estate was not so much to provide her with a cash income as to place royal patronage at the disposal of a *de facto* queen regnant: *The Royal Demesne in English History* (1971), pp. 54-55.
2. J.L. Kirby, *Henry IV of England* (1970), pp. 17-18.
3. Ibid., pp. 135, 137-38.
4. J.H. Wylie, *History of England under Henry the Fourth* (4 vols., 1884-98), I,260-62, 308.
5. Ibid., p. 310; Kirby, op.cit., p. 135.
6. Wylie, op.cit., I, 260; III, 100.
7. Kirby, op.cit., pp. 120-22.
8. J.H. Wylie and W.T. Waugh, *The Reign of Henry V* (3 vols., 1914-29), I, 158-59, 411, 419; III, 187, 203, 268-69, 393.
9. The question of the statute and Queen Catherine's remarriage is fully dealt with in R.A. Griffiths, 'Queen Katherine of Valois and a missing statute of the realm', *Law Quarterly Review,* XCIII (1977), 248-58.
10. J.J. Bagley, *Margaret of Anjou, Queen of England* (1948), pp. 24, 38; *Wars of the English in France during the Reign of Henry VI, King of England: Letters and Papers,* ed. J. Stevenson (2 vols., RS, 1861), I, 443.
11. C. Ross, *Edward IV* (1974), pp. 84-85, 91.
12. Ibid., p. 95.
13. Ibid., pp. 146-47.
14. S.B. Chrimes, *Henry VII* (1972), pp. 22, 51, 65-67.
15. Wolffe, *Royal Demesne,* p. 56.
16. Ibid.; H. Johnstone, 'The Queen's Household', in T.F. Tout. *Chapters in the Administrative History of Mediaeval England* (6 vols., Manchester, 1920-33), V, 278, 281.
17. *CPR, 1401-5,* p. 213.
18. Wolffe, op.cit., pp. 80-81.
19. *CPR, 1401-5,* p.234. Mansfield and the manor of Linby, co. Notts., were surrendered in 1406 for equivalent sums *(ibid., 1405-8,* p. 157).
20. R. Somerville, *History of the Duchy of Lancaster, 1265-1603* (1953), p. 165; *CPR, 1401-5,* pp. 259, 328, 347, 364, 463. Hertford castle was resumed by the king in 1415 in exchange for King's Langley, and she was granted custody of the other third of the Stafford lands during the minority of the heir, Humphrey, in December 1404.
21. Wylie, op.cit., I, 409; II, 27, 286; *CPR, 1401-5,* pp. 402, 405, 454, 501.
22. *Ibid., 1405-8,* p. 438.
23. Kirby, op.cit., pp. 222-23; *CPR, 1413-16,* pp.164, 341.
24. A.R. Myers, 'The Captivity of a Royal Witch: the household accounts of Queen Joan of Navarre, 1419-1421', *BJRL,* XXIV (1940), 264-65, 272.
25. Somerville, op.cit., pp. 207-8.
26. Stevenson, op.cit., II, pt. 1, 264-66.
27. Wolffe, op.cit., p.95.
28. Somerville, op.cit., pp. 208-9; A.R. Myers, 'The household accounts of Queen Margaret of Anjou, 1452-3', *BJRL,* XL (1957-58), 80-84.
29. Somerville, op.cit., pp. 238-39.
30. *Materials for a History of the Reign of Henry VII,* ed. W. Campbell (2 vols., RS, 1873-77), I, 338, 347; *CPR, 1485-94,* pp. 75-77.

31. Campbell, op.cit., II, 148, 319, 322, 555; *Privy Purse Expenses of Elizabeth of York*, ed. N.H. Nicolas (1830), pp. lxxvi-lxxxi; *CPR, 1485-94*, p. 302.
32. Somerville, op.cit., pp. 188, 191.
33. Myers, 'Household of Margaret of Anjou', pp. 95-96; C. Rawcliffe, 'Baronial Councils in the Later Middle Ages', in *Patronage, Pedigree and Power in Late-Mediaeval England*, ed. C. Ross (Gloucester, 1979), p. 99.
34. Myers, 'Household of Margaret of Anjou', pp. 92-94; *The Household of Edward IV: The Black Book and the Ordinance of 1478*, ed. A.R. Myers (1958), pp. 92-93. Kings and queens seem to have spent an average of about six months in each year together, often more before an heir was born or less if the couple did not get on. It has been estimated that Henry VII and his queen spent about seven or eight months each year together.
35. G.L. Harriss, 'The Royal Household, 1437-1460' (Oxford D. Phil. thesis, 1954), quoted in Myers, *Household of Edward IV*, p. 7.
36. A.R. Myers, 'Some household ordinances of Henry VI', *BJRL*, XXXVI (1953-54), 463-64.
37. Myers, 'Household of Margaret of Anjou', pp. 391-430.
38. D.H. Jones, 'A Household Account of Queen Elizabeth Woodville' (Liverpool M.A. thesis), quoted by Myers, *Household of Edward IV*, p. 38.
39. Myers, 'Household of Margaret of Anjou', p. 98; A.R. Myers, 'The Household of Queen Elizabeth Woodville, 1466-7', *BJRL*, L(1967-68), 212, 214, 451; idem, 'The Jewels of Queen Margaret of Anjou', *BJRL*, XLII (1959-60), 113.
40. Johnstone, 'The Queen's Household', in Tout, *Chapters*, V, 265-67; Ross, *Edward IV*, p. 100. M.A. Hicks, 'The Case of Sir Thomas Cook, 1468', *EHR*, XCIII (1978), 95, touches on this point, but does not fully make it.
41. Nicolas, op.cit., pp. ci-ciii, xciv; A. Strickland, *Lives of the Queens of England*, II (1857), 429, 437-38.
42. Myers, 'Joan of Navarre', pp. 268-72.
43. Wylie, op.cit., II, 44, 286-87; Stevenson, op.cit., I, 165-67, 183-84; Myers, 'Household of Margaret of Anjou', p. 92; M.M. Condon, 'Ruling Elites in the Reign of Henry VII', in *Patronage, Pedigree and Power*, p. 114; Chrimes, op.cit., pp. 302-4.
44. For a full discussion of the Lancastrian dynastic problem, see R.A. Griffiths, 'The Sense of Dynasty in the Reign of Henry VI', in *Patronage, Pedigree and Power*, pp. 13-36.

3. English Coastal Defence: some Fourteenth-Century Modifications within the System

J.R. Alban
City Archivist
Swansea

In 1966, in a remarkable study of *The Organization of War under Edward III*, H.J. Hewitt drew attention to many aspects of late-medieval warfare which hitherto had largely been neglected by historians. As its title suggests, the book dealt chiefly with Edward's preparations for foreign wars and highlighted topics such as the raising of armies, the transportation of troops overseas, commissariat arrangements and, perhaps most significantly, the involvement of the 'non-combatant' in medieval war. It was in his treatment of the last of these areas that Hewitt touched upon the important question of home defence during the Hundred Years' War. Defence, however, formed only a small part of the work, which, moreover, concentrated only on the period from 1338 to 1362. But in 1971, Hewitt extended his study of home defence into the fifteenth century in an article on 'The Organisation of War' in a collection of essays on the Hundred Years' War.[1] It is mainly from these two pioneering works, which raise many important issues, that the accepted picture of the system of home defence in late-medieval England has been drawn. The aim of this paper is to investigate certain of the land-based measures taken by the crown for the defence of the English coasts within the period 1337-89.[2]

That there was a need for coastal defence during this period is evident. With the exception of the 1360s, every decade from the 1330s to the 1380s saw instances when the English coasts were harassed, or at least threatened, by hostile naval forces.[3] In the early 1330s, the Scots had been vigorous in their attacks on English coastal places and on shipping.[4] War with France from 1337 onwards meant a general intensification of naval hostilities, the immediate results of which were raids on a large number of places on the south and east coasts between 1337 and 1340. There was also the very real threat of full-scale invasion in 1338 and 1340. The degree of concern in England at this time is clearly reflected in the extent of defensive measures taken, in frequent repetitions in royal defensive writs of dire warnings, such as 'our enemies of France have a great fleet at sea and have attacked various towns and places on the coast, . . . and they are now at sea in these parts', and in regular complaints in parliament that 'because of the want of a navy at sea . . . the Navy of France has done many ills by sea and land'.[5]

There was some reduction in the level of actual attacks in the 1340s and 1350s. Nonetheless, the threat of attack was ever present, so much so that in almost every year when open hostilities against France occurred, precautionary measures for home defence were taken. These precautionary measures reached significantly high levels in those years in which the English planned large campaigns in France. Edward III well appreciated the danger of leaving his realm unprotected during his absence, as the stringent defensive measures of 1346-47, 1356 and 1359-60 clearly show.[6]

The first phase of the Hundred Years' War ended in 1360 as it had begun, with serious enemy threats to the English coast. The years 1359-60 saw widespread fear in England of a French invasion, although actual attacks did not take place until March 1360, when the French descended upon Winchelsea.[7] The events of 1359-60, however, demonstrated that the mere *threat* of invasion could cause untold disruption in England.

The truce of Brétigny brought respite in the 1360s, but when hostilities were resumed in 1369, they were accompanied by an escalation of French naval involvement. The 1370s witnessed coastal attacks of far greater intensity and frequency than ever before. Using fast-moving galleys, the French, by means of their hit-and-run raids, caused widespread damage along the south, east, and west coasts of England, while the government's apparent impotence to counter such attacks provoked bitter complaints in parliament and throughout the country.[8] Most years in this decade saw serious attacks. The list of places pillaged in 1377 will serve as an impressive, if alarming, example: in June, Rye was taken, held for a short while, then burnt as the attackers withdrew; in August, the Isle of Wight was invaded, Carisbrooke castle besieged, and the attackers departing only after a ransom of 1,000 marks had been paid, leaving many places in the island 'utterly destroyed'; other places attacked or threatened included Gravesend, Hastings, Rottingdean, Stonor, Winchelsea, and Yarmouth.[9]

If the hit-and-run raids of the 1370s had given cause for concern, they were overshadowed in gravity by threats of full-scale invasion in 1385 and 1386. The aim of these threats, according to one contemporary French poet, was to repeat the Norman conquest, while the English crown viewed them as intended to 'destroy the English tongue . . . and imbue the realm with a new tongue'.[10] Although these projected invasions came to nought, they caused widespread panic in England. Final release from the menace of naval attacks only came with the commencement of peace negotiations in 1389.

Thus, for a period of over fifty years, the English coasts had been regularly subjected to the threat of naval attack. There was, therefore, a need for some defensive machinery to counter this menace. The system employed by the English crown for the defence of the coasts in this period had not, however, been developed in response to the contemporary threat. Instead, it was a system which had gradually evolved over the preceding centuries to meet the realm's increasing need for protection. The system was rooted in traditions harking back to the Anglo-Saxon fyrd. These had been modified by statute, experiment, and custom during the twelfth and thirteenth centuries, so that by the 1290s the system of defence employed by Edward I was substantially that which was later to be employed by Edward III and Richard II.[11]

The standard picture of the organization of coastal defence in the fourteenth century has been outlined by Hewitt in the two works mentioned above. Broadly speaking, these are its main points.[12] For the defence of the coasts — the *garde de la mer* — the crown relied essentially upon the obligation of every male between sixteen and sixty to provide military service for the protection of his homeland, the force raised by this obligation being led by local defensive officials appointed by royal commissions.[13] Before 1369, there were two principal sets of royal commissioners responsible for defence. The chief of these were the keepers of the maritime land (*custodes terre maritime*), who were in charge of the overall organization of defence on land within the coastal areas, and who had wide control in such matters. Hewitt gives a 'typical statement' of their duties: they were to guard the coast and the whole of the maritime land of the county; to resist invaders whether they came by sea or land; to take all steps necessary for the safety of the realm; to make suitable appointments; to require that, after due warning, the sheriff should parade the *posse* before them. Other duties included setting up beacons and the occasional arraying of men. To aid them in their duties, they were empowered to compel men to perform service by arrest of person or distraint of goods and chattels. They could prevent men and victuals from leaving the coastal area in time of danger, and could compel all men to be intendant to them.[14] In short, they were overall commanders within the coastal shires, backed by royal writ and by the intendance of the sheriff and arrayers of the county.

Responsible to the keepers of the maritime land were the commissioners of array, who actually raised the fencible men of the shires, and then placed them at the disposal of the keepers. Hewitt suggests that this two-tiered system lasted until the end of the first phase of the war, in 1360. After the resumption of hostilities in 1369, the keepers of the maritime land disappeared, and their functions in the coastal shires were transferred to commissioners of array, who thus received wider powers and became the principal royal local officials concerned with defence.[15]

The keepers of the maritime land (and the post-1369 arrayers) operated within a coastal zone known as the *terra maritima* or maritime land, which extended six leagues inland from the shore. Over this zone they had complete control in defensive matters, and no men, victuals, or arms could be taken from it at times of danger. Indeed, the keepers' power stretched further afield, since they could command the arrayers of certain inland counties to send them reinforcements when needed. To facilitate this, inland shires were grouped with coastal shires to form defensive units.

This, then, is the picture drawn by Hewitt. It is an accurate portrayal of the general framework of the system of coastal defence in fourteenth-century England. Indeed, in its *basic* structure, this system saw very little change between 1295 and the militia reforms of 1558.[16] However, like many other aspects of medieval royal administration, defensive organization underwent constant internal changes, particularly in the fourteenth century, under the influence of the prolonged threat of attack from France. A close analysis of several aspects of the system will show this to be the case.

As we have seen, at times of danger from abroad, the crown appointed certain officials to mobilize the local levies and take charge of the defence of coastal areas. Throughout most of the period under consideration, the bilateral system involving keepers of the maritime land and commissioners of array prevailed. However, this system did not disappear in 1369, as Hewitt suggests, but continued for some years into the 1370s. Moreover, from time to time — usually on occasions of extreme danger — other, extraordinary defensive officials made a brief appearance. For instance, in July 1338, special overseers of commissions of array were appointed, while in 1359-60, commissions of array which included the duties of the keepers of the maritime land were issued.[17] Such measures, however, were probably experimental, and the usual practice in time of danger was for the crown to issue simultaneously patents *de custodienda terra maritima*, which appointed keepers of the maritime land, and commissions of array.

The basic duties of the keepers of the maritime land — as principal defensive officials — from the late 1330s onwards have been described above, but points of detail in their commissions varied. The powers of the keepers were often strengthened by the inclusion of a clause *de intendendo*, binding on all the inhabitants and other officials within the area of the keepers' jurisdiction.[18] Often, the keepers' commissions were modified by the inclusion or omission of other powers. A commission of April 1339, for instance, added the supervision of towns, villages, 'and other maritime places', burdened the keepers with the responsibility of fortifying them or repairing existing defences, and of keeping the chancery apprised of all works undertaken in this respect.[19] While powers such as these were not a permanent feature of the commissions, it is possible that they reflected existing duties carried out by the keepers *de facto* in the course of their work.

More frequently included was a clause empowering the keepers to make direct arrays themselves, a feature which would become common in defensive commissions of the 1370s and 1380s. In 1337, the keepers in the palatinates of Chester and Durham were commissioned 'both to guard and to cause to be guarded all the ports and sea shores in which ships land or will be able to land, and all the maritime land . . . and to assess to arms (*assiduendos*) and array all the fencible and capable men of the same counties'.[20] In 1338, the keepers of the maritime land in Devon were similarly given powers of array, while commissions of 1344, 1346, and later gave like powers to keepers in all English maritime counties.[21]

Conversely, on a number of occasions before the 1370s, the commissioners of array in coastal shires received powers usually granted to keepers of the maritime land. In March 1360, for example, the arrayers of inland counties were ordered to array their fencible men 'to be ready to march towards the several parts of Hampshire or elsewhere . . . upon the king's warnings or that of the Hampshire arrayers'.[22] In the following month, the arrayers had powers to compel local landholders to find 'men to abide on the sea shore during the present perils'.[23] Such functions, particularly that of compelling men to remain in defence of the coast, were usually the prerogative of the keepers of the maritime land. The later part of the 1350s, however, witnessed a tendency towards some overlapping of the functions of commissions of array and commissions *de custodienda terra maritima*, especially at times of acute danger.

Occasionally, the keepers were empowered to arrest workmen and supplies, if required, for defensive works, and could compel by distraint if necessary.[24] Less frequently, powers of arrest were extended to shipping and crews, although this task was normally carried out by other officials, such as royal sergeants. However, the arrest of ships had been included in commissions of keepers of the maritime land in 1324, and this power reappeared intermittently in some commissions of 1335, 1346, and later.[25]

Another duty frequently imposed upon the keepers was responsibility for beacons. The keepers had been involved with beacons from at least the reign of Edward II: the inquisition into the beacons on the Isle of Wight in 1324 had been held before the keepers of the maritime land there, while in the same year, commissions *de custodienda terra maritima* gave keepers the responsibility for erecting beacons.[26] The care of beacons was entrusted, from time to time, to other officials, such as constables of hundreds, sheriffs, or commissioners of array.[27] Nevertheless, although the keepers of the maritime land had this responsibility in 1337, and on several later occasions,[28] its inclusion was not a permanent feature of their commission during the fourteenth century.

As there were occasional modifications in the duties of the keepers of the maritime land, so the number of keepers named in each commission was subject to variation. Commissions *de custodienda terra maritima* before the 1370s usually appointed between two and four keepers in each maritime county. The commissions of March 1338 and those of 1371 and 1373 were more or less the same size.[29] In March 1346, however, commissions varied between four and twelve members, while the sheriff of each maritime shire was also named as a keeper.[30] Such large commissions were exceptional before the 1370s, while the inclusion of the sheriff, though not usual at this date, heralded the practice of including him in the enlarged commissions of array which were issued from the late 1370s onwards.

The keepers were usually magnates or other notable persons with substantial holdings of land in the shires in which they operated. The New Ordinances of 1311 had decreed that wardens of the coasts and keepers of castles near the sea were to be local men *de la terre mesmes*,[31] and although the Ordinances had been repealed, it is clear that the concept of appointing local men held good in practice throughout the fourteenth century. The appointment of local men as keepers, moreover, was an extension of the principle that men should be enjoined to go to their estates near the coast whenever danger threatened.

Between the 1290s and the early 1370s, the commissioners of array played an important subordinate role within the bilateral system of defensive officials. It was the arrayers who did the actual work of mobilizing the fencible men of the shire — the *jurati ad arma* — who were to serve in the maritime land under the control of the keepers. The commission of array was also the main medium through which the king raised troops for service overseas. It is, however, clear that a distinction should be made between commissions of array issued for this purpose and commissions of array issued for home defence. The distinction hinges around the practice of selection in the making of the array. Many historians, from Stubbs onwards, have noted the appearance in the fourteenth century of select arrays and have assumed that the selective array gradually replaced the general array — the *levée en masse* — of the whole *posse comitatus*. Several reasons have been adduced for this, the chief of them being that it would have been impractical and impracticable to remove all the fencible men from a county to fight elsewhere, while the fighting force raised by a *levée en masse* would, in their training, discipline, and armaments, be hopelessly unsuited to offensive warfare against professional troops.[32]

Documentary evidence makes it clear that although selectivity did occur in arrays of men for overseas service in our period, general arrays were not superseded. When arrays were made for home defence — when it was weight of numbers rather than quality of troops which mattered — no selectivity occurred. The difference is apparent in the wording of two typical commissions issued in 1337. The first ordered the array of men to serve with the king overseas, and ran:

> Rex dilectis et fidelibus suis Roberto de Hagham, Edmundo de Durresme, Johanni de Haveryng, et Johanni Grifford, salutem. Cum assignaverimus vos, coniunctim et divisim, ad elegandos in comitatu Essex', exceptis villis de Waltham, Colcestre, et Chelmsford, *viginti homines pedites et centum et sexaginta sagittarios de validoribus et potencioribus comitatus illius,* tam infra libertates quam extra . . .[33]

It may be seen how the numbers, types, and quality of the troops required are carefully set out. There is a sharp contrast between the terms of this commission and those of a commission issued in the same year for the internal defence of the west riding of Yorkshire:

> Rex dilectis et fidelibus suis Johanni de Eland, Nicholao de Worteley, Willelmo Soryail, et Ranulpho filio Radulphi, salutem. Cum assignaverimus vos ad arraiandos *omnes homines defensabiles, tam milites quam armigeros, quam alios de Westrithingo in comitatu Eborac',* tam infra libertates quam extra . . . iuxta statum suum . . .[34]

The differences are plainly seen. When troops were needed for overseas service, the king could be discriminating in his choice. But when the threat of enemy attack presented a danger to the realm itself, the full *posse comitatus* was arrayed.

The commission of array for defence was, in its simplest form, an order 'to array all the fencible men and to lead them to the keepers of the sea ports for resisting the king's enemies'.[35] Often, the commission further instructed that the men be arrayed and armed according to their status, as prescribed by the statute of Winchester, and sometimes also specified that they should be organized into millenaries, centaines, and vintaines.[36] Commissions occasionally bestowed upon the arrayers additional powers, such as responsibility for the beacons.[37]

Having mobilized their levies, the arrayers were then obliged to hold them in readiness to march wherever the keepers of the maritime land should direct, and, as we have seen, the order to do so was amplified by a clause in the commission enjoining the intendance of the arrayers to the keepers.[38] Thus, in the early part of the war, a clearly defined hierarchy of royal defensive officials is evident: arrayers actually raising troops, and keepers of the maritime land responsible for their overall command and deployment in the coastal shires. Below the keepers of the maritime land and the arrayers was a hierarchy of lesser defensive officials, at the apex of which were the constables of hundreds. Beneath them were the constables of boroughs and vills, while the leaders of the smallest units of the *jurati ad arma* were the centenars and vintenars. These lesser officials did not hold commissions from the crown but looked to the local communities for their appointment.[39] Investigation of the functions of these non-royal officials therefore falls outside the scope of this paper; nonetheless, they had important subordinate roles to play within the system of defence.

The two-tiered structure of royal defensive officials before the 1370s is not, however, the whole story. The crown was always seeking to improve the efficiency of its defensive machinery. For instance, in the period of war up to 1360, there were several innovations which seem to have been experimental and short-lived. These innovations did, however, pave the way for the more lasting reforms of the 1370s.

The first experiment took place in the 1330s, although it may have been tried already in 1324.[40] In July 1338, for the greater security of the realm, the crown appointed overseers of commissions of array.[41] These officials appear to have been intermediate in status between the keepers of the maritime land and the arrayers, and their role was a partial combination of the duties of these two sets of officials. They had supervisory powers over the making of arrays, while at the same time they were 'to be ready to repel invasions of the French at the request or summons of the keepers of the coast'. By the scheme of July 1338, the English counties were arranged into seven large groups, two or three overseers being appointed within each group to supervise arrays made by the commissioners of array in the constituent shires of the group.[42] By August, there had been some reorganization of the new system: the number of overseers in each group increased, while the number of shires in each group decreased, and the total number of groups was raised to ten.[43] Such officials were appointed again only in January 1339 and November 1359.[44] The appointment of these overseers clearly represented attempts by the crown to improve the efficiency of the defensive system. Their appointment in 1338 and 1339 was almost certainly a reaction to French naval activity which had intensified from the spring of 1338. Failure of the defensive system had resulted in Portsmouth being attacked and burned in March, while throughout the year there was a fear of invasion prevalent in England.[45] Whether the introduction of these new officials improved the system of defence is debatable, since the raid on Southampton in October 1338 underlined certain deficiencies and prompted a royal investigation into the negligence of the defenders. Moreover, in the latter half of the year, a large number of coastal places was damaged by the French.[46] It is, perhaps, no small wonder that the appointment of such overseers was soon abandoned, and was only resurrected once, in 1359, when again there was an acute fear in England of impending invasion.

The 1330s and 1340s witnessed experiments in other directions. One of the most frequent was the amalgamation of commissions of array with commissions of the peace. The joining of a judicial commission to another with military functions was not as illogical as might at first appear. Contemporaries saw an indisputably close connexion between measures taken for the keeping of the peace within the realm and those taken for the defence of the realm from external threats. The statute of Winchester, so frequently referred to in the terms of commissions of array, was basically a peace statute, and the forces raised under the statute were liable for both police and defensive duties.[47]

The first joint commission of array and of the peace was issued in July 1338. It made reference to the statutes of Winchester and Northampton and contained instructions 'to array the men of the counties for the defence of the realm against the French, to keep the peace, and to hear and determine trespasses'.[48] A clue to the reasons for the amalgamation is found in similar joint commissions issued in August of the same year, when the commissioners were to array the men of the county and keep the peace, these duties being necessary since the king had heard that 'many suspected persons run from county to county to avoid the commissioners'.[49] The suspects were probably criminals, but may also have included 'draft dodgers' seeking to avoid military service. Further joint commissions on similar lines were issued in April 1347 and February 1350, but in the 1350s the crown reverted to the former practice of issuing separate commissions for array and for keeping the peace.[50] Although in November 1371, the *custodes pacis* and the sheriffs were given powers of array and of enforcing the statute of Labourers, such joint commissions were rare after the renewal of war in 1369.[51]

The association of the commission of array with that of the peace was a sensible arrangement. The two commissions were similar in many respects, including size. In the 1330s and 1340s, the three, four, or five *custodes pacis* in a typical commission of the peace resembled the numbers of arrayers named in each commission of array. Each commission, moreover, already possessed some of the aspects of the other: arrayers had powers of arrest and imprisonment while justices, in theory at least, were empowered to deal with those who defaulted against the military provisions of the statute of Winchester.[52] The merger, however, should probably be viewed as experimentation with the office of the keepers of the peace rather than as an extension of the powers of the arrayers. Certainly, the rise in the crime rate and in the level of enemy attacks during the period contributed to the merger, while the rare appearance of such joint commissions after the late 1350s may possibly be attributed to the decline of the keepers of the peace in the 1350s and 1360s and the cessation of enemy attacks in the latter decade. The crown also tried mergers with other commissions. In July 1340, for example, a joint commission of array, of the peace, and of oyer and terminer was issued.[53] But such unions may well have proved unsuitable since, when war was resumed in 1369, the commission of array veered towards another type of commission with which it had close affinities in the military sphere: the commission *de custodienda terra maritima*.

Despite the temporary appearance of new officials and the occasional merging of commissions, the bilateral system of keepers of the maritime land and arrayers was the usual method of defence adopted by the crown in the period of war before the treaty of Brétigny. This bilateral system continued for some time after the renewal of war in 1369, although the line of demarcation between the keepers of the maritime land and the arrayers was becoming increasingly blurred. This is reflected in the wording of commissions of the early 1370s. For instance, in May and October 1371, keepers of the maritime land were appointed in certain coastal shires with the usual powers, together with that of array. Those issued in May for Kent and Sussex also included responsibility for beacons.[54] In May, June, and July 1372, commissioners of array were appointed in inland shires, while in certain coastal shires keepers of the maritime land, with responsibility for arrays and beacons, were appointed. The inland arrayers were to be intendant to them.[55] Keepers of the maritime land were also appointed in 1373. The keepers' commissions in Norfolk, Suffolk, and Devonshire of May and June combined arraying with the usual duties of keeping the coast, while the keepers appointed in Hampshire in July were further empowered to array both laymen and clergy.[56] This evidence would seem, at first sight, to suggest that it was becoming the practice to retain commissioners of array in inland shires while the keepers of the maritime land took over the functions of arrayers in coastal shires. However, in June 1372, arrayers were appointed for the defence of thirteen coastal shires. Arrayers were also active in Devonshire in July and in Kent in August of that year.[57] The personnel of these commissions of array was different from that of commissions *de custodienda terra maritima* issued in the same year.

From 1375, however, it was customary to issue for the coastal shires commissions which embraced the keeping of the maritime land and also the direct arraying of fencible men. These commissions were henceforth known in the chancery rolls as *commissions of array*, although their format was identical with that of the commissions *de custodienda terra maritima* with extended powers issued to keepers of the maritime land between 1371 and 1373. For instance, the keepers of the maritime land in Kent in July 1372 were to see to the defence of all places where ships could land; to array all the fencible men and knights according to their status, within and without liberties; to compel all who owed service to perform it, by distraint or by such other means as they saw fit; to arrange horsemen into constabularies and footmen into centaines and vintaines, and to lead them to wherever the enemy might land; to erect beacons; to arrest and imprison all rebels; and to do all else expedient for the defence of the realm.[58] The terms of this commission compare closely with those of commissions of array issued in May 1375 and July 1376, whereby arrayers in the coastal shires were to guard all ports and sea-shores in the county where ships could put in; to resist and destroy all persons wishing to invade the realm by land and sea; to array all the fencible men of the county, furnish them with arms according to their estate, and to lead them against enemies who entered the realm; to raise beacons to give the alarm; to depute others to help where necessary; to arrest and imprison rebels and to seize their lands and property.[59]

The similarities of these two commissions show that the only real difference between them is in their titles: the keepers of the maritime land in 1372 and the arrayers in the coastal shires after 1375 performed the same duties. Clearly, in the early 1370s, the crown, concerned with setbacks in the naval war, sought to experiment with defensive commissions, the result being an amalgamation of the two main ones into a single, all-purpose commission which, after 1375, it chose to call a 'commission of array'. Thus, in the coastal shires, the arrayers became the main local officials concerned with defence, responsible not only for raising and mobilizing the fencibles of their own shire, but for controlling all matters relating to defence, and with powers to call upon inland arrayers for reinforcements when needed.

A feature of these new commissions in the maritime shires was that they had more members than the earlier commissions of array. The amalgamation of commissions naturally resulted in an immediate increase in the number of commissioners appointed, but commissions of array for defence had, in fact, been gradually getting larger since the 1330s. In October 1335, for example, only two men were named in each county commission. In October 1359, the average was four, while after 1369 thirteen, fourteen or fifteen members were usual in each commission.[60] Indeed, the crucial years 1385-86 saw commissions consisting of twenty-five and twenty-six members in the vulnerable county of Kent, but such large figures were exceptional.[61]

The size of commissions after 1369 was doubtless influenced by the intensification of the naval threat, but there was an additional factor which contributed to such an increase. After March 1369, the sheriff was also specifically included in the commission of array for each county.[62] To an extent a retrograde step — the sheriff had lost many of his military powers to royal defensive commissioners in the thirteenth century — his inclusion in the commission was evidently intended to improve liaison between the crown's chief administrative officer in the shire and the royal commissioners charged with defence. Indeed, during the fourteenth century, the sheriff had given strong support to arrayers and keepers of the maritime land in matters of defence, and had always worked in close conjunction with them. He usually issued proclamations on matters of defence and he often purveyed arms and victuals for the defensive forces, while the crown, by writs of intendance, frequently ordered him to give all support to the defensive commissioners.[63] Indeed, before 1369, the sheriff had occasionally been empowered to make arrays himself. In February 1360, for instance, the sheriff of Wiltshire was ordered to array men for the defence of the castles of Old Sarum and Marlborough, while sheriffs frequently arrested workmen and seamen for defensive purposes.[64] Thus, the inclusion of the sheriff in commissions of array from 1369 was a logical move which, in theory, would lead to greater defensive efficiency. His position as an arrayer was confirmed in 1377 by an ordinance which declared that the arraying of the *jurati ad arma* and the watching of beacons should be the responsibility of the sheriff, constables, and other ministers of the crown.[65]

The enlarged defensive commissions of array of the 1370s and 1380s probably also underwent changes in their internal structure. Patents of appointment did not specify the allocation of duties within each commission, but a hierarchy of what may be termed senior and junior arrayers is discernible. Defensive commissions of array in these two decades contained a small number of high-ranking magnates, while the bulk of the arrayers were gentry with lands in the shire covered by the commission.[66] It is likely that the highest-ranking officials acted as commanders of the forces actually raised by the subordinate members of the commission. In effect, the senior arrayers may have thus carried out the functions formerly performed by the keepers of the maritime land, who, in the days of the bilateral organization, had usually been men of higher social standing than the arrayers. Before the 1370s, there had been no distinction between senior and junior arrayers in commissions of array.

While there is no direct evidence concerning the allocation of duties within the enlarged commissions of array of the 1370s and 1380s, such a practice was not unknown. There are earlier examples of defensive commissioners sharing the duties of their commissions and each specializing in one particular aspect of them. In 1335, for example, keepers of the maritime land in south Wales were responsible for the defence of the coasts and the arrest of ships. One keeper concerned himself solely with defence on land, while the other concentrated exclusively on the impressment of vessels.[67] We know also, from the evidence of muster rolls, that arrayers delegated many of their functions — particularly those of mobilizing men and arranging them into fighting units — to the constables of hundreds and their subordinates.[68] It is therefore likely that in the commissions of the 1370s and 1380s, the senior arrayers delegated certain of the roles of their commissions to their more junior colleagues.

Now let us turn to the area which was defended by these officials. By the fourteenth century, a concept had developed whereby the belt of land running parallel to the coast and extending several miles inland was a special area with an individual identity in defensive matters which set it apart from the rest of the county in which it lay. This zone was known as the *terra maritima*. Inhabitants of the zone were exempt from performing military service outside it, and in time of war no men, victuals, or arms were to be removed from the area.[69] Modern historians have long accepted that this maritime land extended six leagues inland from the coast, although it had 'a boundary conventionally and traditionally understood rather than mathematically defined'.[70] It is quite clear from documentary evidence, however, that contemporaries did not regard the extent of the maritime land as fixed. In 1346, the limit of the *terra maritima* was indeed defined as six leagues. In April of that year, the arrayers in Somerset and six other coastal counties were told that all persons residing within this distance from the sea were to be exempt from military service elsewhere.[71] In August, the sheriff of Sussex was instructed that if Stephen Power were found *cum toto posse suo* 'on the safeguarding of the maritime land within six leagues of the sea', he was to be released from a distraint to contribute to the cost of men-at-arms for the king's overseas expedition.[72] The release of Richard Danvers and John Keene from a similar distraint was ordered in April 1348. Both men, 'whose lands and tenements are within six leagues of the sea in the county of Hampshire', were serving there in compliance with a royal order which stated that 'with the agreement of our council, we shall have arranged that men having lands and tenements within six leagues of the sea . . . should remain on the sea coasts in those parts for the defence and protection of those parts against the hostile incursions of enemy aliens'.[73] This limit of six leagues occurred frequently, again in 1353 and 1371.[74]

However, in a writ of 6 April 1338, the commissioners of array in Kent were ordered not to choose men living within *twelve* leagues of the sea for service outside the county. At the same time, purveyors of victuals and sheriffs were instructed not to take any supplies except wine from within twelve leagues of the coast, since the enemy's fleet was at hand.[75] The twelve-league limit was used occasionally thereafter, as in 1347.[76] This variation in the extent of the maritime land may have been influenced by prevailing conditions: factors such as the degree of external danger, or the demands of recruitment of troops and supply of provisions for overseas campaigning may have had some effect. This may explain the twelve-league limit in 1338, when invasion was feared, and the six-league limit in 1346, when the king's Crécy expedition had involved recruitment on a large scale. If this is indeed the case, then it emphasises the fact that for English kings it was often vital to maintain a nice balance between attack and defence for the well-being of the realm.

As well as the two common limits mentioned, there may have been other distances involved from time to time. For instance, the well-known writ of November 1338 concerning the ringing of church bells to warn of the approach of enemies applied to churches situated within seven leagues of the sea.[77] In 1346, a distraint on the men of Lewes for their failure to provide troops for the king's expedition was relaxed because the town was 'at a distance of four leagues from the sea on the safeguarding of the maritime land'.[78] Whether these distances can be taken as limits of the maritime land is uncertain: both, of course, fell within the more customary distances of either six or twelve leagues.

Whatever the extent of the maritime land, the removal of men and, occasionally, arms and victuals from the coastal tract was normally prohibited in time of danger. But whereas this practice prevailed in the area defined as *terra maritima,* it did not necessarily apply to the whole of the coastal shire. Men living in the inland parts of a coastal county, *outside* the belt of maritime land, were indeed liable for service beyond the county's borders. For instance, whereas in June 1347 the fencible men of the Kentish maritime land were declared exempt from performing military service elsewhere, in August of that year the arrayers of Kent raised a force of archers from the non-maritime parts of the county for service at Calais.[79] This was a common state of affairs which reflects the practice of the northern border shires, where a distinction was made between the 'march', or part of the county adjoining the national frontier and under the control of the wardens of the march, and the remainder of the shire.[80]

As we have seen, while the keepers of the maritime land (and the later arrayers) were pre-eminent in defensive matters within the coastal zone, their powers stretched further afield, since they were able to command the obedience of the inland arrayers. By the 1330s, a clear principle was in operation whereby persons living in inland shires were bound by their obligation to provide defensive military service within the maritime land of neighbouring coastal shires, if need should arise.[81] For this purpose, shires were grouped together, two or three inland ones sending their levies to serve in the maritime land of a specified coastal shire. The groupings were sometimes fairly rigid — Surrey men always served in Sussex, Wiltshire men in Hampshire — but the groupings did change slightly from time to time. While, for example, the groupings of June 1337 and March 1338 were identical, those of March 1346 showed slight variations in arrangement, whereas in March 1360 the pattern was one of larger groups on the south and east coasts.[82]

By and large, changes in the groupings were slight, but they did occur. In May 1351, for instance, Dorset, Hampshire, Somerset, and Wiltshire were linked, but this was an unusual arrangement.[83] However, by the 1370s and 1380s, there was a tendency towards the formation of large groups. In arranging counties into such associations, the crown attempted to ensure that men would be available in sufficient numbers for the defence of the coastal belt. On a more cynical plane, it is possible that the crown also used this practice as a means of achieving the maximum defensive service owed to it by drawing men from unthreatened areas, where their service would not be needed, to the coast, where their service could be utilized to the full.[84]

Finally, let us look at the men who defended the coasts. The bulk of the defenders were drawn from the fencible men of the shires, raised by commission of array under their defensive obligations. But although the crown relied heavily upon the *jurati ad arma* of the shires to perform the *garde de la mer*, county levies were by no means the only kind of troops involved in defence. Many coastal towns, for example, enjoyed the privilege of arraying their own burgesses for self-defence, a right always jealously guarded. In February 1339, for instance, the civic officials of thirty-six cities and towns were ordered to array their inhabitants for their own protection, while during the great invasion scare of 1385, separate commissions of array were issued to a number of important coastal towns, including Canterbury, Gloucester, Lynn, and Norwich.[85] It made sense for strategically important towns to array their own inhabitants: standards of arming in towns were generally higher than in rural districts — a clear reflection of the greater wealth of urban communities — while urban levies, sharing a common bond of coming from the same municipality and fortified by civic pride, formed more tightly knit and versatile defensive units than their rural counterparts.[86]

Moreover, the pattern of enemy naval attacks during the fourteenth century meant that the right of self-array was an important one for coastal towns. Towns near the coast were the natural targets for hit-and-run raiders: it was there that the greatest concentrations of wealth were to be found, which made for richer pickings; it was there also that the English had the most to lose, not just economically but from the point of view of prestige, in the event of a successful attack. Because of this, as a further precaution the defence of many important towns, such as Portsmouth, Southampton, and Yarmouth, was entrusted to a keeper with a garrison of indentured troops serving under him at the king's wages for a specified period.[87]

Coastal castles, each with an indentured constable and garrison, played key roles in defence. Some, such as Corfe and Portchester, not merely acted as strongpoints or blockhouses, but had specific responsibility for the security of the coastal area surrounding them.[88] In time of acute danger, the garrisons of coastal castles and towns could be reinforced by units of *jurati ad arma* raised by commissions of array in rural parts of the shires. Thus, Warin de l'Isle's garrison at Portsmouth was strengthened by the arrival of county levies from Bedfordshire, Buckinghamshire, and Northamptonshire in August 1369.[89] Conversely, rural levies serving on the *garde de la mer* outside towns were sometimes reinforced by contract troops when danger was imminent. This practice was especially common in the 1380s, when the defence of long stretches of open coastline was frequently entrusted to indentured retinues.[90]

The fourteenth-century phase of the Hundred Years' War covered a long period, during which the ever-present threat of attack, and the burdens of defence resulting from it, often stretched English resources to the limit. This was particularly the case in the years after 1369. The changes within the defensive system between 1337 and 1389 serve to show that, in response to external danger, there was continuous experimentation in the organization of defence which reflected the crown's desire to improve efficiency and make the realm more secure. As well as the changes which we have seen, significant modifications occurred in other aspects of defence during the period: there were, for instance, revisions in defensive obligations, and changes in the organization of defence at sea and in the methods of financing war. To deal with these adequately would require separate treatment. As it is, one can see that the system of home defence in fourteenth-century England was not as straightforward as the currently accepted picture suggests: instead, the traditional defensive organization, which had evolved over several centuries, was subjected to continuous modification, albeit, in most cases, modest changes of no lasting consequence.

Despite all, the basic framework of the system remained intact: the crown continued to rely on the general obligation of all adult males to provide military service for the defence of their homeland, and applied this obligation to the *garde de la mer* under the control of royal defensive commissioners. The only major lasting change was the replacement of a bilateral system of royal defensive officials with a one-tier system in the mid-1370s. This was the system which was to survive, in its basic form, into the fifteenth century, when it continued to experience constant minor modification in much the same way as it had done during the fourteenth century. It was not until the militia reforms of the Tudor period that the organization of defence in England underwent any great and lasting changes.

NOTES

1. *The Organization of War under Edward III, 1338-62* (Manchester, 1966) (hereafter *Organization . . . Edward III*); 'The Organisation of War', in *The Hundred Years War*, ed. K.A. Fowler (1971), pp. 75-95 (hereafter 'Organisation', Fowler).
2. For reasons of space, this paper omits measures taken for the defence of the northern shires against the Scots, and naval defence at sea. Other important aspects of defence, such as finance and defensive obligations, have also been ignored for the same reasons.
3. On the history of naval attacks on England during this period, see W.L. Clowes, *The Royal Navy. A History from Earliest Times to the Present* (7 vols., 1897-1903); N.H. Nicolas, *A History of the Royal Navy from the Earliest Times to the Wars of the French Revolution* (2 vols., 1847); C.G.B. de la Roncière, *Histoire de la Marine Française* (6 vols., Paris, 1899-1934); H.P.A. Terrier de Loray, *Jean de Vienne, Amiral de France, 1341-96* (Paris, 1877).
4. R. Nicholson, *Edward III and the Scots. The Formative Years of a Military Career, 1327-35* (Oxford, 1965).
5. E.g., PRO, C61/50, m. 9, 11; *RP*, II, 104.
6. E.g., PRO, C76/23 m. 3v, 16, 19v, 25v; *Foedera, Conventiones, Litterae, etc.; or Rymer's Foedera*, ed. A. Clarke, J. Caley, J. Bayley, F. Holbrooke, and J.W. Clarke (4 vols., RC, 1816-69), III, i, 77-78, 87; III, ii, 105-7; PRO, C76/34, m. 9, 9v; *CCR, 1354-60*, pp. 209, 214-15.
7. *Chronicon Angliae ab Anno Domini 1328 usque ad Annum 1388, Auctore Monacho quodam Sancti Albani*, ed. E.M. Thompson (RS, 1874), pp.40-41; *Chronicon Henrici Knighton*, ed. J.R. Lumby (2 vols., RS, 1889-95), II, 109; *Thomae Walsingham Historia Anglicana*, ed. H.T. Riley (2 vols., RS, 1863-64), I, 287.
8. E.g., *RP*, II, 306-7, 311, 314, 319-20. On the long-term effects of defensive burdens, especially after 1369, see E. Searle and R. Burghart, 'The Defence of England and the Peasants' Revolt', *Viator: Medieval and Renaissance Studies*, III (1972), 365-87.
9. *Chronicon Angliae*, pp. 151-52, 166-68; Walsingham, *Hist. Ang.*, I, 340-42; *Eulogium Historiarum sive Temporis Chronicon ab Orbe Condito usque ad Annum Domini 1366; a Monacho quodam Malmesbiriensi Exaratum*, ed. F.S. Haydon (3 vols., RS, 1858-63), III, 340; *CCR, 1385-89*, p. 356; *CIM, 1377-86*, pp. 78, 205-6.
10. *Oeuvres complètes d'Eustache Deschamps, publiées d'après le Manuscrit de la Bibliothèque Nationale*, ed. A. de Queux de Saint-Hilaire and G. Raynaud (11 vols., Paris, 1878-1903), VI, 74; L. Mirot, 'Une tentative d'invasion en Angleterre pendant la Guerre de Cent Ans', *Revue des Études Historiques*, LXXXI (1915), 249-87, 416-66; G. Templeman, 'Two French attempts to invade England during the Hundred Years' War', *Studies in French Language, Literature, and History presented to R.L.G. Ritchie*, ed. F. Mackenzie, R.C. Knight, and J.M. Milner (Cambridge, 1949), pp. 225-38.
11. For a description of defensive organization in 1295, see A.Z. Freeman, 'A Moat Defensive: the Coast Defense Scheme of 1295', *Speculum*, XLII (1967), 442-62.
12. *Organization . . . Edward III*, pp. 3-27; 'Organisation', Fowler, pp. 77-78.
13. The nature of this obligation has been examined in M.R. Powicke, *Military Obligation in Medieval England. A Study in Liberty and Duty* (Oxford, 1962).
14. *Organization . . . Edward III*, p. 7. Hewitt calls the keepers 'keepers of the maritime lands', although contemporary documents always refer to *terra maritima* in the singular.
15. 'Organisation', Fowler, pp. 77-78.
16. See L. Boynton, *The Elizabethan Militia, 1558-1638* (1967), pp. 7-12; C.G. Cruickshank, *Elizabeth's Army* (Oxford, 1966), pp. 5ff.
17. *CPR, 1338-40*, pp. 134, 139; *CPR, 1358-61*, pp. 324, 416. See below p. 64.
18. E.g., PRO, C61/50, m. 7; C76/22, m. 24; /30, m. 4, 5.

19. PRO, C76/14, m.9.
20. PRO, C61/49, m. 24.
21. *CPR, 1338-40*, p.184; BL, Cotton MS. Julius C. IV, f.129v; PRO, C76/22, m. 30; /23, m. 15v, 20, 24; /54, m. 8.
22. *CCR, 1360-64*, pp. 97-98. The italics are mine.
23. Ibid., p. 19.
24. E.g., PRO, C61/49, m. 26; /50, m. 7-11; C76/22, m. 25, 30.
25. *Parliamentary Writs and Writs of Military Summons, with Records and Muniments relating to Suit and Service to Parliament*, ed. F. Palgrave (2 vols., RC, 1827-34), II, ii, 660 (1324); PRO, E101/19/13; /612/34 (1335); C76/22, m.25, 30 (1346). This power to arrest ships was a vestige of the powers of the thirteenth-century wardens of the sea-coast (F.W. Brooks, *The English Naval Forces, 1199-1272* [1933], pp. 168ff.; Powicke, op. cit., p. 84)
26. *CIM, 1307-49*, p. 209; *Parl. Writs*, II, ii, 661.
27. E.g., constables of hundreds, E. Coke, *Fourth Institutes* (1664), p. 151 (1325); sheriffs, *Foedera*, II, ii, 1055 (1338), III, i, 72 (1346); arrayers, *CPR, 1324-27*, pp. 216-19 (1325), *Foedera*, II, ii, 636-37 (1326), PRO, C76/34, m.9 (1356), *Foedera*, III, ii, 947-48 (1372); sheriffs and arrayers, *CCR, 1369-74*, p. 436 (1372).
28. E.g., *CCR, 1337-39*, pp. 137, 179; *Foedera*, II, ii, 996 (1337); PRO, C76/23, m. 20; C81/1758/3 (1346); *Foedera*, III, i, 239; PRO, C76/30, m. 4, 5 (1352); /34, m. 9 (1356); BL, Cotton MS. Julius C. IV f. 129v (1373).
29. PRO, C61/50, m. 7 (1338); C76/54, m. 8; BL, Cotton MS. Julius C. IV, f. 129v (1371 and 1373).
30. PRO, C76/22, m. 24, 25.
31. *SR*, I, 160.
32. E.g., W. Stubbs, *The Constitutional History of England in its Origin and Development* (3 vols., Oxford, 1874), II, 283. On commissions of array, see A.E. Prince, 'The Army and Navy', in *The English Government at Work, 1327-36*, ed. W.A. Morris, J.F. Willard, J.R. Strayer, and W.H. Dunham (3 vols., Cambridge, Mass., 1940-50), I, 332-93; Powicke, op. cit., pp. 118-65, 182-209. The Superiority of professional troops over local levies has been revealed by archaeological evidence from grave-pits at Visby (B. Thordeman, *Armour from the Battle of Visby, 1361* [2 vols., Stockholm, 1938-40], I, 22-25, 225-29).
33. PRO, C61/49, m. 29v. The italics are mine.
34. Ibid., m. 26. The italics are mine.
35. Ibid., m. 26.
36. E.g., PRO, C76/22, m. 23; /23, m. 20; *CPR, 1334-38*, pp. 137-39.
37. See n. 27.
38. E.g., PRO, C61/50, m. 7, 11; C76/22, m. 23-25.
39. On these lesser officials, see H.M. Cam, 'Shire Officials: Coroners, Constables, and Bailiffs', in *English Government at Work*, III, 143-83; Powicke, op. cit., pp. 127-29; H.B. Simpson, 'The Office of Constable', *EHR*, X (1895), 625-41; J.R. Alban, 'National Defence in England, 1337-89' (Liverpool, Ph.D. thesis, 1976), pp. 132-66.
40. *Parl. Writs*, II, ii, 661.
41. *CPR, 1338-40*, p. 134.
42. See Appendix 1.
43. *CPR, 1338-40*, pp. 141-142. See Appendix 2.
44. PRO, C76/14, m. 16v (1339); *CPR, 1358-61*, p. 324 (1359).
45. *Chronicon Domini Walteri de Hemingburgh*, ed. H.C. Hamilton (2 vols., English Historical Soc., 1848-49), II, 315; *Knighton*, II, 3; Walsingham, *Hist. Ang.*, I, 200.
46. *Chronicon Galfridi le Baker de Swynbroke*, ed. E.M. Thompson (Oxford, 1889), pp. 62-63; *Chronicon Angliae*, p. 5; *Knighton*, II, 7-8; *Chronica Adae Murimuth et Roberti de Avesbury*, ed. E.M. Thompson (RS, 1889), pp. 87-88.

47. W. Stubbs, *Select Charters and other Illustrations of English Constitutional History* (9th edn., Oxford, 1913), pp. 423-29.
48. *CPR, 1338-40*, pp. 135-36.
49. Ibid., p. 141.
50. *CPR, 1345-48*, p. 301; PRO, C47/2/45/26.
51. *CPR, 1370-74*, p. 34.
52. E.g., PRO C76/14, m. 16v; /21, m. 23; /23, m. 25v; /24, m. 31v; B.H. Putnam, 'Shire Officials: Keepers of the Peace and Justices of the Peace', in *English Government at Work*, III, 213-14; E. Moir, *The Justice of the Peace* (Harmondsworth, 1969), p. 20.
53. *CPR, 1340-43*, p. 12.
54. *CPR, 1370-74*, pp. 107-8; PRO, C76/54, m. 8.
55. PRO, C76/55, m. 14, 16, 27, 34-37.
56. Ibid., /56 m. 9, 21.
57. Ibid., /55 m. 16, 27, 38.
58. Ibid., m. 27.
59. Ibid., /59, m. 12, 19; *CPR, 1374-77*, p. 152.
60. *CPR, 1334-38*, pp. 137-39; *Foedera*, III, i, 448; *CPR, 1377-81*, pp. 38, 471, 574.
61. *CPR, 1381-85*, p. 588; *ibid.*, *1385-89*, p. 176.
62. *CCR, 1369-74*, pp. 18, 36.
63. E.g., PRO, C47/2/45/29, C76/15, m. 7v, 17; /16, m. 26 (proclamations); /30, m. 12; E358/3, m. 11v; *Organization . . . Edward III*, pp. 63-73 (purveyance); PRO, C61/50, m. 10 (intendance).
64. *CCR, 1360-64*, p. 9 (1360); PRO, C76/34, m. 18 (seamen); E364/4, m.3; *CCR, 1339-41*, p. 411 (workmen).
65. *RP*, III, 384.
66. E.g., *CPR, 1381-85*, p. 588.
67. J.R. Alban, 'The Impressment of two Ships at Swansea for the Defence of South Wales, 1335', *Gower. The Journal of the Gower Society*, XXIX (1978), 67-71.
68. E.g., PRO, C47/2/23/42; Greater London Record Office (Middlesex Records), Acc. 1085, F.P. 9, m.2 (Newdegate Papers: muster roll for Spelthorne hundred, Middlesex, c. 1338).
69. For the history of the development of this zone and its officials, see Powicke, op. cit., pp. 57-62, 84-85, 91-93.
70. *Organization . . . Edward III*, pp. 6-7.
71. *Foedera*, III, i, 81.
72. PRO, C76/23, m. 16v.
73. PRO, C76/26, m. 17v.
74. *CCR, 1349-54*, p. 545; *ibid., 1369-74*, p. 229.
75. *Foedera*, II, ii, 1025-26.
76. PRO, C76/24, m. 24v.
77. *Foedera*, II, ii, 1066.
78. PRO, C76/23, m. 16v. See also ibid., 22, m. 30 (Holderness).
79. *Foedera*, III, i, 130.
80. E.g., *Rotuli Scotiae in Turri Londoniensi et in Domo Capitulari Westmonasteriensi asservati, 19 Edward I — Henry VIII*, ed. D. Macpherson, J. Caley, W. Illingworth, and T.H. Horne (2 vols., RC, 1814-19), I, 140-41; R.R. Reid, 'The Office of the Warden of the Marches: its Origin and early History', *EHR*, XXXII (1917), 485.
81. *Organization . . . Edward III*, pp. 8-9.
82. PRO, C61/49, m. 26 (1337); /50, m. 7 (1338); C76/22, m. 24, 28, 30 (1346); C54/198, m. 39v (1360). See Appendix 3.
83. PRO, C76/29, m.9.

84. On royal attempts to obtain maximum service, see Powicke, op. cit., pp. 138-61, 182-210; G.L. Harriss, *King, Parliament, and Public Finance in Medieval England to 1369* (Oxford, 1975), pp. 87-97.
85. PRO, C76/14,m. 4; *CPR, 1381-85*, pp. 597-98.
86. Compare the urban musters in PRO, C47/2/23/42; /2/58/23; and W. Hudson, 'Norwich Militia in the Fourteenth Century', *Norfolk Archaeology*, XIV (1900-1), 236-320, with the rural musters in PRO, C47/2/45/22; /2/58/18-24; Greater London R.O. (Middlesex Records), Acc. 1085, F.P. 9.
87. E.g., *CPR, 1367-70*, p. 304 (Portsmouth & Southampton); Southampton Record Office, SC13/3/1-3 (Southampton); PRO, C76/54, m. 8 (Yarmouth). The functions of keepers of towns and castles are discussed in T.F. Tout, *Chapters in the Administrative History of Medieval England* (6 vols., Manchester, 1920-33), III, 21ff.; W.O. Ault, 'Manors and Temporalities', *English Government at Work*, III, 13, 14, 29.
88. E.g., PRO, C76/24, m. 16. Defensive responsibility could also extend to the arrest of fighting men, ships, and enemy aliens, and the making of arrays (e.g., *CPR, 1377-81*, pp. 2, 536 [men]; PRO, E403/508, m. 1 [ships]; *CCR, 1346-49*, p. 131 [aliens]; PRO, C76/64, m. 25 [arrays]).
89. PRO, E364/3, m. 4v, 5v.
90. E.g., PRO, E101/531/40; E403/508, m. 4.

APPENDIX 1
Overseers of Commissions of Array: Shire Groupings and Numbers of Overseers appointed, July 1338.

Shire Groupings	No. of Overseers
i. Hants, Berks, Surrey, Sussex, Oxon, Kent	2
ii. Glos, Worcs, Heref, Salop, Staffs, Warw, Leics	2
iii. Cornwall, Devon, Somerset, Dorset	2
iv. Essex, Herts, Cambs, Hunts, Norf, Suff, Bucks, Beds, Midd	3
v. Yorks	3
vi. Lancs, Northumb, Cumb, Westm	3
vii. Lincs, Northants, Rutland, Notts, Derb	2

APPENDIX 2

Overseers of Commissions of Array: Shire Groupings and Numbers of Overseers appointed, August 1338.

Shire Groupings	No. of Overseers
i. Hants, Berks, Wilts, Surrey, Sussex, Kent	5
ii. Norf, Suff, Cambs	4
iii. Glos, Heref, Salop	5
iv. Worcs, Warw, Oxon	5
v. Cornwall, Devon, Dorset, Somerset	5
vi. Cumb, Westm	4
vii. Essex, Herts, Hunts, Beds, Bucks, Midd	5★
viii. Notts, Leics, Derbs, Staffs	3
ix. Yorks, Northumb, Lancs	4
x. Lincs, Northants, Rutland	4

★ Plus a further two overseers in December.

APPENDIX 3

Inland Shires linked with Maritime Shires for Coastal Defence, showing the fluctuations of the Shire Groupings.
Maritime shires to which men from the inland shires of the group were sent for service are shown in capitals.

a)   *25 March 1338*
i.   CORNWALL.
ii.   DEVON.
iii.   DORSET, SOMERSET.
iv.   HANTS, Berks, Wilts.
v.   SUSSEX, Surrey.
vi.   KENT.
vii.   GLOS, Heref, Worcs.
viii.   ESSEX, Herts, Midd.
ix.   LANCS, Salop, Staffs.
x.   NORF, SUFF, Cambs, Hunts.
xi.   LINCS, Leics, Northants, Rutland.
xii.   YORKS, Derb, Notts.

b)   *10 March 1346*
i.   CORNWALL.
ii.   DEVON.
iii.   SOMERSET.
iv.   DORSET.
v.   HANTS, Berks, Oxon, Wilts.
vi.   SUSSEX, Surrey.
vii.   KENT.
viii.   GLOS, Heref, Worcs.
ix.   ESSEX, Herts, Midd.
x.   LINCS, Leics, Northants, Rutland.
xi.   NORF, SUFF, Cambs, Hunts.

c)   *2 March 1360*
i.   CORNWALL, DEVON, DORSET, SOMERSET, GLOS, Worcs.
ii.   HANTS, Berks, Bucks, Oxon, Wilts.
iii.   KENT, SUSSEX, Beds, Midd, Surrey, City of London.
iv.   ESSEX, NORF, SUFF, Cambs, Herts, Hunts.
v.   LINCS, Derb, Leics, Notts, Rutland.

4. John Beaufort, duke of Somerset and the French expedition of 1443

Michael Jones
University of Bristol

The confused events leading to the collapse of English fortunes in France at the end of the Hundred Years' War were the cause of much bitterness and recrimination. A major complaint was that of a malign influence in policy-making and the management of the war; those close to the king like William de la Pole, duke of Suffolk, and the Beauforts were principal targets. In 1440 Humphrey, duke of Gloucester had, in a list of grievances, criticised the role of Cardinal Beaufort in foreign affairs. Ten years later Edmund Beaufort was to receive even more stringent denunciations from Richard, duke of York for his involvement in the final loss of Normandy as an example of 'inordinate negligence, lacchesse and covetyse'.[1] Whatever the particular justification for these complaints, they were symptoms of a more general ill arising from the king's own government and management of the realm. Henry VI's conspicuous lack of interest in taking command of an army himself was compounded by a failure to provide a firm delegation of authority. The political uncertainty underlying his sense of patronage can be seen in the military expedition of 1443. Here Edmund Beaufort's brother John, specially created duke of Somerset before the campaign, acquired an independent command that unquestionably altered York's own existing authority as king's lieutenant-general in France.[2] The expedition received financial priority at the exchequer at the expense of York's own annual salary.

Much was hoped from this new war effort. In the event little major success resulted from it; a more prudent course might have been to reinforce Normandy.[3] It was the expedition's apparent aimlessness that caused the chronicler Thomas Basin (who was in Normandy at the time) to ridicule Somerset's conduct. The duke's idea of generalship, he remarked, was secrecy: 'in fact it remained a secret at the end of the campaign whether he himself had found out his intentions'.[4] How did the expedition come about? Why was it operating separately from the English war effort in Normandy? These puzzling questions offer an opportunity to look at the most enigmatic member of the Beaufort family, John, duke of Somerset, the army's commander.

John Beaufort, eldest surviving son of the first earl of Somerset,[5] had spent much of his life imprisoned in France. While still a minor he had been captured at the battle of Baugé where his step-father, Thomas, duke of Clarence, was slain. It was not until 1438, over seventeen years later, that he was finally released. He served briefly in France in the summer of 1439 and was prepared to lead a considerable army to Normandy at the start of the new campaigning season. He remained abroad for most of 1440, taking temporary command of the duchy before York arrived as the new lieutenant-general. But the expedition of 1443 was to be a difficult test, an independent commission operating outside Normandy in areas where the English presence was at best uncertain.

This responsibility for an important and expensive military initiative[6] was a reflection both of dynastic and political circumstances. The Beauforts' closeness to the royal family may have been consciously strengthened by Henry by the 1440s;[7] it was certainly proper that high command should be delegated to those 'of the blood'. As such, John's position as the heir of the first earl made him a natural choice for responsibility in France. Moreover, the Beauforts had done Henry good service in matters of foreign policy. At the time of John's arrival in Normandy in 1439 the cardinal was heading the important peace negotiations at Calais. His younger brother Edmund had served regularly in France since 1427, a particular success being his relief of Calais in 1436, for which he was later created earl of Dorset. John's other brother Thomas had died at the siege of Louviers in 1431, only a year after his release from captivity.[8]

With Henry's own participation in politics the Beauforts began to benefit from grants of land and office in France. In 1436 Edmund was granted the important *comté* of Harcourt in eastern Normandy, held in the royal demesne after the death of the duke of Bedford. Two years later he received the governorship of Anjou and Maine.[9] As interest in the war effort declined among the higher aristocracy, Henry looked more and more to the Beauforts to take on responsibility. In 1443, when he contacted Somerset to find out his intentions regarding the new expedition, he reminded him of his willingness to do him service 'the which he hath alle tymes redyed hymself to'.[10]

John Beaufort is a shadowy and rather difficult figure with whom to come to grips, and it is worth dwelling on his background and the particular problems associated with it. At the age of seventeen he and his younger brother Thomas had been taken prisoner after Baugé.[11] His initial captor was a Scot, Lawrence Vernon. At first there were hopes of a speedy release for the Beauforts in exchange for John, count of Angoulême, who was held by their mother, Margaret; however, this plan was vetoed by Henry V himself. Meanwhile, in 1423 the Dauphin Charles bought

Somerset from Vernon and transferred his custody to the countess of Eu, to serve as a bargaining counter for the release of the countess's son, captured at Agincourt.[12] Years of frustration were to follow. Although the council had been willing, in 1427, to release the count of Bourbon on the condition that he secured the freedom of John, who was now of age as earl of Somerset, and his brother Thomas, Bourbon failed to achieve this.[13] Thomas was finally released in 1430, but John remained in captivity. The stumbling block was probably that the council was not prepared to release the count of Eu himself, a high-ranking Agincourt prisoner, until Henry VI came of age. Petitions from John to the duke of Bedford and Humphrey, duke of Gloucester had little effect.

However, with the king's entry to politics the picture changed. Although the minority was not formally terminated till November 1437, Henry became involved in state affairs over two years before this.[15] From the first the cardinal and Edmund were working closely with the young king to secure John's release: it expressed Henry's own feelings of clemency to war prisoners as well as Beaufort family interests. In February 1435, on Henry's orders, the custody of the count of Eu was transferred from the constable of the Tower of London to the keeping of Edmund Beaufort.[16] After a number of meetings, arrangements were made whereby Somerset's attorneys purchased the count from the crown.[17] By April 1437 negotiations with the French were underway, and Edmund and the earl's receiver, Thomas Sutton, journeyed to France with their captive. Somerset was finally released in 1438 for 'an immense sum of money'.[18]

By Somerset's own statement his ransom was £24,000. It included payments to the English exchequer, to his captor in France, his original custodian, Vernon, as well as, no doubt, the extra expenses of his long period of captivity.[19] The financial position of John Beaufort was thus a difficult one. His landed estates were relatively small. After the death of his elder brother Henry, and a period of wardship by the crown, on coming of age in 1425 he inherited manors scattered over five or six counties. These included the lordship of Corfe, where the castle had become the family residence; and the forfeited lands of Owain Glyndŵr in Wales, which had been granted to John's father in 1400. On the death of his uncle, Thomas, duke of Exeter, he inherited those lands that had not been sold off to pay outstanding debts.[20] The principal sources of his income were annuities, both from the petty customs of the port of London (£500) and from the exchequer (500 marks); and these formed the bulk of the valuation of the estate made by the earl's receiver in 1436 (at £1,000).[21]

The costs of estate administration during Somerset's imprisonment must have mounted up considerably.[22] In 1433 he petitioned parliament concerning a claim made against his lands in south Wales. The action was taken by John Scudamore, who had married Glyndŵr's daughter and heir,

Alice. Somerset's own rights to inheritance were safeguarded, but his brother Edmund made doubly sure by gaining Scudamore's dismissal from royal service on old charges, based on a statute made at the time of Glyndŵr's rebellion.[23] The Beaufort brothers were to co-operate closely in matters that concerned their family's position.

The size of his ransom meant that Somerset was impoverished at the time of his release. However, on the death of his mother Margaret, duchess of Clarence, in January 1440, he inherited custody of a valuable French prisoner.[24] This was John, count of Angoulême, younger brother of Charles, duke of Orléans. Angoulême was not a war-prisoner; he was taken as surety for the large indemnity pledged by Orléans and others at Buzançais in 1412 for Thomas, duke of Clarence and his captains to leave Gascony.[25] Clarence, as master of the captive, had the right to negotiate his deliverance. On his death at Baugé, Beaufort's mother Margaret, duchess of Clarence inherited the custody and the unfortunate count spent his next seventeen years in continuous exile in Maxey (Northants.), Groombridge (Kent) or London, writing poetry or studying the lives of the saints. On Margaret's death John himself became heir to the large sum of money,[26] a sum that might offset the costs of his own ransom. Negotiations were underway with the French in 1442: by assignments on this pledge Beaufort secured the release of John Bastard of Somerset, and paid off a debt to his original captor, Vernon. In 1444 Angoulême was taken over to France and terms were signed in May for an immediate payment to Somerset of 12,000 *saluts d'or* with sureties for another 60,000. But Somerset himself died before he could receive any of this.[27]

In the meantime his financial position remained very difficult. Family jewels were pledged to raise loans from London merchants; and money was borrowed from other sources.[28] The earl's shortage of ready cash made even small sums important.

In December 1439 Somerset, soon to embark with a relief army for France, made use of captains' rights to claim priority at the exchequer for outstanding government debts due to him as a private person. At the time of his indenture, the earl submitted a petition concerning sums still owed to him.[29] This concerned the annuity from the exchequer. The original grant, of an annual value of £500, had been made to John's father by Henry IV. Two-thirds had been assigned to John's elder brother Henry, the other third to his mother. After Henry's early death John himself inherited the larger amount (500 marks) on coming of age. This, it seems, was the area of contention. His seisin of his inheritance took place on 24 September 1425. Somerset, however, claimed that his proof of age before the escheator had been delivered late, and that arrears of another 500 marks were owed him.[30] This matter had still not been settled by the time of Somerset's expedition in 1443, when he was again sueing for the arrears.[31]

We know little about Somerset himself. By 1440 he had married Margaret, the sister of John Beauchamp of Bletsoe. Their only child, a daughter Margaret, was born in May 1443.[32] Considering his long years in captivity, he must have had mixed feelings about returning to serve in France. A reference to a petition of his concerning the inheritance due to him on the death of his mother mentions '. . . as soon as he was delivered from captivity he was sent again to France and made no delay'.[33] By 1443 he was already in poor health, and with no son the future of his estate was uncertain. These circumstances provide an important background to his hard bargaining with the crown over the terms of the expedition.

Since the death of Bedford and the Burgundian alliance with the French in 1435 the English military position had steadily worsened. Within a year Paris and the Île de France had been lost, and French forces had captured both Harfleur and Dieppe in upper Normandy. Not only was Rouen more vulnerable to attack, but there were new dangers to western Normandy from the south. In 1439 troops of the duke of Alençon gathered at Angers, marched through Maine and Normandy and besieged the important fortress of Avranches. Only a determined counter-attack led by Edmund Beaufort and Talbot saved the situation. The English presence in Maine itself had become increasingly precarious. In 1440 French troops had won the fortresses of St. Suzenne and Beaumont-le-Vicomte. By 1443 the English feared a major new offensive from the east, threatening Rouen, or from the south, attacking Le Mans or Avranches.

Despite the uncertainties of fighting in France at this stage in the war, it is significant that soon after his release Somerset was prepared to serve there. He seems to have arrived in Normandy by April 1439, when he was appointed captain of Renneville. In May he and his brother formed part of the governing council created after the death of Warwick, the lieutenant-general.[34] Two months later he saw his first action when he raised a considerable relief force to aid the beleaguered garrison at Meaux. By this time he had taken over several important captaincies: Cherbourg from his uncle the cardinal, and Avranches and Tombelaine from Suffolk. These, and others he received in 1440, he was to hold until his death.[35] By September he had left Rouen and returned to England.

In December he agreed with the king to recruit a sizeable new army, which he took to Normandy in February 1440. This force, 100 men-at-arms and 2,000 archers, was intended for a counter-offensive by the English; clearly Somerset had been entrusted with an important command.[36] Many more troops joined him on his arrival in Normandy *au recouvrement de certains places et autrement sur les champs*. With this army he led a raid into the Santerre district of eastern Normandy. This seems to have been very successful: Folleville and Lihons were captured and much plunder taken.[37]

North-west France in the Mid-fifteenth Century.

Meanwhile, the king and council were deliberating on the important question of the new lieutenant-general in France. This post was first offered to Humphrey, duke of Gloucester. As Gloucester required a considerable amount of time to raise a new army, Somerset, who was now in the field, had been given a temporary command as *Lieutenant et gouverneur general sur le fait de la guerre,* which gave him civil as well as military powers. His commission and salary were to stand until the arrival of his permanent successor. Gloucester himself seems to have passed over the office, for in July Richard, duke of York was appointed for a five-year term. York did not reach Normandy with his army till the spring of 1441; in the interim Somerset remained the king's representative in the duchy.[38] His appointment was marked in May 1440 by a grant of an annual farm of 3,000 *saluts d'or* from the appanage of St. Sauveur Lendelin in the Norman Cotentin from a grateful Henry. This was made *en consideration de ses services,* with especial respect to *pertes inconveniens et dommages qu'il a eus a cause de son service par longues detention de prison es mains des ennemis.*[39]

During the summer the two Beaufort brothers worked closely in the investment of Harfleur, which was still held by the French. In this major military operation Edmund Beaufort took command of the siege and a large force assembled under him in June and July. A French relief army was being raised and Somerset gathered more troops to cover the siege. He was in the field during August and September and Fécamp was reinforced. By late September he was back at Rouen taking artillery and more troops up for the last stages of the operation.[40] The French were unable to break through and by the beginning of November the garrison was ready to surrender. After the town's capitulation — a major military success — both Beauforts returned to England; this was probably the occasion of Somerset's creation as knight of the garter in recognition of his services.[41]

Between the death of Warwick and the arrival of York, Somerset had been the highest-ranking peer in Normandy. Consequently he and his brother had enjoyed a considerable amount of authority. But after the arrival of York he took no further part in the defence and running of the duchy, though he continued to draw on the salaries of his French captaincies during his absence.[42] But late in 1442, with a royal army under Charles VII making considerable inroads in Gascony, there was need for a new major expedition to be sent to France. Somerset appears to have agreed to take the command. Here the records peter out, but no indentures were sealed that year. Perhaps a lack of funds prevented anything more definite being undertaken.[43]

At the start of the new campaigning season, Gascony was still one of the main priorities. Charles's troops had only re-crossed the Dordogne in January. However, there were growing fears of a new offensive against Normandy. At the beginning of February the king and council discussed whether to send an army to Gascony, Normandy or both. The outcome was inconclusive, the possibility of two relief forces being dependent on the necessary financial resources being available. Later Henry was in touch with Somerset, who was at this stage suffering from illness, to discover his intentions.[44]

Two important considerations spring to mind concerning the background to Somerset's conditions of service. The first was the general lack of enthusiasm among the higher nobility for the war in France. In March the king had little success in trying to persuade the recalcitrant earl of Devon to lead an army to Normandy.[45] Other peers, such as the duke of Norfolk, showed no interest in the war effort. It seems there were few contenders, apart from Somerset himself, for the new command. The second was the question of finance. Since parliament had made no allocation for a new offensive the money had to be raised by other means. An appeal for funds was sent round the country in March but finally the expedition depended on a massive new loan from Cardinal Beaufort. After the council had approved Somerset's terms, £10,000 was contributed towards the first quarter's wages. Another £10,000 followed in May, and a month later a further £1,000 covered additional costs of the shipping.[46] This, the last major loan the cardinal made, was the crucial factor that enabled preparations for this important army to go ahead.

It is necessary here to say a word about the sources for the origins of this campaign. The main printed source is Nicholas's collection, which, as is pointed out by B.P. Wolffe, provides important but often meagre and incomplete references to council meetings.[47] The detail of the entries varies enormously. There fortunately survives considerable information about the important council meeting of 30 March, in which Somerset's terms of indenture were discussed, although this creates the impression that his proposals were presented to the council as a *fait accompli*. In fact, there are very brief references in council meetings early in March to messages passing between Henry VI and Somerset. Their delivery on at least one occasion by Adam Moleyns, clerk of the council,[48] suggests the proposals were being considered by the council well before the terms of indenture were presented.

This is substantiated by two important documents. The first is a draft by the council clerk, Henry Benet, of Somerset's articles for his appointment and the king's replies. It was drawn up for Chancellor Stafford for the same council meeting of 30 March. Several entries in the margin show that the council had already been deliberating on some of the articles: the extent of Somerset's authority in his commission, for example.[49] The second is filed among the collections of indentures, but does not appear to represent the final terms of service. Rather it seems to have been a working-copy, an original draft, with alterations and additions by members of the council and Somerset himself.[50] After the word 'John' a gap was left, presumably because of an unsureness as to whether Somerset was to be styled earl or duke. The draft of the articles suffers from a similar uncertainty, sometimes describing Somerset as earl and sometimes as duke. This matter will be discussed more fully later, but suffice it to say that this probably dates the copy before 30 March, when Somerset's new rank was confirmed by the king. The length of time of these deliberations before the indenture was finally sealed is almost certainly a reflection of the important demands Somerset was making.

The official terms of indenture do not survive. The draft copy indicates it was finally signed and sealed on 8 April. From the warrants, on the same date, for the payment of the first quarter's wages, it appears that Gascony was to be relieved only if Charles launched a new campaign there. The army was to be paid at normal, not Gascon, rates.[51] Instead a new initiative was proposed, crossing into French territory from the north, and waging 'most cruel and mortel werre'[52]

Where did this new plan of campaign originate? The suggestion may well have come from Somerset himself. In his articles of service he had requested a virtual *carte blanche* in either Gascony or other parts of France, to lead his army where he 'shall thinke beste and most necessarie after his own conceite' with the intention of the 'destruction of our said souvrain lords ennemyes And ye recouvrement of his inheritance'. The power and authority he wished was declared in a minute attached to the articles.[53] This no longer survives but was probably referred to in an important insertion made at the foot of the draft of the terms of indenture. While the terms were in English, the insertion was in French and was signed by Somerset. It clearly refers to a separate document kept with this copy, probably some form of commission of service; it reads:

Avons baillie la charge et gouvernement de notre Arme et lui avons donne tout pour le bien de notre Reaume de France et de notre duchie de Normandie et de Guyenne pour aler et mener notre dit Armee en notre dit Reaume de France et duchie de Normandie es pais occupies et tenez par notre adversaire et lui faire guerre et pour Reduire et mettre en notre obeissans la plus diceulx pars qu'il pourra y les moions qu'ils mieulx verra estre a faire pour notre honeur et bien En lui donnais et ottroions plain pouvoir et auctorite et mandement especiall par ces patentes pour pugnire et corriger toux ceulx tout de notre dit Arme et despais qu'il Reduira en notre obeissance qu'il trouva delinquence en Aucun manere selon l'exigence de leur cas en selon sa discretion Et mesmements de leur en faire grace.[54]

These wide-ranging powers were amplified in the final commission of service that was enrolled on 4 June. This gave Somerset his important military and civil authority over newly captured towns, the assembly of estates-general, administrative and clerical appointments, and the raising of further taxes. Copies were sent to administrators in Gascony and Normandy.[55]

It was apparent that Somerset himself did not regard the needs of Gascony as the main military priority. He wished to ship 'at ye narowesse sea' for fear of storms or delay on the 'brode sea'. Thus, the port of embarkation was fixed for Portsmouth, an indication that a crossing to Cherbourg was likely. It was from Normandy that Beaufort was proposing a new offensive, requesting a 'suffisante puissance of men' to go against his adversary. In the margin it was noted: 'the kyng and he have been accorded of ye nombre of ye armee'.[56] A large aristocratic contingent was hoped for, though there was some uncertainty as to how many would actually join: 'as many as he may gete unto the nombre or undre of four barons, eight bannerets and thirty knights'. A later provision established that no charge would be made for any difference between the numbers specified above and those who actually mustered, merely that the second quarter's wages would be altered accordingly. This hope for a substantial army was reflected in the discussion over the number of men-at-arms needed. A note on the draft of the indenture revealed that Somerset had originally proposed a figure of 1,000 or even more, 'trustyng rather to have hade greater nombre thannes lesse such ye necessitee of help daily increaseth', though he left the final number to the decision of king and council. By 8 April, 800 had been decided upon. This again was a sign of the considerable force that was felt necessary for the new campaign, comparable with York's own army two years earlier.[57]

Somerset had gained an unusual degree of personal discretion in the arrangements for a large provision of ordnance. Several of his articles referred to this. He was allowed to appoint as many men as he wished for either construction or maintenance at the crown's expense. Items of equipment that Somerset himself had requested included twenty carts of 'ribauldequins', a 'newe ordonnance', and, significantly, a bridge of barrels 'that hath be desired for him maad and carried with him at ye kyng's cost to passe ye Ryvers with that he shal fynde in his way', suggesting an intended crossing of the Loire or its tributaries.[58]

On several occasions Somerset referred to the urgency of providing help, '. . . ye grete distresse, perill and danger that ye saide Reaume and Duchie standeth isne', adding 'it was never so greet need to doubte as it is now'. This was his justification for a landing in Normandy instead of at Bordeaux. The longer crossing would take too long. A new offensive was needed urgently. With this in mind it seems that Somerset himself altered on the draft of the indenture the date of the muster from 17 June to 'withinne two months'. However, when the indenture was finally sealed the original date had been kept to. At the beginning of May he again requested an earlier date, 3 June, provided the necessary shipping could be made ready in time.[59]

The major political consideration that arose from this was the implicit challenge to York's authority as lieutenant-general. Somerset had insisted that his own articles of service be enrolled under the great seal of England. He wished York's 'contentment and goodwill', seeing that his own new power 'that he should have in his voiage myght be vallable nor effectual considered that my said lord of York hath ye God power before of all ye saide Reaume and Duchie'.[60] Somerset needed the king's sanction for York to accept the terms of commission. If he was able to take his army where he wished it was clearly necessary for York to be told what the expedition intended to do.

The king undertook to write to York, and this letter, presumably under the royal signet, delivered by the garter-at-arms, informed him '. . . it is seemed ful behoveful and necessaire that the maner and conduit of the werre be chaunged'. The letter continued with the assurance that Somerset's army, which would be crossing York's own area of jurisdiction, '. . . shal passe the sea by a part of Normandie (and so passe) over the water of the Leyre into ground occupied by the ennemyes and therre use most cruel and mortel werre.'[61] Thus, the expedition, by forming 'a shelde' to York, was intended to divert the attention of the French by striking across the Loire. The wording of this letter suggests the English were fearing a new French offensive from Anjou, as well as the possibility of an attack on Rouen. The retaining of Somerset with a new army while York remained in Normandy must have seemed the best solution. All this may well have caused York considerable concern. The official enrolment of Beaufort's commission for a year's term of service referred to his power in . . . *notre Reaume de France es parti en notre trescher et tresame cousin le duc de York actuellement n'exerce le pouvoir a lui depar nous donner.* But significantly Somerset had only agreed to serve on condition that his own authority was final, stating that he should not be commanded 'neither in this Reaume nor beyonde ye sea' to take on any enterprise against 'his own will and entent'.[62]

Because of the importance of the expedition and the high command Beaufort held, he could expect important marks of royal favour. Some of the gains he made are well known. For the better obedience of the king's subjects and to instill fear into his enemies, Henry granted his request 'to exhalte ye saide Erle into ye estate of Duc'. In an important article of service Somerset had wished this promotion to be approved before the indenture was sealed. This was officially confirmed in the council meeting of 30 March, when he was given precedence over the duke of Norfolk. His investiture took place at Windsor on St. George's Day.[63] The important link between the new duke's conditions of service and his creation may have reflected a desire for parity with York's position.

Along with this promotion, 'for to maintain that estate withalle', Somerset requested a certain livelihood declared in a bill attached. This has been lost, but from the account of the same council meeting on 30 March it seems likely that it was for lands of an annual value of 1,000 marks. The king agreed to 600 marks' worth. The acquisition of such an estate was of great importance to Beaufort. At his only recorded attendances at the council, on 28 May and 21 June, he chose from the king's livelihood the earldom of Kendal, which had come into the crown's hands on the death of Bedford in 1435.[64]

The expedition marked a new dispersal of royal authority in France. One of Somerset's articles made reference to an agreement to appoint him governor of Anjou and Maine when his brother's own term of office expired. Edmund Beaufort, now himself created earl of Dorset, had been captain and governor there since 1438; he was appointed early in that year, before he led the relief army from England on a campaign into Maine.[65] In this case the new arrangement would have taken effect from early in 1445. Of great importance was Somerset's wish that Dorset's original grant, which had been authorised under the seal of France, should now be held under the seal of England. Instead of holding an office, as had previously been the case, subordinate to York's authority as lieutenant-governor, Edmund would now have control of this area in his own right. Henry agreed to this: York was informed in the same signet letter of this re-definition of his authority.[66] This was the key to the new expedition: both Beaufort brothers now held commands in France that allowed them to exercise their own discretion both in military and political matters independent of the government in Normandy.

Somerset was concerned over his landed position in France. He had petitioned the king in respect of the grant of St. Sauveur Lendelin, which was unable to yield an annual rent of 3,000 *saluts d'or*. Henry and his council agreed to his request to hold the title and right to the appanage in the same manner as had the duke of Orléans, its original owner, unless another grant of similar value was made. This provision was perhaps a precaution against any land settlements that might be made in a truce.[67]

In addition, Somerset had wished for a grant of 'ye countee of Alençon to have holde and in alle wise and manyers to rejoyce it as he that hath called himself Erle thereof had it. Notwithstanding that it be of ye kynge's ancien demaine or appliqued thereto'. The reference to 'he that hath called himself Erle' almost certainly was to the duke of Alençon, whose widespread estates in southern Normandy and Maine had remained unalienated since the death of Bedford. This was the last major body of land at the disposal of the crown in France. The particular article concludes with a reservation that 'yif a good pease finally be maade And it like ouresaide souvrain lorde to give him . . . ye said Countee agayne be it in name of Duchee or Countee Oure said souvrain lorde in that case to so do therewith as shall please him best'. This possibility of a restitution of lands to Alençon is interesting in that it indicates Henry was already considering territorial concessions in order to obtain a peace. In the margin, instead of the usual 'it is graunted' was the rather more ambiguous comment, 'My saide lorde knoweth hereinne ye kynge's answer'.[68] Since there is no record of such a territorial grant being made one must assume that Henry intended to keep these lands for his own purposes.

As far as the expedition itself was concerned, the king had allowed the revocation of his own customary right to possession of conquered territory. The draft of the indenture contained the clause that as principal captain Somerset 'shal have and dispose al such contrees landes townes castelles fortesses and places as he shal gete within ye saide reaume and Duchie or elles where which he shal reduce into ye kynge's obeissance our said souvrain lord out of his ennemis hand. And applique hem to himself and his herres . . .'[69] The king had also, on Beaufort's request, revoked his rights to war profits, the thirds and thirds of thirds. According to Somerset, this was to cover such extra costs as the employment of spies, guides and messengers. If the campaign went well he could hope to profit from this rebate, which included plunder and prisoners' ransoms.

All this was given preferential treatment at the treasury. The wages for the first six months were paid in advance; the remainder was to be paid on the basis of monthly musters in France.[70] Payment for transport and shipping of the army and the construction and carriage of the ordnance received priority at the exchequer. This large outlay was at the expense of York's own annual salary, as well as any large-scale assistance for Normandy.

These negotiations over the terms of service ended in a final acceptance by king and council early in April. As well as delegating considerable responsibility for the new offensive to Somerset, they offered the possibility of further gains if the expedition was successful. As such they marked a change in the direction of the war effort. Neither of the Beauforts had served in France since York's arrival as lieutenant-general in 1441. Clearly John was only prepared to lead an expedition if a new area of authority were created for him that would allow him to use the army in the way he himself saw fit.

During May we find Somerset attending to his own affairs before the start of the expedition. His bastard daughter Tacyn was made a denizen, which suggests he was planning to leave property or goods to her. Meanwhile, orders were being issued along the south and east coasts for shipping to be arrested and to rendezvous at Camber.[71] The train of ordnance was being assembled in London. John Dawson, the duke's master of ordnance, and a team of men under him were busy throughout May working on what seems to have been a particularly substantial supply and artillery train, including a large number of culverins. Preparations were noted by contemporaries: a 'grete ordinaunce of gones, Brigges, and scalyng ladderis and many more other thinges'.[72]

Unfortunately, problems were developing with the recruitment of the army. At the end of May Somerset requested a reduction in the number of men-at-arms for which he was contracted, to be replaced by bowmen due to a 'lakke of barons, bannerets and knights'. Men of rank had refused to join; by July there was only one banneret, Sir Thomas Kyriel, and six knights.[73] The circumstances of this lack of interest remain mysterious: who, for example, were the four barons who had been anticipated? Perhaps the new purpose of the expedition was distrusted by some of the nobility. Of the captains that had joined, some, like James Standish, had connections with Somerset's brother Edmund. Others had served with Talbot's force a year earlier.[74]

Something seems to have gone badly wrong with Somerset's own preparations. Instead of his original intention to move the muster date forward, he was forced to seek a postponement. A new date, 3 July, was agreed upon. When the musters were taken they revealed many cases of fraud and malpractice by his captains. Beaufort himself claimed that the musters had been taken 'in divers places whereinne both he and his captains were disseived'. Faced with new delays, the king's relations with Somerset began to sour. In a detailed communication to the duke, Henry reminded him that he 'shall fulfill the tenure of the said endenture'. After mentioning the charges against some of his captains, he pointed to the lavish grants he had received, '. . . more largely than he hath do to any man in cas semblable in his dayes', adding, '. . . he merveilleth gretely and noght withoute cause the long abood of his saide cousin on this side of the see and the grete and long delays of his passage to the Kynge's ful gret hurte . . .'[75]

These complaints may well have been brought to Henry's attention by the council; Adam Moleyns had been one of the musterers. But the information could also have come from a number of Henry's own household who were serving on the commission.[76] A firm command that, 'alle excusacons cessing', the duke assemble his forces on 17 July, saw the musters finally taken near Portsmouth.[77] The delays had meant new expenses for keeping ready the large amount of shipping which had been waiting near Portsmouth since June.[78] The second quarter's wages had been paid out on 6 July for a force of one banneret, six knights, 592 men-at-arms and 3,949 archers. The whole amount was not paid: a further £800 was paid to Somerset's servant Thomas Gerard on 26 July, just before the expedition finally set sail. Whether this was due to a shortage of money or to some irregularity concerning the musters we cannot tell. But early in August the council ordered royal officials to take the musters again when the troops landed in Normandy.[79] Thus, Somerset's expedition was already under a cloud before it left for France. As one chronicler remarked, he 'moustred at Portesmouth diverse tymes and might not have redy passage which was grevous to ye contree'.[80] These circumstances assured that the conduct of the campaign would be regarded critically from England.

Attempts to reconstruct the campaign depend largely on chronicle sources. Some important documents survive, though these are for the most part limited to events of concern to Normandy itself. A wide variety of chroniclers can be made use of, English, French, Breton and Burgundian.[81] Some clearly had little idea of what was going on;[82] comparison with others reveals contradictions in chronology, and details left out or added. Although some points can be substantiated, there are certain times during the course of the expedition when we cannot really be sure what was happening.

By 12 August the army had finally reached Cherbourg. Somerset's first action was to levy a 'charroy', a transport tax, in the Cotentin. This again is an indication of the size of his artillery and supply train. Robert Byote, the *vicomte* of Coutances, and other local officials were instructed to bring the proceeds from the parishes, payable in money or practical help, to John Dawson, Somerset's master of ordnance. Some carts and their drivers were sent to Cherbourg to meet the army; others mustered in towns further south.[83] Much detail on this tax survives because of a royal inquiry some two years later, by which time the English government's attitude to the expedition was pretty bleak. A letter to the Norman treasurer in December 1445, on the occasion of the grant to the new queen of all Somerset's outstanding debts, accused him of having extorted this money; the cash for his ordnance, it was claimed, had been fully provided already. The reality is less clear. Somerset, in his articles of service, had been granted the carriage of his ordnance at the crown's expense. The exchequer, however, had provided payment to Cherbourg but no further. The duke himself clearly felt justified in seeking an aid for the transport of his army as it marched towards enemy territory.[84] Some carters were retained for a few days; other seem to have accompanied the army for several months. Further assessments were carried out in the *comtés* of Avranches and Mortain as the troops moved southwards. At some stage it seems that the army was joined by Beaufort's brother Dorset, governor of Anjou and Maine, and the captain Mathew Gough. Gough, who had had much experience of warfare in Maine, had served under Somerset during the siege of Harfleur three years earlier. Perhaps, too, Somerset took reinforcements from his garrisons at Avranches and Tombelaine.[85]

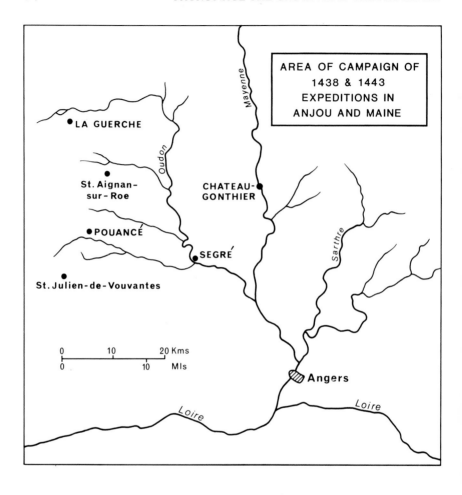

The sequence of events as the army moved into enemy territory becomes far less clear. The generally accepted version, outlined by the chroniclers Basin, Berry and, to a certain extent, Waurin, is that the army, moving down the marches of Brittany and Maine, first captured the Breton town of La Guerche and then laid siege to Pouancé in northern Anjou. A force was despatched to defeat an assembling relief army (mentioned by all the chroniclers except Basin), but after remaining outside the town for around two months Somerset raised the siege and marched back north. However, the much fuller detail provided by the Breton sources presents a rather different picture. Somerset and his troops marched through Maine and Anjou laying waste to the countryside up to the very walls of Angers itself. The army's captains lodged in the nearby abbey of St. Nicholas of Angers. The English then swung northwards through Segré and encamped outside Pouancé.[86] It was at this stage that Somerset had intelligence of a French relief force assembling at Chateau-Gonthier. A strong detachment under Mathew Gough routed the French troops in a surprise attack and a number of prisoners were taken.[87] After staying outside Pouancé for between two and three weeks while many of his soldiers dispersed, plundering the surrounding countryside, Somerset then moved on to La Guerche, a few miles away in the Breton marches.[88]

The closely related accounts of the Bretons Le Baud and D'Argentré provide some valuable detail on this episode. Although just inside Brittany, La Guerche belonged to the French duke of Alençon as part of the seigneurie of Beaumont. As such it was held as a fief from the Breton dukes.[89] Its undeniably partisan status had caused problems in the past. In 1432 Jean V had had to make a special agreement with the captain of the town, one of Alençon's men, to prevent breaches of the truce with the English. It had remained a base for raiding French troops and, significantly, Edmund Beaufort had launched an attack on it during his campaign in Maine in 1438.[90] Upon the arrival of Somerset's army the inhabitants decided to surrender; the place was occupied and all those of pro-French sympathy were arrested.[91]

According to the Breton chroniclers, Somerset justified his action by claiming that the truce had lapsed and that the town belonged to the duke of Alençon. The truce referred to had been negotiated with the previous duke, Jean V, in June 1440 by Somerset himself as the king's representative in France. One of the clauses concerned a Breton agreement not to shelter any enemies of the English.[92] Negotiations between the new duke, Francis II, and Somerset ended with Francis buying the English out of the town upon payment of an indemnity of 20,000 *saluts d'or*. Fortunately the quittance for this survives. It is dated 16 October and is on receipt of 10,000 *saluts* paid by Francis's treasurer, with an obligation for the other 10,000 after Christmas. In return, Somerset agreed to a prolongation of the truce.[93]

This incident undoubtedly discredited Somerset in the eyes of both the king and his council. The Breton ambassadors, in the process of discussing a renewal of the truce, protested about the conduct of the English army, *exploiz de guerre moult creux et enormes*. The council, after discussing these complaints, referred them to the king. Henry, who had taken a personal interest in maintaining good relations with Francis's brother Gilles, one of the principal ambassadors, must have been shaken by the affair. A letter was dispatched to Beaufort ordering him to make restitution for any damage done and to refrain from such activities in the future.[94]

We cannot be sure what Somerset's intentions had been. According to French accounts, his troops had pillaged the town. But the Breton chroniclers, who describe the incident in much greater detail, make no mention of plunder. There remains the possibility that to a commander in the field, faced with the uncertain situation in the Breton marches, the action seemed militarily justified. The council, already critical of Somerset's management of his army, took it ill; on his return to England the duke was accused of treachery.[95]

For most chronicle accounts this marked the end of the campaign. We know, however, from the fuller version of the Burgundian chronicler Waurin, and from surviving manuscript evidence, that the army remained in the field until late December. It is Waurin who refers to the expedition's last important action, the capture of Beaumont-le-Vicomte in Maine. It seems likely that by early December Somerset had returned to western Normandy to gather reinforcements.[96]

By this stage of the war the English position in Maine was extremely precarious. The French occupation of the fortress of Beaumont-le-Vicomte, which commanded the main road from Alençon to Le Mans, both of which were Edmund Beaufort's captaincies, was a considerable nuisance to the English position. Several surviving documents indicate that the capture of this town was seen as an important military operation. Somerset was clearly expecting a French relief force to arrive. Further modest reinforcements were taken from the garrison of Fresnay and another force under Sir Richard Harrington was raised in Normandy to join the army in Maine.[97]

In the event, no French army appeared and the garrison of the fortress agreed to surrender. After bringing the surrounding area back into English obedience and reinforcing the frontier garrisons, Somerset returned to Normandy. By now the six months of service were up, but no further money was made available, and by the beginning of January, he seems to have disbanded his army and returned to England.[98] It is possible that any further funding of the army was at the discretion of the Norman treasury, under York's jurisdiction.

From a number of chronicles, both French and English, it is clear that Somerset faced a very hostile reception on his return to England. It was felt that he had done little of use; the king himself was angered and may well have banished him from court.[99] More than this we do not know, as no formal charges were brought against him.[100] We know little about the remainder of his life. In March he seems to have been engaged in the final negotiations concerning the release of his captive, John, count of Angoulême.[101] According to Basin, he succumbed to illness; he died on 27

May at Wimborne in Dorset.[102] The duke's death, so soon after his disgrace, even gave rise (according to the Croyland chronicler) to rumours that he had hastened his own end rather than live out a life in banishment.[103] But the nature of this illness, and how much it might have affected his prosecution of his last campaign, remain an open question.

In an age very aware of dramatic falls from fortune, Somerset's disappointing expedition, his disgrace and subsequent death, all so soon after his investiture as duke, seem to have had a mysterious fascination for contemporaries.[104] Even now it is difficult to unravel what went wrong. Beaufort's insistence on a command resting completely on his own terms and authority rebounded badly on him. But about the campaign itself much uncertainty remains. Was Somerset's own conduct at fault, or were the English being unrealistic in expecting a major success to be achieved at this stage of the war? This chevauchée had after all waged 'cruel and mortel werre' in enemy territory; the new offensive under Charles VII that the army was supposed to counter had never materialised.

Again, one would like to know more about the atmosphere of political uncertainty that surrounded the expedition. Somerset was only willing to serve in France if a new area of command were created for him. There is no evidence that this command was used in an attempt deliberately to undermine York's authority. Even so the circumstances of the campaign may well have worsened relations between the Beauforts and York and his followers in Normandy. The hostile account of the chronicler Thomas Basin made great play of the secrecy of the campaign, criticising Somerset for not co-operating more with the captains at Rouen. Clearly he must have got this from somewhere; it might reflect resentment felt in Normandy about the new army's independent field of operations. If so, this would form an unhappy prelude to the recrimination following the final military collapse in 1449-50.

I am grateful to Professor Charles Ross and Mr. James Sherborne for their criticism of earlier drafts of this paper; to Miss A. Curry for her advice on the French archives and to Miss M. Condon for her help on PRO material; also to Dr. Christopher Allmand, Andrew Baume and others for suggestions and advice.

NOTES

1. *The Paston Letters*, ed. J. Gairdner (1904), I, lxxvii.
2. His commission as lieutenant- and captain-general of Aquitaine and France 'in the parts where the duke of York does not exercise the power committed to him' was enrolled 4 June 1443: PRO, C76/121/1.
3. Dieppe was relieved by the dauphin in August 1443; Granville was also reinforced despite English efforts. E. Cosneau, *Le Connétable de Richemont* (Paris, 1886), pp. 343-45.
4. Thomas Basin, *Histoire des règnes de Charles VII et Louis XI*, ed. C. Samaran (Paris, 1933), pp. 280-85.
5. *CP*, XII, pt. 1, p.45.
6. By 6 July 1443 John Beaufort had been paid £25,488 for the first two quarters' wages. Another £800 was paid out for the second quarter on 26 July, making a total of £26,288. On 6 July £2,634 was paid out for shipping: PRO, E403/748 m.l8; /749 m.11,20. Between May and July nearly £2,000 was spent on equipment; jewels were pledged for some of this; PRO, E403/749 m.6-12; E101/335/30.
7. Somerset's creation acknowledged his nearness of blood as well as the services he was about to perform: *PPC*, V, 252-53. Creation took place in three stages: an oral or written confirmation by the king, the act of investiture and the issue of the charter. I have chosen to take the date of Somerset's promotion as 30 March 1443 when his rank was confirmed by king and council. This was a response to Somerset's own petition to be made duke before his terms of indenture were sealed: PRO, C47/26/28, art. 14.
8. PRO, E404/28/298; *CChR*, VI, 34. Edmund had also been made knight of the garter by May 1436: *CP*, XII, pt. 1, p.50.
9. He had received Harcourt by January 1436: AN, Collection Dom Lenoir 104 mi 14, f.75. He was appointed governor of Anjou and Maine in March 1438: BL, Add. MSS. 11542 f.90.
10. *PPC*, V, 226.
11. The Latin *Brut* in C.L. Kingsford, *English Historical Literature in the Fifteenth Century* (Oxford, 1913), p.320. There is no evidence that Edmund was at the battle.
12. Dupont-Ferrier, *La Captivité de Jean d'Orléans* (Paris, 1896), p.5; BL, Add. Ch. 306; AN, K168 f.92.
13. *PPC*, III, 225; PRO, C30/9/14; C49/17/2. Bourbon was unable to raise sureties for the Beauforts' ransoms and died in captivity.
14. PRO, SC8/141/7018; SC8/188/9354. This policy of the council would be following the instructions of Henry V's will which forbade the release of either Orléans or Eu until Henry VI came of age.
15. K.B. McFarlane, in *Cambridge Medieval History*, VIII, 398.
16. *CCR, 1429-35*, p.331.
17. For 12,000 marks, 6,000 to be paid immediately by Somerset's attorneys, the other 6,000 to be held against his inheritance: PRO, E404/56/329.
18. T. Rymer (ed.), *Foedera, conventiones, litterae . . .* (20 vols., 1727-35), X, 664, 697.
19. *CPR, 1436-41*, p. 515; *PPC*, V, 112-13. These were the sums specifically paid for his release. The total of £24,000 must have included all the additional expenses of his captivity, which would have been considerable.
20. Anne Marshall, 'The role of English War Captains in England and Normandy, 1436-49' (Wales M.A. thesis, 1975), pp.208, 215. K.B. McFarlane, 'At the death-bed of Cardinal Beaufort', in *Essays in medieval history presented to F.M. Powicke* (Oxford, 1948), p.424; *CFR, 1422-30*, pp.176-77.
21. H.L. Gray, 'Incomes from land in England in 1436', *EHR*, XLIX (1934), 615.
22. For repayment of sums due to Somerset's attorneys, see PRO, E404/51/304.

23. *RP*, IV, 440; R. Somerville, *The Duchy of Lancaster* (London, 1953), p.647.
24. Clarence had left the sum for which Angoulême stood as surety to his wife Margaret, and on her death to her son Henry (Beaufort) and his heirs male.
25. Dupont-Ferrier, op.cit., pp.2-3.
26. A.N., P1403 xxxii; Dupont-Ferrier, op. cit., p.25.
27. Ibid., p.26. By the 1440s the rate of exchange was about 9 *livres tournois* to the English pound. The *salut d'or* was worth 30 *sous tournois*.
28. For the Duchess Margaret's attempts to recover some of her husband's pledged jewels after his death, see PRO, C1/24/230. For a loan from Margaret, countess of Devon, *RP*, V, 22.
29. *PPC*, V, 112-13.
30. PRO, E404/42/165; *PPC*, V, 112-13; PRO, 404/56/154.
31. PRO, C47/26/28 art. 18; E404/59/157.
32. *CP*, XII, pt. 1, p.48.
33. *CPR, 1436-41.* p.515. Before the expedition sailed he was making arrangements for the drawing up of his will: *PPC*, V, 225.
34. BL, Add. Ch. 3878; Add. MSS. 11542 f.78.
35. Somerset was styled captain of Avranches and Tombelaine in June 1439: BN, pièces originales, 65 f.22. He received Cherbourg from Henry Norbury by July 1439: BN, Clairambault 186/7. By 1440 he also held Falaise.
36. On 13 December 1439 Somerset indentured to serve in France for six months with 4 knights, 100 men-at-arms and 2,000 archers. £5,271 was paid out for the first quarter's wages, another £5,152 was paid after the army had mustered at Poole in February 1440, consisting of 3 knights, 97 men-at-arms and 1,980 archers. Shipping and ordnance were being prepared throughout January: PRO, E404/56/155; E403/736 m. 10-18.
37. J. Waurin, *Receuil des Croniques*, V (RS, 1884), 266-73; AN, K65/1/19.
38. For the powers held by Somerset, see BL, Add. MSS. 11542 f.81, discussed in E.M. Burney, 'The English Rule in Normandy, 1435-50' (Oxford B. Litt. thesis, 1958), pp.132-33. York was appointed on 20 July 1440: ibid., f.79.
39. AN, Collection Dom Lenoir 104 mi 26, no.27024.
40. Edmund Beaufort was given command with a force of 500 men-at-arms and 1,500 archers, to be supplemented by further troops. Somerset had a subsidiary force of 100 men-at-arms and 300 archers: AN K66/1/26. His original term of indenture expired in August; the troops that were in the field with him in August and September consisted of 400 men-at-arms and an unspecified number of archers. Somerset was back in Rouen by 24 September. More troops and artillery were brought up to Harfleur by October: AN, Collection Dom Lenoir 104 mi 27, no. 27311; K66/1/54
41. *CP*, XII, pt. 1, p.47.
42. E.g., a quittance for 300 *l.t.* for wages as captain of Falaise in May 1442: BN, nouvelles acquisitions françaises 7628 p.535.
43. *PPC*, V, 218.
44. Ibid., pp.223, 226-27.
45. Ibid., p.240.
46. McFarlane, 'At the death-bed of Cardinal Beaufort', p.424.
47. 'The Personal Rule of Henry VI, in *Fifteenth-century England, 1399-1509*, ed. S.B. Chrimes, C.D. Ross and R.A. Griffiths (Manchester, 1972), p.46; *PPC*, V, 251-56.
48. *PPC*, V, 234; PRO, E404/59/157.
49. PRO, C47/26/28; ibid., art. 9.
50. PRO, E101/71/4/916.
51. Ibid.
52. *PPC*, V, 260.

53. PRO, C47/26/28 art. 11, 8.
54. PRO, E101/71/4/916.
55. PRO, C76/125/1.
56. PRO, C47/26/28 art. 7, 5; E404/59/163.
57. The actual number recorded on the issue roll was 758 men-at-arms: PRO, E403/748 m.18. York's force in 1441 consisted of 2 earls, 4 barons, 6 bannerets, 30 knights, 900 men-at-arms, 2,700 archers: PRO, E 404/57/130.
58. PRO, C47/26/28 art. 8.
59. Ibid., art. 5; E101/71/4/916; E404/59/163; PPC, V, 267.
60. PRO, C47/26/28 art. 23, 4.
61. PPC, V, 260.
62. PRO, C76/125/1; C47/26/28 art. 11.
63. Ibid., art. 14; G.L. and M.A. Harriss (eds.), 'John Benet's chronicle for the years 1400 to 1462', in Camden Miscellany, XXIV (1972), p.189; J.S. Davies (ed.), An English Chronicle, 1377-1461 (Camden Society, LXIV, 1855), p.60.
64. PRO C47/26/28 art. 14; PPC, V, 253. He was created earl of Kendal on 28 August 1443: CChR, VI, 37.
65. BL, Add. MSS. 11542 f.90. Edmund Beaufort's commission, as captain-general and governor, was under the seal of France, dated 22 March 1438. He was to take a new army to Maine two months later.
66. PRO, C47/26/28 art. 22; PPC, V, 259-63.
67. This grant is filed in PRO, E28/73.
68. PRO, C47/26/28 art. 15.
69. PRO, E101/71/4/916.
70. PRO, E404/59/163.
71. PPC, V, 237, 277.
72. N.H. Nicolas and E. Tyrrell (eds.), Chronicle of London (1827), p.151.
73. PRO, E101/54/5.
74. For a sub-contract of Standish's, recruiting men in Lancs., see HMC, 10th Report, Appendix IV (1885), p.227; Marshall, op.cit., pp.133-40, provides a detailed analysis of the composition of the army based on the muster roll of 17 July. Experienced professional captains included Kyriel and Sir Robert Vere, who both had large retinues.
75. PPC, V, 304, 409-14.
76. CPR, 1441-46, p.201. Members of Henry's household who were serving as commissioners included John Vavasour, John Yerde and John Debington: PRO, E403/749 m.12.
77. PRO, E101/54/5. Musters were taken at Portsdown and Calgmore (Southampton).
78. The accounts of John Hexham (PRO, E101/54/4) reveal that some ships were in service from the end of May. On 18 June another £1,000 had be⌐ ⌐ower from Cardinal Beaufort for payment of shipping: E404/59/277.
79. PRO, E403/749 m. 12. 20; CPR, 1441-46, p.202.
80. 'Bale's Chronicle' in Six Town Chronicles, ed. R. Flenley (Oxford, 1911), p.116.
81. Waurin, op.cit., pp.375-77; Basin, op.cit., pp.280-85; G. Gruel, Histoire d' Arthur III duc de Bretagne, comte de Richemont (Paris, 1837), pp.181-82; Berry, 'Histoire Chronologique de Charles VII', in Histoire de Charles VII, ed. D. Godefroy (Paris, 1653) p.424; P. le Baud, Histoire de Bretagne, ed. d' Hozier (Paris, 1638), pp. 490-91; B.D'Argentré, Histoire de Bretagne (1618), p.627.
82. Some English chroniclers thought most of Somerset's troops had been slain when he returned after disbanding his army: e.g. 'A Short English Chronicle', in Three Fifteenth Century Chronicles, ed. J. Gairdner (Camden Soc., XXVIII, 1880), p.64; 'Gregory's Chronicle' in The Historical Collections of a London Citizen, ed. J. Gairdner (Camden Soc., XVII, 1876), p.185.

83. Byote was excused from the Norman estates meeting in August and September *comme retenue par le duc de Sommerset*: J. Felix, *Inventaire de Pierre Surreau* (Rouen, 1892), p.93; AN, K68/19 f. 49, 67, 73.
84. The inquiry revealed that a sum of 5,210 *l.t.* had been collected: AN, Collection Dom Lenoir 104 mi 9, f.286; *PPC*, V, 257; PRO, C47/26/28 art. 6; Burney, op. cit., pp. 206–10.
85. Gruel, loc. cit., describes the chief commanders of the army as Somerset, Dorset and Gough. D'Argentré and Le Baud, loc. cit., also mention Dorset and Gough. The presence of Edmund Beaufort (created earl of Dorset in August 1442, though his rank had been confirmed by the king as long ago as 1438) is significant. For Gough serving under Somerset in 1440, see J. Stevenson (ed.), *Letters and Papers Illustrative of the Wars of the English in France* (RS, 1864), II pt. 2, p.314.
86. Printed in S.Luce, *Chronique du Mont-Saint-Michel*, II (Paris, 1883), extracts from *pièces diverses*, pp.157–60. Reference was made to Pouancé in the instructions to local officials concerning the *charroy*.
87. Gruel, loc. cit.; Le Baud, loc. cit.; D'Argentré, loc. cit. In March 1444 Louis de Beuil, one of the French prisoners, was given a safe-conduct to Cherbourg on matters concerning his ransom: *Rymer*, XI, 17.
88. Berry, loc. cit., says Somerset was outside Pouancé for about two months; Gruel, loc. cit., places it at about three weeks. There is a major division over the sequence of events. Waurin and the French chroniclers cite the attack on La Guerche as the army was on its way down to Pouancé. However, the Breton chroniclers, Gruel, Le Baud and D'Argentré, loc. cit., who go into considerably more detail about the capture, place it after Somerset had left Pouancé. I have chosen to follow the Breton order of events since the one piece of documentary evidence, a quittance from Somerset concerning the surrender of La Guerche (Arch. Dép. du Loire-Atlantique, E122/48/18), is dated 16 October, which seems to fit the latter account.
89. Ogee, *Dictionnaire de Bretagne* (Rennes, 1843), I, 420.
90. Berry, op.cit., pp.400, 404; C.L. Kingsford (ed.), *Chronicles of London* (Oxford, 1905), p.145. The course of Edmund Beaufort's campaign in Maine in 1438 is similar to the 1443 expedition. It may have been Edmund himself who suggested the attack on La Guerche.
91. D'Argentré, loc.cit.; Le Baud, loc.cit.
92. *Rymer*, X, 803.
93. Archives Départmentales du Loire-Atlantique E 122/48/18. It seems unlikely that the other 10,000 *saluts* were ever paid. By December the English government had renounced Somerset's actions. See A. Bourdeaut, 'Gilles de Bretagne entre la France et l'Angleterre', in *Mémoirés de la société d'histoire et d'archéologie de Bretagne*, I (1920), 59–61.
94. *PPC*, VI, 12–13, 17–18, 22–23.
95. *Continuation of the History of Croyland*, trans. H.T. Riley (1854), p.399.
96. Waurin, op.cit., p.377. Proclamations for garrison troops *vivans sur le pays* to join Somerset were being made in Caen and the Vire in early December: AN, K67/21/9, 10. Again Edmund Beaufort may have suggested this operation.
97. R. Triger, 'Le Chateau et la ville de Beaumont-le-Vicomte pendant l'invasion anglaise (1417-50)', *Revue Historique et Archéologique du Maine*, L (1901), 59–60; Stevenson, op.cit., II, i, 59–60. Harrington had previously served under Somerset as lieutenant of Falaise.
98. Waurin, loc.cit., Osbert Mundeford, Edmund Beaufort's captain at Le Mans, took over the captaincy at Beaumont: BN, MS. fr. 26074 no. 5295. Somerset was back in England around the beginning of January: 'Benet's Chronicle', p.189.

99. Ibid.; *Incerti scriptoris chronicon Angliae de regnis Henry IV, Henry V et Henry VI*, ed. J.A. Giles (1848), p.31; 'Brief Notes, 1440-3', in Kingsford, *English Historical Literature,* p.341. Basin and Berry also mention the duke's disgrace.

100. The letter to the Norman treasury two years later says: *il congedia son armee avant le temps et ne rendit rien.* Were the accounts not returned? No further reference survives. See AN, Collection Dom Lenoir 104 mi 9 f. 286.

101. A quittance signed by Somerset discharging Angoulême of some of his debt is dated 16 March 1444: BL, Add. Ch. 12211. Angoulême was then taken across the channel to France while Suffolk finalised arrangements for his release.

102. Basin, op.cit., p.284; *English Chronicle*, p.60.

103. *Continuation of Croyland*, p.399.

104. E.g., the poem 'On the mutability of worldy change', in Kingsford, *English Historical Literature*, p.396; or the prophecy in *Continuation of Croyland*.

5. Herefordshire, 1413-61: Some Aspects of Society and Public Order*

Ailsa Herbert
St Albans

The records of the court of king's bench are a bulky and extensive series of documents which illustrate several aspects of the nature of English government and society in the fifteenth century.[1] As the court's main concern was with serious crime which had been accompanied by violence, they highlight many disruptive influences and points of tension within society. They also indicate the degree of efficiency achieved in the punishment of criminals by one of the highest judicial institutions of the realm. As such, the records of this court present a valuable basis for regional studies during a period when concern was expressed at the fragility of public order and when society's bonds were being loosened during the approaches of civil war.[2]

Numerous instances of violent crime in Herefordshire during the reigns of Henry V and Henry VI are described in the records of king's bench and, supplemented by other sources, they provide material for a survey of the condition of public order in the county. Such an analysis must be limited in its scope for several reasons. First, although king's bench dealt with major breaches of the peace, much petty crime came within the jurisdiction of the justices of the peace or sheriffs, but their proceedings are rarely extant.[3] Secondly, while the plea rolls of king's bench are complete for the period 1413-61, many of its ancient indictments are missing.[4] Thirdly, some — perhaps many — crimes may not have been reported to the courts; the remoteness of Herefordshire from the centre of legal activity at Westminster may have been a significant factor in this respect. As a result, an apparent decline in the crime rate may really mask a period of increasing lawlessness and disrespect for judicial authority.[5] Conversely, an increase in litigation, particularly in privately-initiated lawsuits, may reflect hopes of justice and strong government.[6] Again, many lawsuits which appear in the plea rolls inadequately describe the nature or omit the date of the alleged offence. Finally, it is worth remembering that some private prosecutions may have been purely malicious in their intent.

Despite these limitations, some indication may be given of the incidence of crime in Herefordshire.[7] The early years of the reign of Henry V reveal little recorded crime in the county. Yet a petition in parliament in 1414 complained of thieving raids by Welshmen in the counties adjoining the Welsh Marches, while both neighbouring Shropshire and nearby Stafford-shire are known to have been particularly lawless at this time; it is possible that Herefordshire shared their disturbed condition but that few crimes were recorded.[8] Consequently, a higher incidence of crime in the years after 1417 may only demonstrate that the courts were now more widely respected and used by victims of crime and hence indicate the extension of royal authority in that area. A temporary sharp increase in the number of lawsuits in the early years of the reign of Henry VI suggests a higher crime rate, and a petition in parliament confirms that south Herefordshire was particularly disturbed at this time.[9] Yet a measure of expectation and hope in the new minority council may also be reflected in this increase. The years between 1430 and 1456 saw a continuous though gradual rise in the number of recorded crimes in Herefordshire. By 1438 the people of the area had acquired the reputation of a 'stubborn and fierce nature'.[10] The frequency and serious extent of raids by Welshmen into the county at this time is attested by a series of petitions in the parliaments of 1442, 1445 and 1449.[11] In 1452 and 1456 the city of Hereford was the scene of two major demonstrations by the associates of Sir Walter Devereux, the chief sup-porter of Richard, duke of York in the shire. The investigations into these incidents have brought to light a large number of offences perpetrated by this gang.[12] After 1456 recorded crime lessens. Yet these were years of sporadic fighting when two battles took place in Herefordshire.[13] A break-down in the administration of justice and the rule of force rather than the rule of law may therefore be indicated. When the commons in the Coventry parliament of 1459 named twenty-five of the most notorious disturbers of the peace in England, five Herefordshire gentlemen were included among them; this was the largest group from any one county.[14] The disturbed atmosphere of these last years of Henry VI's reign cannot be doubted, even if precise details are lacking. Herefordshire may not have been the most lawless area of England during the fifteenth century — this distinction was probably earned by the northern shires — but public order in this Welsh border county was never easily preserved, while in the years after 1450 major breaches of the peace with political implications posed serious challenges to the government's authority.[15]

Responsibility for the commission of crime was shared by all classes of society in Herefordshire: gentry, clerks (from dean to curate), trades-men, craftsmen, rural labourers, even a number of women were accused of offences. The rôle of the gentry may be considered of particular significance. As men of often considerable landed welath, they could exert influence over tenants and servants, while some exercised authority as the crown's local agents and others as the estate officials of magnates or the lesser nobility. Some illustrations of this group's interests and use of influence are afforded in the records of king's bench.

Many of Herefordshire's gentry called on the assistance of tenants and servants in the commission of crime and the pursuit of quarrels; feudal loyalties may still have been a vital social force. Thus, a murder in 1416 was allegedly committed by a gang led by William Walwayn and three of his gentry kinsmen; it included at least fifty-four labourers and tradesmen from their estates in Ledbury, south-east Herefordshire and the neighbouring areas of Gloucestershire and Worcestershire.[16] Feuds between neighbouring gentry might result in clashes between rival bands of tenants: a murderous affray at Kinnersley in west Herefordshire in 1433 was the culmination of a quarrel between the local landowner, Sir Richard De la Bere, and Henry Oldcastle of nearby Almeley.[17] A gentleman-led group could also effectively intimidate a complaining victim or his friends, particularly if they were of lower social status. Petitions to the chancellor allege many obstructed prosecutions in the common law courts.[18] John Abrahall allegedly murdered William ap Hywel in 1419 and then threatened Philip Maidstone, a surety in the widow's prosecution of Abrahall.[19] Even the dean and chapter of Hereford Cathedral were afraid to bring an action at law against Thomas De la Hay the younger and Henry ap Gruffydd, who had terrorised the tenants of church property at Madley and Canonbridge.[20]

With justices of the peace, sheriffs and coroners all drawn from their ranks, the gentry had considerable responsibilities in the maintenance of law and order. Yet a criminal record was no disqualification from service in local administration, as the careers of Thomas De la Hay, the elder, and his namesake son well illustrate. The father, who served as justice of the peace, sheriff, escheator and M.P. at various times between 1416 and 1440, faced a charge of mayhem; the son, despite accusations of rape, assault, mayhem, being an accessory to murder and causing a breach of the peace, was appointed sheriff of Herefordshire in 1426 and coroner in 1430.[21]

A number of magnates retained gentry from Herefordshire as their estate officials and councillors. Among them were Richard, duke of York, who held the largest complex of magnate estates in Herefordshire as well as the neighbouring marcher lordships of Wigmore, Clifford, Builth, Radnor, Ewyas Lacy and Maelienydd; John, Lord Talbot and Furnival, later earl of Shrewsbury, who had estates in south Herefordshire; and Humphrey, earl of Stafford and duke of Buckingham, the marcher lord of Huntington and Brecon.[22] Indeed, magnate-gentry connections were at the root of a number of major breaches of the peace. In some cases, the retainer acted on his lord's behalf; in 1452, for instance, Sir Walter

Devereux staged a demonstration in Hereford in support of Richard of York, and a second rising in 1456 may have been similarly contrived.[23] In another case, a quarrel between a magnate and his retainer led to serious disturbances. A petition in the parliament of 1423-24 complained of the extortions, oppressions, murders, evictions, abductions, thefts and other crimes in south Herefordshire which had acompanied the dispute between John, Lord Talbot and his former retainer, John Abrahall, each supported by his gang.[24] Abrahall would seem to have been particularly violent by nature, for he had already been cited in the courts of king's bench and chancery for a number of serious crimes.[25] His association with the Talbot family was already close in 1413 when he assisted John, then Lord Furnival, in a dispute with Thomas, earl of Arundel in Shropshire and by 1421 he had become the Talbots' receiver-general.[26] His dismissal from this post by Talbot preceded their quarrel; his fall from favour may have been precipitated by violent disputes with Thomas Barre, Talbot's brother-in-law, and Dafydd ap Rhys, another of Talbot's retainers.[27] But before his death in 1443 Abrahall had been reinstated in Talbot's favour and had become one of his councillors, while he had also secured the patronage of a second magnate, Humphrey, duke of Buckingham, whom he served from 1439 as steward of the marcher lordship of Brecon.[28] Despite earlier public service as escheator and M.P. for Hereford, Abrahall held no office in Herefordshire from the early 1420s until 1437, when he was appointed to a commission of the peace; further government service then follows.[29] His absence from office may be attributed to his loss of noble patronage, whilst his return may indicate a reconciliation with Talbot or a developing association with Buckingham. Abrahall's career illustrates well both the operation and importance of 'good lordship' and the disruption of an area which could be caused by a member of the gentry and his affinity.

The decade after 1450 witnessed a higher incidence of crime among the gentry of Herefordshire, in which the rôle of Sir Walter Devereux and his associates was of particular significance.[30] The Hereford demonstration of 1456 was staged by Devereux, his Welsh son-in-law, Sir William Herbert, a large band of gentry from the county and the Marches and some citizens.[31] Later that year, the same gang marched through south and west Wales and seized the castles at Carmarthen and Aberystwyth in support of York's claim to the constableship of both[32] Devereux's twenty associates from Herefordshire's gentry in these ventures had already been responsible for many other crimes in the county — five members of the Monnington family, for example, were accused of a long series of thefts — and it would seem that the Devereux-Herbert faction was the source of much serious crime in the county in this decade.[33] Instances of extortion and intimidation occur more frequently in these years, and there were attempts to interfere with the administration of justice.[34] In March 1456 a coroner's inquest and a session of the peace were forced by the Devereux-Herbert gang to declare that Walter Vaughan, a kinsman of Sir William Herbert, had been murdered by some of Hereford's tradesmen; after the justices had allowed the desired verdict, the intruders, who had already served as the jury, acted as executioners and hanged their victims.[35] In this way the Devereux-Herbert gang used the law in all its stages for their own purposes, and their activities suggest a serious disrespect for the law among at least some of the Herefordshire gentry.

The size of Devereux's following undoubtedly reflects his personal influence and political ability; it can also be partly explained by personal quarrels among the gentry themselves. Some of Devereux's associates had previously been engaged in feuds with supporters of the Court party in the shire, and this suggests that political divisions between gentry families arose in some cases from private disputes. Examples may be found in quarrels over property between the Lyngen family (Devereux men) and Thomas Fitzharry (attainted in 1461 for his Lancastrian activities) and in a similar dispute between Devereux himself and Thomas Cornwall (who was also attainted in 1461).[36] But it is also apparent that few of Devereux's supporters had previously served in the county's administration, though a number of them were to become trusted and regular government agents in the reign of Edward IV; it may be conjectured, therefore, that some gentry gave their support to Devereux because of their failure to gain office under the Lancastrian régime.[37] So the conflict between those who enjoyed power and position and those who did not may be reflected in distant Herefordshire.

While the gentry were answerable for their misdeeds in English courts of law, Welshmen who committed crimes in Herefordshire and the other English border counties lived beyond the common law's jurisdiction and presented a serious problem to successive régimes during the fifteenth century. Complaints of damage to property, theft and the abduction of Englishmen for ransom by Welsh raiders were frequent subjects of parliamentary petitions, while criminal associations between men from the marcher lordships and inhabitants of Herefordshire are commonly alleged in the records of king's bench. This co-operation between men from both sides of the border illustrates the contacts which could exist between English and Welsh in the marcher region; Celtic place-names and Welsh-named inhabitants both testify to the presence of Welsh influences in Herefordshire and show the hybrid ancestry of border society.[38]

The rôle of Welshmen in crime in Herefordshire may be seen as one expression of the unrest in the Marches during the fifteenth century. Welsh bitterness after the suppression of Owain Glyndŵr's rebellion found an outlet in lawlessness which was often directed against the inhabitants of neighbouring English shires; a petition in the parliament of 1414 bemoaned the extent of such Welsh raids.[39] By 1442 marcher disturbances had become the concern of the very highest authorities: the king ordered the marcher lords to curb riots in their own lordships and threatened that he would intervene if they did not do so.[40] But the problem remained and was exacerbated by the failure of absentee marcher lords to fulfil their judicial responsibilities through the increasingly frequent suspension of their great sessions in favour of a composition fine.[41]

Abduction and theft by Welshmen in the border counties were declared high treason in 1442 and 1449, and these may be presumed to be the offences which they most commonly committed.[42] The records of the court of king's bench and of the commissions of *oyer* and *terminer* of 1452 and 1457 suggest that cattle-stealing raids were particularly frequent. Wales was a breeding-ground for cattle for English markets; cattle-droving was in progress there during the fourteenth century, and in the early fifteenth Welsh cattle were used to feed soldiers in France.[43] Cattle stolen in the border counties may have been used to further the Welsh cattle-trade either through their direct sale to the English or by their use in breeding for this purpose.[44]

Until about 1450 men from the lower ranks of Welsh society were chiefly responsible for raids; occasionally they were accompanied by a member of the gentry from Herefordshire or the Marches.[45] But the decade after 1450 saw more extensive criminal activity by Welsh gentry, in which Sir William Herbert of Raglan was particularly prominent. Herbert, who served the house of York and received rich rewards for his service from Edward IV, was closely involved with his father-in-law, Devereux, in the incidents in Hereford and west Wales during 1456; twenty-one of his Welsh gentry associates participated alongside Devereux's affinity.[46] This gang also carried out many thieving raids in Herefordshire at this time: James ap Rosser ap John of Abergavenny was indicted of nineteen offences, while sixteen similar accusations were made against Sir William's brother, Richard Herbert.[47] So a disruptive element in Herefordshire again had close connections with one of York's retainers, and it may be conjectured whether Devereux and Herbert deliberately encouraged their lawless followers in order to advance their own, or indeed their lord York's, political ends. Yet York in his second protectorate had shown some concern for the problems of Wales and the Marches; the sharp contrast presented by the actions of his retainers highlights both his problems and the limitations of his political power.[48]

As English common law had no jurisdiction in the magnate-controlled marcher lordships and as the marcher lords in practice frequently shed their judicial responsibilities, Welshmen who committed crimes in the border shires rarely faced punishment. The extent of the problem facing the authorities may be illustrated from the records of the Herefordshire commissions of *oyer* and *terminer* of the 1450s. These extraordinary bodies are generally considered to have been more effective than the permanent common law courts; yet their success in punishing Welsh offenders was minimal.[49] In 1457, for example, only sixteen out of 123 Welshmen indicted before the commissioners (13%) actually appeared in court, in contrast with 149 out of 274 accused Englishmen (54%). One possible solution to this problem lay with the court of chancery, whose writ *sub poena* could penetrate the franchises and offered a means of enforcing royal justice.[50] But the growing popularity of chancery's equitable jurisdiction in the fifteenth century, particularly in the field of uses, meant that it heard fewer common law cases; consequently, this possible loophole in marcher inviolability was infrequently exploited.[51] Only three Herefordshire men sought a remedy against their Welsh attackers in this court between 1413 and 1461, but with uncertain success.[52]

The border counties' representatives in parliament made a number of attempts to end the virtual sanctuary of the Marches.[53] As a result of their petitions, justices of the peace were given limited statutory powers to deal with Welsh offenders in 1414 and again in 1442, when certain crimes were declared treason, and in 1445 the sheriff was instructed to arrest all Welsh outlaws who re-entered Herefordshire.[54] Yet a certain reluctance may be discerned behind the measures of the 1440s. The statute of 1442 had a limited life of six years; a request that it should be made permanent was rejected in 1449 and it was extended for only one year.[55] Henry VI preferred to rely on traditional means of law enforcement and on the responsibility of the marcher lords to maintain public order rather than introduce novel and far-reaching measures.[56] The new statutes appear to have had little effect in reducing the Welsh crime-rate in the borderland. The problem of Welsh raids in the border counties therefore remained. The inadequacy of English common law in this area is evident, as is also the inability of the Lancastrian régime to devise novel and effective solutions. It was left to the Yorkist and Tudor monarchs to bring a new approach to the ancient problem of marcher disorder.[57]

Some indication of the survival of Welsh influences in Herefordshire may be seen in the contemporary adoption of the names 'Welsh' and 'English' to describe the factions which seriously disrupted the city of Hereford in the years around 1450. The background to these disturbances may be found in the considerable tension which existed between the governing merchant class and the city's tradesmen and craftsmen; a comparison may be drawn with similar conflicts in other English towns (for example, Norwich) during the fifteenth century.[58] Hereford's government was in the hands of a small merchant oligarchy.[59] Charges of corruption were levelled at several mayors; if true, they reveal abuse of office; even if exaggerated, they suggest a measure of dissatisfaction with the city's rulers.[60] Richard Green, mayor in 1447-48, was allegedly the most corrupt holder of this office, and during his mayoralty he was said to have taken bribes to release prisoners, to have participated in a murder and to have corruptly forwarded his own business interests.[61] Green's alleged malpractices may have brought the citizens' discontent to a head, for the first outbreak of civic unrest occurred during the election of his successor in October 1448, when a gang of intruders forcibly ensured the election of their own nominee.[62] Their choice of another merchant, who may be presumed sympathetic to their grievances, suggests that opposition to the ruling oligarchy was broad-based. A similar violent demonstration interrupted the mayor's election two years later.[63]

In 1450 the arrest of a tradesman, Philip Corveser, provoked a demonstration and rescue attempt by his friends who called on all the 'Welsh' in the city to rise in rebellion with them against the 'English' mayor and his party:

> . . . the Welsh rose to help them, and so there was a division between the English and Welsh in the city as in a land at war, each faction taking the part of its own country against the other, in breach of the peace.[64]

The existence of tensions which set Hereford's disturbances apart from those experienced in most other towns is thereby suggested. The names 'Welsh' and 'English' do not imply a strict racial distinction, for many of the 'Welsh' faction bore English names; the division was rather between those who supported the city's government (the 'English') and its opponents (the 'Welsh'). While it is possible that the name 'Welsh' was applied to anyone who had close contacts with Welshmen, two such groups may be shown to have had particular cause for dissatisfaction with the civic government. First, it has been suggested that any comparative newcomers to the city from the west were called 'Welsh'; their exclusion from the city's government by older residents could have caused considerable resentment.[65] Secondly, stringent laws had restricted the rights of Welshmen in the border shires after the Glyndŵr rebellion; their implementation would have made second-class citizens of any Welsh settlers in Hereford, and some practical discrimination may still have persisted in mid-century.[66] The adoption of the names 'English' and 'Welsh' to describe the factions in dispute may in fact highlight some of the tensions which still existed in border society between the two peoples. The demonstrators of 1448 and 1450 were therefore drawn from tradesmen who wished to participate more extensively in their city's government and from men with Welsh connections who also found themselves excluded from civic power and were, perhaps, still accorded inferior status in the community.

After 1450 events in Hereford were dominated by the intervention of Sir Walter Devereux. He extended his patronage to the 'Welsh' faction by illegally giving livery to thirty-one tradesmen and craftsmen on 4 January 1452. On 5 February his retainers made a pact to support each other in any dispute. An armed demonstration was planned in Devereux's presence on 28 February and it was put into effect a week later, on 3 March.[67] This rising, master-minded by Devereux, was timed to coincide with Richard of York's march to Dartford; similar demonstrations took place in other English towns where York's supporters had influence.[68]

Four years later a second major demonstration took place in Hereford. The murder of Walter Vaughan on 13 March 1456 brought unrest to a head;[69] Vaughan was a kinsman of Sir William Herbert, and the events which followed his death may be seen in part as the prosecution of a blood-feud by Herbert and his family in order to avenge the murder.[70] But Herbert was a close political associate of Devereux, and the latter had maintained his contacts in Hereford. So on 15 March Herbert, Devereux's son, and a large number of their affinity advanced on Hereford and took control of the city for thirty-six hours. They unlawfully interrupted the sessions of the peace to secure the execution of the men whom they considered responsible for Vaughan's death; they threatened the 'English' mayor and many citizens and generally disrupted life in the city.[71] There is no evidence of a concerted effort by the citizens to eject the invaders; the alliances of 1452 had ensured a favourable reception for Devereux's party by a substantial number of citizens. Indeed, many 'Welsh' citizens may have welcomed the overthrow of mayoral government, however short its duration. The fact that the demonstration took place shortly after the end of the duke of York's second protectorate may give the rising some political importance.[72]

The involvement of Sir Walter Devereux in Hereford's internal disputes gave them a significance which extended far beyond the walls of the city. He also attempted, but with less success, to build up a following in Leominster, the second largest of the county's towns.[73] Consequently, the events of 1452 and 1456 suggest that Devereux's strategy was to gain control of the towns of Herefordshire, perhaps as a preliminary to controlling the county, or even part of south Wales, on behalf of Richard of

York; the attack made by Devereux and Herbert on Carmarthen and Aberystwyth Castles in August 1456 would support this latter contention. Devereux's actions emphasise his rôle as the most influential member of the Herefordshire gentry and as one of York's most zealous and effective supporters in the Welsh Marches.

A study of the cases from Herefordshire heard in king's bench between 1413 and 1461 suggests that this court had little success in punishing crime. Convictions were rare in cases initiated by the crown and even more unusual in private prosecutions. The accused were convicted and hanged in only one case of felony — when the use of force secured the verdict.[74] Crown prosecutions for trespass yielded a small number of convictions and fines, but fewer than ten private cases reached such a conclusion. In contrast, acquittals outnumber convictions; as the majority took place in the crown division, the inability of the civil sector of king's bench to complete cases is again suggested. The purchase of a pardon or the discovery of an error in legal procedure often resulted in the dismissal of a case before a verdict was returned. Many cases, however, never resulted in a trial at all. Private prosecutions were often abandoned once the accused had failed to answer several summonses to appear in court. Numerous accused must have accepted the outlawry which resulted from repeated non-appearance in court with equanimity, if not contempt.[75] There is no evidence to suggest that arbitration was widely used in Herefordshire to settle deadlocked lawsuits.[76] In short, prosecutions in king's bench rarely produced a verdict and frequently failed even to secure the presence of the accused before the justices. Private lawsuits fared even worse than crown cases. The court's efficiency was no greater in the reign of Henry V than under his weaker son. Yet paradoxically, the business of the court continued to expand during the first half of the century, while the early years of civil war witnessed a decline, but not a complete cessation, in litigation. Contemporaries may thus have considered the mere process of registering a grievance in court to be a worthwhile tactical advantage in a dispute and adequate reward for the expense.

The virtual paralysis of this supreme criminal court may be partly ascribed to the nature of English common law in the fifteenth century. Enmeshed in its own complexities, it demanded correct procedure at all times, to the extent that one small error in the wording of the writ or the description of the crime could annul an indictment.[77] Legal processes were complex, long-winded, even leisurely; they must have daunted all but the most patient of plaintiffs, and it is small wonder that so many lawsuits were abandoned. The distance of Herefordshire from the court of king's bench at Westminster made an already tedious process even more time-consuming and further hindered proceedings. Again, some legal processes had become largely ineffective. The futility of outlawry is all too apparent; many received this punishment for contempt of court, but few sought its reversal. The outlaw could no longer be killed on sight by the more law-abiding members of society, nor was he even a social outcast. The imposition of outlawry meant, at most, a slight inconvenience which could easily be remedied by the purchase of a pardon.[78] This mitigation of the penalties of outlawry meant that the law had no real strength against those who chose to disobey its writs, and a major reason for the ineffect-iveness of king's bench is thereby highlighted.

The weakness of this court was also due to the actions of those respon-sible for upholding the law. First, the king could curtail normal legal procedure by granting a pardon. Originally intended to protect the innocent from conviction after wrongful or malicious accusation, the system was much abused in the fifteenth century. General pardons had been issued periodically since 1377; at a cost of 16s. 4d. the recipient could ensure legal immunity for virtually all types of offence committed before a specified date.[79] Henry V granted two such general pardons, while six were issued in the years of Henry VI's personal rule; they were purchased by 292 men from Herefordshire and used by 121 of them to terminate prosecutions in king's bench.[80] Four general pardons were issued in the troubled decade after 1450; while intended as conciliatory measures — which also brought in welcome revenue — they merely afforded many criminals an easy escape from justice. Sir Walter Devereux, pardoned for his rôle in the Hereford rising of 1452, repeated his offence four years later.[81] While it is true that punishment was rare, the sale of pardons made a mockery of the legal system by providing anyone who could afford one with an easy termination to a lengthy lawsuit. In particular, the frequent issue of general pardons by Henry VI in the years after 1450 contributed to the ineffectiveness of king's bench at this time, and a system initially intended to ensure justice paradoxically helped to weaken the authority of the law.

Furthermore, the court of king's bench relied on officials drawn principally from the gentry to enforce its writs in the shires, but the ef-ficiency of local men was often open to question. The sheriff's responsi-bility to arrest offenders, return writs and empanel jurors formed only a part of his wide-ranging administrative duties, and it is perhaps not sur-prising that twenty-three of Herefordshire's forty-seven sheriffs between 1413 and 1461 were fined for not carrying out the orders of king's bench. Regular complaints of shrieval malpractices were made in parliament in the fifteenth century, and accusations in the parliaments of 1431-33 that the sheriffs of Herefordshire had been guilty of extortion and encroach-ment at their tourns must be seen against this general background.[82]

Individual offences by Herefordshire's sheriffs at this time are not specified, but the petitions single out inquiries into breaches of the statute of Labourers, while the records of king's bench show that several sheriffs had exceeded their jurisdiction by taking indictments for murder in their tourns.[83] One later sheriff, Thomas Parker, certainly used his term of office to line his own pockets through extortion and illegal imprisonment for ransom.[84]

Local officials were also susceptible to bribery or intimidation by men of higher social status whose influence was more immediate and threatening than that of the distant government. King's bench frequently referred cases for trial before the justices of assize in the county where the case originated. Acquittals regularly followed such trials and may conceal the bribery or intimidation either of the jurors or of the sheriff to produce a submissive jury.[85] The use of violence to influence jurors is vividly described on two occasions in 1456 when the Devereux-Herbert gang interrupted both a session of the peace and a coroner's inquest.[86]

The weakness of the administration of justice at local level is clear. Gentry officials were too easily swayed from impartiality either by abusing the privileges of office or by a more powerful member of their own class. The important rôle of the gentry in society is again emphasised; at local level they could make or break the efficiency of the agencies of law enforcement.

The crown sometimes met the challenge of a particularly serious disturbance by issuing a commission of *oyer* and *terminer*; two such commissions visited Hereford following the Devereux-inspired risings of 1452 and 1456.[87] These commissions had jurisdiction over a wide range of offences in a specified area; their sessions were held in the place where the disturbances had occurred and they were presided over by professional justices and influential magnates who were clearly less open to bribery and intimidation than local gentry.[88] With these advantages, commissions of *oyer* and *terminer* should have been well equipped to punish crime. Yet it has been suggested that although their sessions showed greater speed and efficiency, they did not always use their powers to the full because they concentrated on political offenders.[89] The records of the two Herefordshire commissions also suggest the intrusion of political faction into the operation of the legal system.

The commission of *oyer* and *terminer* which visited Hereford in August 1452 held sessions in several other English towns and was part of the crown's response to the series of risings in the early months of that year in support of Richard of York.[90] With York's arch-enemy, the duke of Somerset, as its most influential member, the commission may have started its work in a partisan spirit. There is some evidence to suggest that jurors were carefully chosen; certainly no known associate of Devereux served in this capacity. The most serious charges recorded by the commission relate to Devereux's demonstration in Hereford and the preceding civic disputes; the majority of indictments allege only minor incidents of theft and assault, but as many as one-third of these were perpetrated by the associates of a second retainer of the duke of York, Henry ap Gruffydd.[91] The commission achieved little success in the punishment of crime. Only a quarter of the accused appeared before its justices; a number were fined but rather more purchased pardons. Indeed, the chief offender, Devereux, had received a pardon on the day prior to its first session.[92] But a majority of the men who did appear in court were associates of Devereux and Henry ap Gruffydd and this again suggests that the commission was chiefly concerned with the trial of York's lesser supporters. While this apparent preoccupation with York's associates may simply reflect the disruptive rôle played by this group in Herefordshire in the early 1450s, the possibility cannot be ruled out that the commission was partisan in its attitude and deliberately sought to indict associates of York in order to continue Somerset's feud with him in a legal context.

A second commission of *oyer* and *terminer* visited Hereford in April 1457; again its chief concern was with the disruptive activities of York's retainers. The most serious charges heard before the justices related to the Hereford rising of March 1456 and the march through south and west Wales in August; but in all, 285 of the 397 men (72%) who were accused before the commissioners were associates of Devereux, Herbert or of members of their affinities, and they allegedly committed 114 of the 191 recorded crimes (60%). After the initial session of the commission, the court of king's bench took over the trials and dealt with 165 (41%) of the accused. But the weaknesses of the permanent court affected the proceedings resulting from the commission's indictments, and while some men were fined, the majority escaped punishment. Devereux was imprisoned but later acquitted.[93] It seems that a deliberate attempt was made by the Court party to win Sir William Herbert's support, and his pardon was soon enrolled. But although he did not play a major rôle as one of York's supporters during the next few years and was absent from the Yorkist rout at Ludford in October 1459, it is unlikely that his political allegiance changed.[94] The majority of men tried in king's bench were again associates of Devereux and Herbert. While it may be argued that the recurring theme of the Devereux-Herbert gang in the proceedings of the commission merely reflected the seriousness and extent of their disruptive activities in the shire, there are several factors which suggest a partisan attitude in the commission. First, the commission was only issued after attempts over several months to deal with Devereux and Herbert had not been successful, and it appears that the authorities were less concerned with the general suppression of disorder in Herefordshire than with the punishment of York's two retainers.[95] Secondly, the justices chiefly represented the interests of the Court party, and it is possible that some juries were packed.[96] Thirdly, contemporary rumour (as reported in William Botoner's letter to John Paston) suggested some false indictments by the commission, while fifty-one men, many of them supporters of the Court party, were unsuccessfully prosecuted in king's bench for conspiracy by the younger Devereux and several of his associates.[97] Although a privy seal warrant in 1459 dismissed the conspiracy charges as malicious, the fact remains that the impartiality of the commission had been challenged in a court of law.[98]

The Herefordshire commisions of *oyer* and *terminer* failed to fulfil the potential of their greater powers. Although probably the most efficient method of law enforcement in fifteenth-century England, they were too dependent on an over-institutionalised legal system to achieve much success. They were also restricted by being the instruments of an increasingly partisan government, and as such, they must have involved the legal system even more directly in political rivalries. Their failure to deal effectively with treason and serious crime clearly illustrates the impotence of late-Lancastrian government in the face of major challenges to its authority.

Crime in Herefordshire was endemic and went largely unpunished during the reigns of both Henry V and Henry VI; this lawlessness was the result of both regional problems, such as the virtual impossibility of punishing criminally-inclined Welshmen who strayed over the border, and more general problems, as exemplified by the inadequacies of the common law courts. Yet the courts experienced an increasing volume of litigation, which must suggest that the law was still respected, and in Herefordshire there were no major challenges to the authority of the law until the 1450s. In this decade, however, a deterioration in public order may be observed. First, there was a higher incidence of crime among the gentry of the county; this posed a potentially serious challenge to law and order on account of their influential position in society and local government. In particular, the emergence, under Devereux's patronage, of a large gentry gang which was responsible for politically-motivated crimes proved particularly disruptive. Second, a change may be observed in the attitude of some members of society to the authority of the law. Bribery and intimidation were probably common earlier in the fifteenth century and represent attempts to influence legal procedure; but the Devereux-Herbert gang actually took the law into their own hands when they violently supervised a coroner's inquest and session of the peace in Hereford in 1456 and held illegal sessions at Aberystwyth Castle later in that year. This group clearly felt that the law no longer protected either their own interests or those of their lord, Richard of York. Another important factor in the deterioration in public order is therefore suggested: the existence of an increasingly partisan government which could and did use the law to further its own interests. This conclusion is supported by an examination of the operation of the commission of *oyer* and *terminer* which visited Hereford in 1457. Again, a faction-dominated government might make a restricted choice of local government officials; and exclusion from office has been suggested as one reason for Devereux's large following among Herefordshire's gentry. The existence of political faction and its incursion into the administration of justice are therefore crucial factors in the deterioration in public order and the drift towards civil war in the late 1450s.

By 1461 Hereford jail was in a state of extreme disrepair, possibly caused by the earlier civic disturbances, but more probably the result of neglect; repairs were carried out in the early years of the reign of Edward IV.[99] An apt parallel may be drawn with the administration of the law in Lancastrian Herefordshire and the task which awaited the Yorkist kings in 1461.

NOTES

* I am grateful to Dr. R.A. Griffiths for critically reading a draft of this paper.

1. The most important classes of this court's records are King's Bench, *coram rege* plea rolls (PRO, KB27) and ancient indictments (KB9). The major studies of this court in the fifteenth century are M. Blatcher, *The Court of King's Bench 1450-1550: A Study in Self-help* (1979), and 'The Working of the Court of King's Bench in the Fifteenth Century' (London Ph.D. thesis, 1936).

2. Complaints of the lack of public order may be found in *RP*, V, 367-68, and again in Hardyng's Chronicle of *c.* 1457: C.L. Kingsford, 'The First Version of Hardyng's Chronicle', *EHR*, XXVII (1912), 745, 749-50.

3. For the jurisdiction and powers of J.Ps., see B.H. Putnam (ed.), *Proceedings before the Justices of the Peace in the Fourteenth and Fifteenth Centuries* (1938). Some cases heard by the justices or sheriffs were transferred to king's bench for trial: ibid., pp. lvii-lxxvii.

4. The ancient indictments contain writs transferring cases from other courts to king's bench for trial, together with their returns; the plea rolls record proceedings on these cases and others in king's bench. The latter generally, but not invariably, include the cases recorded in the former class of documents.

5. For disorder in outlying English shires and disregard of the legal system, especially in the northern counties, see R.L. Storey, *The End of the House of Lancaster* (1966), especially pp. 84-85.

6. King's bench dealt with prosecutions by both the crown and private individuals.

7. For a more detailed study of crime, criminals and attempts to maintain public order in Herefordshire between 1413 and 1461, see A.E. Herbert, 'Public Order and Private Violence in Herefordshire, 1413-61' (Wales [Swansea] M.A. thesis, 1978).

8. *RP*, IV, 52. For disorder in Shropshire, see E.G. Kimball (ed.), *The Shropshire Peace Roll, 1400-14* (Shrewsbury, 1959), pp. 10-11. The court of king's bench held sessions in Shropshire and Staffordshire in Easter and Trinity terms 1414, an indication of their lawlessness: KB27/612, 613.

9. *RP*, IV, 254.

10. *populos non parum natura feroces ac indomitos*: C. Williams (ed.), *The Official Correspondence of Thomas Bekynton* (RS, LVI, 1872), I, 2.

11. *RP*, V, 53, 106, 151.

12. KB9, 34/1, 34/2, 35; see below.

13. The Yorkists were routed at Ludford Bridge on 12 October 1459 and the Lancastrians were defeated at Mortimer's Cross on 2 February 1461.

14. James Baskerville, Robert Whitney, Thomas Monnington, George Monnington, Hugh Shirley: *RP*, V, 367-68.

15. For violence in the north, see Storey, op.cit., ch. VII, VIII, X; Storey, 'The North of England' in S.B. Chrimes, C.D. Ross and R.A. Griffiths (eds.), *Fifteenth-century England* (Manchester, 1972), pp.129-144; R.A. Griffiths, 'Local Rivalries and National Politics: the Percies, the Nevilles and the duke of Exeter, 1452-55', *Speculum*, XLIII (1968), 589-632.

16. KB27/620, rex m.12; 621, rex m.12.

17. KB27/691, m.6; 692, m.3d., 75; 694, m.66; C1/11/171 a and b. Henry Oldcastle was the son of the Lollard traitor, Sir John Oldcastle: J.C. Wedgwood, *History of Parliament, 1439-1509. Biographies* (1936), pp. 646-47.

18. For this aspect of the chancery's jurisdiction, see M.E. Avery, 'Proceedings in the Court of Chancery up to *c.* 1460' (London M.A. thesis, 1958), pp. 15, 38.

19. C1/4/128; KB27/632, m.5d., 7d.; for Abrahall, see below.

20. C1/12/161; Hereford Cathedral Library, Dean and Chapter Archives, 2234.
21. The elder Thomas was J.P. in 1416-27 and 1435-40, escheator 1418-19 and 1427-28, sheriff 1433-34, M.P. for the shire 1413, 1422 and 1430: *CPR, 1416-22*, p.453; *ibid., 1422-29*, p.563; *ibid., 1436-41*, p.583; *CFR, 1413-22*, p.263; *ibid., 1422-30*, p.194; *ibid., 1430-37*, p.176; W.R. Williams, *A Parliamentary History of the County of Hereford* (Brecon, 1896), p.30. For the son's appointments, see *CFR, 1422-30*, p.156; *CCR, 1429-35*, p.70. For their crimes, see KB27/608, m.10d.; 678, m.43d., 107; 679, m.37; C1/7/51; 12/161.
22. For York, see J.T. Rosenthal, 'The Estates and Finances of Richard, duke of York', in W.M. Bowsky (ed.), *Studies in Medieval and Renaissance History* (Lincoln, Nebraska, 1965), II; his retainers included Sir Walter Devereux and John Wigmore. For Talbot, see A.J. Pollard, 'The Family of Talbot, Lords Talbot and Earls of Shrewsbury, 1387-1472' (Bristol Ph.D. thesis, 1968), especially appendices I and III; his retainers included John Abrahall and Thomas Barre. For Buckingham, see C. Rawcliffe, *The Staffords, Earls of Stafford and Dukes of Buckingham, 1394-1521* (Cambridge, 1978), especially appendices A-D, and T.B. Pugh, *The Marcher Lordships of South Wales, 1415-1536* (Cardiff, 1963); his retainers included Abrahall, Sir John Scudamore, Miles Scull and Thomas Fitzharry.
23. KB9, 34/1, no.48; 35, nos. 61, 72. Devereux's manor of Weobley was held from York; he had served with York in France; he was York's constable of Wigmore Castle and one of his councillors. Storey op.cit., p.230; Rosenthal, op.cit., II, 181; Anne Marshall, 'The Rôle of English War-captains in England and Normandy, 1436-61' (Wales [Swansea] M.A. thesis, 1974), pp.54, 79, 231; BL, Additional Charters, 6963; Wedgwood, op.cit., p.271.
24. *RP*, IV, 254; see also KB27/666, rex m.8.
25. Ibid. 616, rex m.26; 634, m.110, rex m.12; C1/4/128, 4/181, 69/221; *CCR, 1419-22*, p.24; for a more detailed description of Abrahall's career, see A.E. Herbert, op.cit., pp.54-58.
26. KB27/616, rex m.26; Pollard, op.cit., p.26.
27. Ibid., p.29; *CCR, 1419-22*, p.24; C258/41/23; C1/4/181; KB27/634, rex m.31; 656, rex m. 15d.
28. Pollard, op. cit., p.29, appendix III; Rawcliffe, op. cit., p.222; C85/92/31, no.1. He was also a steward of Bronllys and held other offices in the duchy of Lancaster in that area: R. Somerville, *A History of the duchy of Lancaster, 1265-1603* (1953), I, 650; *CPR, 1436-41*, p.288.
29. *CFR, 1413-22*, p.209; C219/12/3 (unusually, all the electors were county gentry rather than citizens of Hereford, and some irregularity may be suspected); *CPR, 1436-41*, pp.288, 504, 583; *ibid., 1441-46*, pp. 48, 49, 61, 92; *CFR, 1437-45*, p.. 130.
30. In the period 1413-22, 19 gentry were accused in king's bench; between 1423 and 1436, 84; between 1437 and 1449, 43; and between 1450 and 1461, 106.
31. KB9, 35, nos. 44, 61, 72.
32. Ibid., nos. 24, 71; Storey, op.cit., p.179; R.A. Griffiths, 'Gruffydd ap Nicholas and the Fall of the House of Lancaster', *Welsh History Review*, II (1964-65), 225-26.
33. For the Monnington family's crimes, see KB9, 35, nos. 6, 13, 17, 24, 39, 42, 44, 46, 50, 59, 61, 62, 64, 72. For Thomas Monnington, see Wedgwood, op. cit., pp.600-1.
34. KB9, 35, nos. 41, 59, 61.
35. Ibid., nos. 44, 60, 61, 62; 281, no.4; 282, no.31; KB27/784, m.55.
36. Fitzharry married the widow of Ralph Lyngen; for the latter's will, see BL, Harleian Charters, 112 B13. For the quarrel, see CP40/782, m.57; C1/22/107, 26/526-29; KB27/785, m.43, 62; 787, rex m.21d; 804, rex m.27; KB9, 277, no.78; 292, no.4. For their allegiances, see ibid., 35, no.44; *RP*, V, 478, 480. The dispute between Cornwall and Devereux originated in a double grant of the wardship and keeping of the lands of one of Cornwall's kinsmen: *CFR, 1452-61*, pp.30, 32; KB27/774, rex m.22; *RP*, V, 480.

37. For example, Thomas Monnington was sheriff of Herefordshire in 1461-63 and the county's M.P. in 1461-62, 1467-68 and 1472-75. John Lyngen was sheriff in 1465 and 1471, and Hugh Shirley was escheator in 1461. Wedgwood, op.cit., pp.600-1; PRO, *List of Sheriffs of England and Wales* (Lists and Indexes, IX), p.60; *CFR, 1461-71*, p.49.
38. D. Sylvester, *The Rural Landscape of the Welsh Borderland* (1969), pp. 347-77; B.G. Charles, 'The Welsh, their Language and Place-names in Archenfield and Oswestry', *Angles and Britons: the O'Donnell Lectures* (Cardiff, 1963), pp.85-110.
39. *RP*, IV, 52.
40. *PPC*, V, 211-13, 215; R.A. Griffiths, 'Wales and the Marches', in Chrimes, Ross and Griffiths, op.cit., pp.157-58.
41. Ibid., p.153; Pugh, op. cit., pp.36-39.
42. *RP*, V, 53, 151; *SR*, II, 317-18, 351.
43. K.J. Bonser, *The Drovers: who they were and how they went: an Epic of the English Countryside* (1970), p.20; C.Skeel, 'The Cattle Trade between Wales and England from the Fifteenth to the Nineteenth Centuries', *TRHS*, 4th. ser., IX (1926), 137-38.
44. Kimball, op.cit., p.47.
45. E.g., KB27/614, m.89; 698, m.8d.
46. Herbert married Devereux's daughter, Anne, in 1449. For his career, see H.T. Evans, *Wales and the Wars of the Roses* (Cambridge, 1915), pp, 73-81; R.A. Griffiths, *The Principality of Wales in the Later Middle Ages, I. South Wales, 1277-1536* (Cardiff, 1972), pp.155-56; D.H. Thomas, 'The Herberts of Raglan as Supporters of the House of York in the Second Half of the Fifteenth Century (Wales [Cardiff] M.A. thesis, 1967); C.D. Ross, *Edward IV* (1974), pp.75-80; KB9, 35, nos. 24, 61, 71, 72. For examples of Edward IV's grants and commissions to Herbert, see *CPR, 1461-67*, pp.7, 13, 30, 36, 43, 45, 65, 98, 99, 114, 132 — and this is only during the first year of Edward IV's reign!
47. For James ap Rosser ap John, see KB9, 35, nos. 18, 24, 33, 44, 61, 72, 104, 105, 107, 109, 113, 114, 118. For Richard Herbert, see ibid. nos. 4, 5, 18, 24, 26, 44, 61, 72; Griffiths, *Principality of Wales*, p.156.
48. Griffiths, 'Wales and the Marches', p.158; Storey, op. cit., p.164; J.R. Lander, 'Henry VI and the Duke of York's Second Protectorate', *BJRL*, XLIII (1960-61), 46-69.
49. For the Herefordshire commissions of *oyer* and *terminer*, see below.
50. Avery, op.cit., p.203.
51. M.E. Avery, 'The History of the Equitable Jurisdiction of Chancery before 1460', *BIHR*, VII (1969), 129-44, especially p.131.
52. C1/4/63; 6/273; 69/157.
53. *RP*, III, 615, 663-64; IV, 52; V, 53, 106, 151.
54. *SR*, II, 188-89, 317-18, 331.
55. Ibid., p.351.
56. Griffiths, 'Wales and the Marches', p.157.
57. Ibid., pp.159-65.
58. For social conflict in late mediaeval towns, see C.Platt, *The English Medieval Town* (1976), pp.141-50; for disputes in Norwich, Storey, op.cit., appendix III.
59. Indications of the existence of an oligarchy may be found in the fact that only a small group of men held the office of mayor and acted as mayoral and parliamentary electors in the years 1413-61. For a list of mayors, see J.Price, *An Historical Account of the City of Hereford* (Hereford, 1796, reprinted 1970), pp.254-55. Parliamentary electors are listed in C219; mayoral electors in 1448 are given in KB9, 34/1, no.5.
60. C1/10/181; 13/159; 15/17; 70/180; KB9, 34/2, no.29; KB27/715, m.6.
61. Ibid., 754, m.35d., rex m.8; KB9, 997, no.15.
62. Ibid., 34/1, no. 5. For disturbances during mayoral elections in other English towns, see Platt, op.cit., p.149.

63. KB9, 34/1, no.5.
64. Ibid.: *publice proclamantes quod omnes Wallici in civitate predicta cum ipsis malefactis contra prefatum nuper maiorem et omnes cives eiusdem civitatis starent et perservarent, cuius proclamacionis accionis pretextu predicti Wallici tunc et ibidem insurrexerunt cum assistencia ipsorum malefactorum et sic divisio inter Anglicos et Wallicos quasi in terra guerrae adtunc et ibidem fuit et terram suam quaelibet pars versus alteram cepit tunc ibidem contra pacem domini regis.*
65. Storey, op.cit., p.229.
66. R. Johnson, *The Ancient Customs of the City of Hereford* (London and Hereford, 1868), p.74, quoting statute of 2 HIV, c.12; Griffiths, 'Wales and the Marches', pp.149-51.
67. KB9, 34/1 nos. 5, 48, 49; Storey, op.cit., appendix V.
68. Ibid., pp.96-100.
69. KB9, 282, no. 31.
70. For genealogies of the Herberts and Vaughans, see Evans, op.cit., pp.113, 228.
71. KB9, 35, nos. 44, 61, 62, 65, 66, 72; KB27/784, m.55.
72. York's second protectorate ended on 25 February 1456; the rising in Hereford took place less than three weeks later. Lander, op. cit., pp.46-49.
73. Devereux's henchman in Leominster was Hugh Shirley, who had represented Leominster when Devereux was M.P. for Herefordshire in 1450: C219/16/1, nos. 32 and 34. In 1456 Devereux retained nineteen men from Leominster: KB27/784, rex m. 22 and d.
74. KB9, 285, nos. 21, 22; KB27/784, rex m.6.
75. Outlawry was a punishment for contempt of court rather than for the crime committed; by banishing the offender from society, it was intended to bring about his acknowledgement and return to the jurisdiction of the courts: Blatcher, 'Working of King's Bench', part II, chapter I.
76. J. Bellamy, in *Crime and Public Order in England in the Later Middle Ages* (1973), pp.117-18, suggests that arbitration was increasingly used to settle disputes by the mid-fifteenth century; Rawcliffe, op.cit., p.181, also believes that private settlements were common by 1500. Two arbitrations involving men from Herefordshire have been found. One followed the murder of Richard Whitton and had the bishop of Hereford as mediator; it also indicates an earlier arbitration in a dispute between Whitton and Edmund Cornwall by Richard of York and three gentry. See A.T. Bannister (ed.), *Register of Thomas Spofford, Bishop of Hereford, 1422-48* (Hereford, 1917), pp. 183-85. In the second case Devereux, Herbert and Thomas Bromwich made a bond with James, Lord Audley, Sir John Barre, Thomas Cornwall and Thomas Fitzharry to abide the award of the bishop of Hereford and the earl of Shrewsbury in a dispute in 1457: Longleat, Devereux Papers 1/15, quoted in Griffiths *The Principality of Wales*, p.151. It is of course possible that other arbitrations were not recorded, or that the records have not survived.
77. E.g., in the prosecution of William Pope for aiding and abetting in the theft of cattle, the case was dismissed because the place where Pope was alleged to have committed the offence was not mentioned: KB27/730, rex m.30.
78. Blatcher, 'Working of King's Bench', part III, ch. II.
79. Storey, op.cit., pp. 212-13. The offences annulled by such a pardon were treasons, murders, rapes, rebellions, insurrections, felonies, conspiracies, common trespasses, offences and negligences, extortions, misprisions, contempts, concealments, deceptions and offences against the crown's feudal rights. They are catalogued at the beginning of each general pardon issued: C67/36-43.
80. Ibid.
81. Ibid., 40 m.21; KB9,34/2 no.43.
82. M. Hastings, *The Court of Common Pleas in Fifteenth-century England* (New York, 1947),

pp.224-30; A.R. Myers (ed.), *English Historical Documents, IV. 1327-1485* (1969), pp. 384-85; R.L. Storey, *Henry VII* (1968), pp.139-40, 143; Bellamy, op.cit., pp. 89-93; *RP*, IV, 380, 401, 406, 450.

83. The sheriff's tourn was considered to have no jurisdiction over cases of murder; yet several such indictments were recorded before sheriffs in the late 1420s and early 1430s: KB27/656 rex m.11d; 690 rex m.5d.

84. KB9,34/2 nos. 14, 19, 20; C1/22/192.

85. For the weakness of the jury system, see Hastings, op.cit., pp. 218-24.

86. See above.

87. *CPR, 1446-52*, p.580; *ibid., 1452-61*, pp. 348-39. The records of the 1452 commission are KB9, 34/1 (indictment file, 54m.) and 34/2 (process file, 184m.). The records of the 1457 commission are KB9, 35 (indictment file, 119m.). King's bench took over the trial of the accused in 1457 and a process file may never have existed.

88. J.B. Avrutick, 'Commissions of *Oyer* and *Terminer* in Fifteenth-century England' (London M.Phil. thesis, 1967), pp. 14-15, 61-68.

89. *Ibid.*, pp.2, 332-35.

90. Storey, op.cit., p.102; Avrutick, op.cit., pp. 115-30, 182-85.

91. Henry ap Gruffydd may have served Humphrey, duke of Buckingham as sheriff of Newport and Wentloog and steward of Machen between 1448 and 1452: Rawcliffe, op.cit., p.214. By 1451 he was York's steward of Usk and Caerleon: BL, Additional Charters 1816. Petitions to the commissioners of 1452 alleged that he was the 'confusyor and destroyer' of one area of south Herefordshire, whose inhabitants had been 'betyn, robbed and despoyled': KB9,34/2 no.13. Many other thefts and assaults were alleged against him, his sons John and Miles, his servants and associates: ibid., nos. 23,27,30; 34/1 nos. 5,21,24,25,27,28,31,33,35,41,51,53.

92. The pardon was dated 8 August 1452 and ratified on 29 August: ibid., 34/2 nos. 33,43,45; C67/40 m.21.

93. KB27/784 rex m.22 and d.; *CCR, 1454-61*, p.223.

94. *CPR, 1452-61*, pp.353,360,367; KB27/791 rex m.1 and d.; Evans, op.cit., p.107; Ross op.cit., p.76; T.B. Pugh, 'The Magnates, Knights and Gentry', in Chrimes, Ross and Griffiths, op.cit., p.92.

95. Devereux and Herbert were summoned to a meeting of the great council at Coventry in September 1456; both attended. Devereux was imprisoned at Windsor but Herbert escaped and returned to the Marches where he allegedly issued a proclamation inciting rebellion. Eventually, on 10 March 1457, he was declared a rebel; the commission had been issued on 8 March.*CCR, 1454-61*, pp.158, 174; KB9, 35 nos. 26,52,102; Storey, op.cit., pp. 180-81.

96. The presiding justices included Humphrey, duke of Buckingham, John, earl of Shrewsbury, John, Viscount Beaumont and James, Lord Audley, who all died while fighting for the Court party at either Northampton (10 July 1460) or Blore Heath (23 September 1459). The grand jury, which dealt with the most serious indictments, included seven gentry closely associated with the Court party in Herefordshire and five little-known and uninfluential members of the same class.

97. 'Manye be endyted, som causelesse, whych makyth Herbert partye strenger' (written 1 May 1457): N. Davis (ed.), *Paston Letters and Papers of the Fifteenth Century* (2 vols., Oxford, 1971-76), II, 171. See KB27/790 m.68d.; 798 m.40d.; 802 m.35d., 68.

98. PSO1/20/1067.

99. E101/565/11/15 (2-11 Edward IV).

6. The Struggle for Power in Mid-Fifteenth-Century Devonshire

Martin Cherry
University of Leicester

On 15 December 1455, the forces of Thomas Courtenay, earl of Devon and those of William, Lord Bonville 'bykered and fought' near Clyst bridge.[1] Bonville's flight from the battlefield unleashed a systematic campaign of assault and looting directed against his associates and tenants in south-east Devonshire. The 'battle' of Clyst, together with the occupation of the city of Exeter by the earl's troops for almost two months, which was preceded by the most notorious crime of the decade, the murder of Nicholas Radford, made the violence of the latter part of 1455 qualitatively different as well as distinct in terms of scale from the chronic disorder that characterised life in the county in the 1440s and '50s. This was civil war. The 'battle' itself had been heralded some weeks before by a formal declaration of hostilities thinly disguised in the chivalric mode of a challenge to a duel. The opening sentences of these documents neatly parodied the customary form of greeting in contemporary letters: 'all due salutacone of frendlyhode leid apart', wrote Bonville; 'all friendly gretyng stond or noght', retorted the earl.[2]

An analysis of the process of polarisation that had been developing within the local ruling class in Devonshire over the previous fifteen years is necessary if we are to understand how conflict and tension inherent in this group degenerated into civil war. Although the leading members of the county establishment frequently used violence in promoting their own interests and indeed relied on its use as a means of social and political control, they nevertheless abhorred and shrunk from civil war. The earl of Devon was similarly reluctant to go to war. He has received a universally bad press from modern historians - 'turbulent and self interested', 'grasping and ambitious', a 'notorious ruffian . . . for years the terror of the south west' — and it is not the purpose of this paper to attempt his rehabilitation for he undoubtedly possessed most of the qualities attributed to him.[3] But even so he embarked on his 1455 campaign only after all other methods of achieving his aims, above all his attempts to influence the policies of various governments towards the west country, had failed. It is now axiomatic that if a lord were to maintain his power in the provinces he had to gain access to crown patronage and influence royal policy in favour of himself and his clients. Earl Thomas failed in this endeavour although it was not through lack of trying. Indeed, his experiences in the 1430s, '40s and '50s could be taken as a case study of the damage that persistent periods of exclusion from power could inflict on a lord's stature in a locality and on his sense of honour. During the late 1430s and early 1440s he took advantage of the powerful backing of his Beaufort relatives in an effort to undermine Bonville's local authority. In the mid-1440s he refused to serve abroad in the hope that he might be able to reinforce his position in the south-west during Bonville's absence in Gascony. In the late 1440s he served abroad himself and increased his attendance at court in order more directly to influence government affairs. These expedients brought with them few tangible rewards. In 1450 he moved with the duke of York into a position of open opposition to the Court circle but this led only to the *débâcle* of February 1452 on Blackheath. At a local level the consequences of political failure were profoundly serious. During the course of the 1440s he lost control over the upper ranks of west-country society, first in Somerset, Dorset and Cornwall and then in Devonshire itself. In the months following Blackheath his leadership over Devonshire gentlemen of even quite modest status began to falter. It was this trend towards political isolation that forced the earl to resort to violence on an unprecedented scale in order to rid himself of his enemies. In this, too, he failed.

The fate of the earl of Devon was of considerable moment to the political community in Devonshire. Despite a significant redistribution of landownership within the county élite over the previous sixty years that had served to narrow the gap between the landed income of the earl and that of other prominent members of the gentry, the earldom remained the largest estate in the county and represented the greatest single source of local patronage. Indeed, the earl's inability to maintain political leadership in the 1440s and '50s appears in striking contrast to the unchallenged regional ascendancy enjoyed in the 1380s by his grandfather, Earl Edward Courtenay. At that time political society in Devonshire, and to a lesser extent the adjoining counties, was centred on the earl, and government had little alternative but to work through him and his affinity when appointing local officials. His was the greatest of local lineages whose influence touched most of the key members of the local hierarchy.[4] By the turn of the fifteenth century, however, this regional dominance was beginning to be eroded largely as a result of a series of family misfortunes. Earl Edward died in 1419 after a long period of political inactivity probably brought about by his own blindness. His successor, Earl Hugh, died prematurely in 1422 leaving as heir a young son whose minority was to last until 1433. The death of Hugh made the problem of finding alternative sources of patronage a matter of considerable urgency for members of the political community. It was during the minority of Thomas, earl of Devon that Sir Philip Courtenay and Sir William Bonville assumed local leadership and together came to form the nucleus of a new configuration of loyalties over which the young earl, when he came of age, could wield little authority.[5] Thus, when Earl Thomas entered his estates he found himself at a considerable disadvantage compared with those men who had been consolidating their position at his expense during the previous decade. Furthermore, at a time when some leading Devonshire land-owners were commanding incomes greater than ever before, the earl's inheritance had been seriously wasted by the administration set up during his minority under the direction of his mother. Income from the comital estate in the late 1420s appears to have dropped by almost one-fifth since 1404-5.[6] This adverse situation was compounded by the longevity of the earl's mother, for when she died in 1441 she was seised not only of her dower portion but also of a large number of estates that had been settled on her by jointures and other devices. Between 1433 and 1441 altogether about two-thirds of the young earl's estates lay outside his control.

The scale of the earl's financial disabilities made it virtually impossible for him to provide members of the local gentry with patronage at a level sufficient to arrest the drift of affinities towards Bonville and his circle. In the circumstances it became imperative for him to seek the backing of a patron influential enough to tilt the local balance of power in his favour. In the early 1430s Earl Thomas had married Margaret Beaufort, the niece of Cardinal Beaufort and sister of John, earl of Somerset. The growing ascendancy of the cardinal and his friends and relations over government and the royal patronage is evident in the years after Henry VI's assumption of power in 1437. At the same time Beaufort protégés and supporters were established in key positions in the provinces. Most of the important west-country appointments during this period were of men closely identified with the Court circle, such as Sir Remfrey and Sir Thomas Arundel, Sir William Beauchamp, John Nanfan and Walter Rodney.[7] The earl of Devon also derived considerable benefit from his association with the Beauforts. In November 1437, he was granted an annuity of £100 for good service 'that he hath doon and shall doo'.[8] In May 1441, he was appointed steward of the duchy of Cornwall.[9] In February 1442, he was given the keepership of the lands late of the Cornish knight, Sir William Bodrugan, and in 1445 the conservancy of the river Exe.[10] The most spectacular demonstration of Beaufort goodwill towards the earl was his appointment as steward of England at the coronation of Queen Margaret in May 1445, a prestigious position to hold at what was not only a major social event but also a carefully orchestrated exhibition of the Beaufort ascendancy.[11]

The benefits that might accrue from Beaufort patronage were not to be

measured solely in terms of offices, annuities and keeperships. John
Beaufort, earl of Somerset was prepared to back his brother-in-law's claim
to the stewardship of the duchy of Cornwall with force, despite attempts
by the council to defuse what was clearly a dangerous situation. Devon's
appointment to this office has been generally recognised as a gross blunder
on the part of the government, for Bonville had been appointed for life to
an almost identical post in 1437.[12] It served to aggravate the tension that
had been building up between Bonville and Devon throughout the
preceding decade and which had already erupted in violence the year
before.[13] In November 1441 the council grew alarmed at reports of
'diverse companies of men . . . arrayed in guise of war' that had 'caused
manslaughter' in the west country and ordered that neither Bonville nor
the earl should occupy the post.[14] However genuine the concern of some
members of the council may have been, the Beauforts were more interested in supporting Devon. Instead of gathering his forces in Gascony, the
earl of Somerset chose to mobilise them in the south-west of England on
behalf of his brother-in-law. Sir Philip Chetwynd, a knight who was to
serve under Bonville in Gascony the following year, alleged before the
council that he and others had been attacked between Bristol and
Hungerford by more than fifty armed men. The motive behind the assault
was that 'some said that they supposed that the said Philip and his men
had been toward Bonville'. Chetwynd himself did not know the identity
of his attackers, but some locals stated that 'they were toward the earl of
Devon' and Chetwynd recognised some of them to be wearing the earl of
Somerset's livery.[15]

   Although valuable in the short term, the alliance between the earl of
Devon and the Beaufort family was also politically dangerous. There was
a growing resentment in the late 1430s and early 1440s of the family's
avarice, and Somerset's ineffective campaign in France in 1443 drew
widespread criticism. Obstacles came to be placed in Somerset's path and
he found it difficult, for instance, to obtain a settlement over his father's
inheritance.[16] The earl of Devon might have been well advised to seek
good lordship from other quarters but, at a time when many of the
personal relationships that held political significance for the future were
being forged among the captains and garrisons of Normandy and
Aquitaine, he was attempting to take advantage of Bonville's absence in
Gascony to reinforce his position at home. Whatever pickings a Beaufort
connection might have afforded him abroad, the earl declined to serve in
France in spite of a royal letter urging him to lead a campaign there in
March 1443.[17] As will become clear, tarrying in the west country did him
very little good for, meanwhile, Bonville was forging an association with
the duke of Suffolk that was to lead to Devon's exclusion from the
counsels of those in power and hasten the erosion of his affinity.

As an executor of Thomas, duke of Clarence, Bonville was implicated in the shady dealings surrounding the ransom of the count of Angoulême from which Suffolk emerged to greatest advantage and which are discussed elsewhere in this volume.[18] His tie with Suffolk was strengthened when he appeared as a member of the ducal entourage at the proxy wedding of Margaret of Anjou.[19] He consolidated this attachment further when he married his daughter to one of Suffolk's henchmen, William Tailboys. Bonville's connection with Suffolk and his circle brought with it certain rewards, above all his summons for the first time as a lord to parliament in January 1449. It was perhaps more than coincidence that during this very parliament Devon lost his case in which he had asserted his precedence against the earl of Arundel.[20] Bonville's growing identification with a faction that was gaining a stranglehold over the royal patronage by the late 1440s presented a major threat to the position of his west-country rival. After Bonville's return from Gascony in 1446 the level of violence in Devonshire markedly increased, but the earl of Devon was not prepared to allow developments at the centre to go unchallenged.[21] In 1446 he had himself served abroad — at last — at Pont L'Evêque in Normandy.[22] In February 1447 he was mingling with the great men of the realm for he acted with Suffolk as one of the earl of Wiltshire's feoffees in a Leicestershire transaction.[23] His need to influence affairs became more pressing when Cardinal Beaufort died in the summer of 1447, for this confirmed Suffolk's position as leader of the court party. From May of that year (just prior to the cardinal's death) Devon attended the court so frequently that it must represent a conscious policy on his part to divert the direction of crown patronage in favour of his own clients.[24]

Devon recognised rather too late that membership of the court circle, or at least access to it, was the key to maintaining leadership over the relatively small number of knightly families which constituted the upper stratum of the local political community and from which senior county officials were customarily drawn. Despite the patronage he had received from his Beaufort kinsmen earlier in the decade, the long-term realignments in regional loyalties brought about by the misfortunes that had beset Earl Thomas and his family made it almost impossible for him to extend his local influence or penetrate the affinities that had been built up by better-connected magnates from among these higher-ranking gentry. A brief perusal of west-country appointments in the 1440s will demonstrate the scale of the problem facing him. In Somerset and Dorset the considerable influence of a senior member of the council in the 1430s, Lord Hungerford, had benefited members of his family: one of his sons-in-law, Sir Philip Courtenay, was able to gain control over the Luttrell estate through Hungerford's good offices, and another, Sir Walter Rodney, served as sheriff of the county in 1439-40 and also as a J.P. there.[25] As

Hungerford's power waned towards the middle of the decade, so local affinities came to group around others who held high office in the government or household, both of which were falling gradually under the control of Suffolk; three members of Lord Stourton's family held key posts in the county administration.[26] Household retainers could be appointed directly to local office: Sir Edward Hille and Thomas Noreys, both sheriffs of Somerset and Dorset, fall into this category.[27] The balance of power in the county was tilted even more decisively in favour of Suffolk's faction when one of his adherents, Sir James Ormond, earl of Wiltshire, inherited a vast west-country estate by virtue of his marriage to Avis Stafford.[28] The Courtenay earls of Devon had never enjoyed an overriding dominance in either Somerset or Dorset, although they were major landowners in both, but the affinities here described maintained a hold over public affairs that almost entirely deprived Earl Thomas of any political role there. A similar pattern emerges in Cornwall. This county was exceptional in that it was dominated by the huge pool of patronage provided by the duchy of Cornwall. As steward with special responsibilities within the county, Bonville figured prominently in its affairs although his authority was undermined somewhat by the disruptive appointment of Devon to a similar post in 1441. Suffolk's interest in Cornwall had developed in the 1430s when he received various keeperships there as well as the wardship of John Arundel who, partly through Suffolk's patronage, became one of the key figures in the county and duchy.[29] The earl of Devon, despite his considerable estates in the eastern parts of the county, could not compete with the massed forces of Suffolk's patronage machine. During the 1440s the death of both Lord Fanhope and the earl of Huntingdon had released vast amounts of duchy bounty in the form of estates and perquisites. Some of this was made over to Arundel, but much more was given to a couple of royal retainers who were to become, in effect, the king's lieutenants there: Thomas Bodulgate and John Trevelian.[30] The sense of solidarity within this élite was strengthened by the formation of marriage ties such as those of Trevelian, who married the daughter of a king's esquire, Thomas Whalesborough, who was also a sheriff of Cornwall and keeper of the king's venison there, and Arundel, who married the widow of Sir William Stafford, thereby carrying ties of affinity across county borders. As in Somerset and Dorset, the earl of Devon found it almost impossible to attract clients from the affinities being built up by those men who were able to capture an increasing share of the limited crown patronage available.

It was in Devonshire itself, however, the traditional centre of Courtenay power, that the earl's need to influence the selection of local government personnel was greatest. Although the death of his mother in 1441 had released resources hitherto unavailable to him, it was still necessary for

Earl Thomas to secure unimpeded access to crown patronage if he were to satisfy the expectations of the leading members of the county establishment. The situation in Devonshire was by no means as desperate as that facing the earl in the adjoining counties. Indeed, as will be shown later, he commanded a striking degree of control over the lesser-ranking gentry throughout the decade. It was the senior members of the political community who had sought and found alternative lordship and felt no compulsion to transfer their loyalties to Devon. The sheriffs of Devonshire in the middle years of the 1440s illustrate this fact: John Cheyne was Bonville's kinsman, maintained his association with Bonville and his circle, and married his daughter to one of Sir Philip Courtenay's sons; John Blewet forged connections with members of the dominant group in Cornwall, men such as Arundel, Bodulgate and Trevelian as well as with Bonville himself, but none with Earl Thomas; while Nicholas Broughton was a peacetime retainer of Lord Harington, a close friend and relation of Bonville.[31] Bonville's social promotion as one of Suffolk's clients, culminating in his elevation to the peerage as Lord Bonville in 1449, forced the earl of Devon, as we have seen, to emerge from the country and fight for patronage and recognition at Court.

If Earl Thomas's self-imposed exile in the west country in the early 1440s had made little impression on the leading members of the county establishment, he was nevertheless able to reinforce his family's traditional control over those gentlemen of lesser status. The social and political horizons of these men were generally more localised than those of the wealthier and more influential gentry. Of the 116 men who attested the Devonshire elections between 1442 and 1455, a group drawn in the main from the lesser gentry, most of those for whom accurate genealogies can be constructed married within the county.[32] Together they provided the crown and local magnates with a substantial pool of administrative expertise and formed a community of considerable political significance. About one-fifth were lawyers, a little over a third were involved in local government and a quarter sat in parliament to represent usually a borough but, occasionally, the county. They were a diverse group in terms of wealth and social standing: some were gentlemen about whom little can be ascertained whilst others, like John Coplestone and Nicholas Radford who were attached to the household of the earl of Devon and Lord Bonville respectively, were men of honour whose status was in part determined by their important connections.[33] It is impossible to calculate how many members of this group of over one hundred were related to each other, but certain key kindred links emerge, and the problems of asserting political control over this body of men lay partly in dominating certain family groupings.[34] In the 1440s Earl Thomas exerted a striking degree of control over the Devonshire electorate of which, of course, the attestors formed a part. It underlines the fact that, however alarming his decline in influence over the upper rank of the gentry may have been, his ability to mobilise public opinion further down the social scale was still impressive. Of those returned to the parliament of 1442, Thomas Carminow, Henry Denbold, Robert Hille, William Henderston, John Serle, John Werthe and Robert Wyse were connected in various ways to the earl.[35] The full results of the 1445 election do not survive, but the county M.Ps. were Henderston, along with the earl's steward, William Boeff.[36] In 1447 Henderston was again returned, together with one of the earl's supporters in the early 1450s, Thomas Wyse, and a considerable number of the attestors were associates of Earl Thomas.[37] The pattern continued into 1449: the January election saw Henderston again returned, along with the earl's second cousin, Thomas Dauney, and William Cruwys, Thomas Dourish and John Deneys, all of whom were associated with the earl or prominent members of his circle.

Devon's command of the Devonshire electorate is most dramatically illustrated in the results of the November 1449 election, which took place against a groundswell of resentment against Suffolk and his faction that was soon to lead to the duke's fall and murder. To this anti-Suffolk parliament the Devonshire electorate returned a body of M.Ps. predominantly composed of the earl of Devon's men. Henderston (representing the county), Dourish (Exeter) and Denbold (Tavistock) have already been encountered. Thomas Calwodelegh (Totnes) was closely related through his mother to a family connected by service to both Earl Thomas and his father.[38] John Hatch (Devonshire) was related to the Cruwys brothers, who were committed adherents of the earl in the early 1450s. John Hobbys (Totnes) was one of the earl's parkers in Tiverton.[39] Thomas Holand (Exeter) came out in support of the earl in 1451 and Robert Hilling (Plympton) was pardoned for having done the same.[40] The electors of Plymouth returned two of Devon's servants, Thomas Welywrought and John Brigham.[41]

Devon's control over the Devonshire electorate remained strong throughout 1450.[42] Even so, access to the royal patronage was a matter of great urgency, particularly during the insecure and unstable months that followed the death of Suffolk. It is not possible to date with certainty the beginning of his association with Richard, duke of York. Possibly it was at some time in September when many men hastened to make their peace with him.[43] By late November he emerged as one of the small number of lords who supported York in his display of strength at the Westminster parliament.[44] Devon was also responsible for saving the duke from acute political embarrassment when he safely delivered the duke of Somerset from the hands of a mob that seems to have been intent on killing him.[45] But the small gains Devon made during the brief ascendancy of York during the last months of 1450 and the early part of 1451 hardly merited the political risks he had run and the expense he had incurred in maintaining a body of liveried familiars in London for two months or more.[46] York's power was in any case illusory: he was not capable of challenging the entrenched position of the court circle ranged around Somerset and his satellites. By May Somerset's authority was established. His faction was able to maintain its control over the distribution of royal largesse and men anxious to find new patrons after the death of Suffolk gravitated towards this group. Bonville was one of these and he developed a connection with the earl of Wiltshire that was to have a damaging impact on west-country political life, for the earl of Devon, who was once again excluded from government, chose to embark on the first of his notorious local wars against both Bonville and Wiltshire.

The character and scale of Devon's Somerset campaign in September 1451 is now well known.[47] It involved Devon and his army marching across the county to Wiltshire's house at Lackham (near Bath) and then, when they found that their prey had flown, marching back again in order to besiege Lord Bonville in Taunton Castle. The siege was called off only when news arrived of the approach of the duke of York accompanied by Sir William Herbert and Lord Moleyns. This induced the belligerents to patch up a hasty and hollow peace.[48] Yet, unlike the earl of Devon's exploits late in 1455, the Somerset campaign was far more than a straightforward attempt to settle old personal scores.[49] When set in the wider context of York's shift towards open opposition to the Court party, of which, of course, both Bonville and Wiltshire were members, a connection between Devon's activities and those of York in September seems probable. The duke's involvement in the activities of his allies struck contemporary observers as being far from disinterested. He moved west in order to lend support to the earl of Devon. The indictments filed against the rebels by a jury of presentment in 1452 stressed the authority wielded by York who allowed Devon to go in peace as if he enjoyed the king's good will, even though York exceeded his authority in doing so.[50] The pro-Yorkist 'Benet's Chronicle' — an important source for these events — states that the king's anger with all those involved in the insurrection was so great that he ordered the internment for one month of Wiltshire and Bonville in Berkhamstead Castle and Cobham and Moleyns (who had moved west with the duke) in Wallingford.[51] The chronicler goes on to relate that, despite repeated royal summonses, neither York nor Devon appeared before the king. The relevance of this detail to the general theme of this paper is that it was largely because Devon's Somerset campaign was seen to be part of a broader expression of grievances against the Court and voiced in particular by the duke of York that it attracted to its banners a respectable number of local gentry. These formed, proportionately, a far larger group than did those gentry who were prepared to support the earl in 1455 when he was operating in a context divorced from wider loyalties and lacking popular objectives.[52] The political isolation of the earl of Devon in 1455, which forced him to attempt to solve his problems by resorting to civil war, was in large measure the result of events on Blackheath in March 1452. As might be expected of nobles deeply resentful of their exclusion from power and influence, York's and Devon's expedition in February and March was an ambitious one that aimed to confront the king and force the removal of the duke of Somerset. Their plan involved the co-ordination of anti-government demonstrations over a wide area of the south midlands and the west country and the junction of York's army with that of Devon moving east from Devonshire and Somerset.[53] These troops encamped near Dartford in Kent impressively arrayed with guns and banners, but the king's duplicity deprived the leaders of their armed support. Henry promised to dismiss Somerset on condition that York and Devon disband their forces. This they did, but the king then refused to reject his favourite, thus leading the way to the humiliating submission of the duke and his allies on Blackheath on 2 March. Whilst neither York nor (at this point) Devon was tried for treason, their submission at Blackheath marked the nadir of their political fortunes.

To all the earl's accumulated and inherited disadvantages was now added the penalty of political disgrace, one consequence of which was a short term of imprisonment.[54] Blackheath also inaugurated a period of eighteen months during which Bonville was to enjoy an unchallenged ascendancy in Devonshire allowing him to make serious inroads into the earl's traditional area of support, the lesser gentry. Bonville enjoyed the backing of the government, which reinforced his local position by means of numerous grants and offices. In February 1452 he was pardoned any offences that he may have committed against the statute of liveries.[55] In March, in order to avoid any ambiguity, he was confirmed in his office of steward of the duchy of Cornwall and in September he received further grants from the duchy.[56] In April 1453 he was appointed keeper and constable of Exeter castle and, provocatively, conserver of the waters of the Exe, a post previously held by the earl and which carried with it powers of enquiry into offences committed within the earl's manor of Topsham.[57] He became extremely active as a J.P. in the west country especially during the summer of 1452, when he was largely responsible for bringing Devon's adherents to justice. The seal was set on Bonville's local supremacy by the king's progress through the south-west that year: not only did Henry VI pass through the earl's borough of Crewkerne (Somerset) and the abbey of Forde (traditionally associated with the Courtenay family), but he was entertained by Bonville at his house at

Shute.[58] The local consequences of these shifts of fortune were considerable. Bonville was able to mobilise support from amongst the more modest-ranking members of the political community, a group which had hitherto been in many respects the preserve of the earl of Devon. The Devonshire electors in February 1453 returned two friends of Bonville to represent the county, Walter Ralegh and Walter Reynell, and furthermore no fewer than a quarter of the attestors at this election had been members of juries that presented against the earl and his adherents in 1452.[59]

The king's illness (which occurred in August 1453) and the imprisonment of Somerset in November threatened to change all this. In fact, Bonville had used his eighteen months of unchallenged dominance in the west country to good effect and was so successfully entrenched there that even the duke of York was unable to dispense with his services during his first protectorate. But Bonville nevertheless took precautions. At some point in January 1454, he and Wiltshire were mobilising their forces in the west and 'maken all the puissance they kan' in a bid (so the correspondent John Stodeley thought) to overawe London.[60] His recent commission to safeguard the sea enabled him to raise shipping as well as land forces.[61] His seizure of shipping early in 1454 antagonised the merchants of both London and Calais. So great was their wrath that the chancellor 'was so dismayed that he coude ne myght no sey to thym for fere'.[62] Bonville's activities in this field angered even the duke of Burgundy, who sent Sir Edmund Mulso to England to insist that 'justice be don uppon the lord Bonevyle, or els that he be sent to hym to do justice by hym self, as he hath deserved, or satisfaccion be made to the value'.[63] Moves against the earl of Devon and, implicitly, the duke of York were being pursued simultaneously on another front. In January indictments relating to the 1452 rising were required to be dispatched from Somerset to London so that they could be used as evidence against the earl of Devon, who was arraigned on a charge of treason.[64] The indictment against the earl implicated the duke of York, who 'conceyved the trouthe of his alliegeaunce to bee emblemyshed and disteigned'.[65] After Devon's acquittal York was to make his protestation of innocence which, being wholly accepted by the lords there present, made possible his appointment as protector on 27 March.

Richard of York's assumption of power did nothing to reduce the political instability in Devonshire. Indeed, it served to aggravate the situation there: feeling unable actively either to undermine Bonville's position or bolster that of the earl, York's régime acted ambivalently and a combination of ineptitude and prevarication led to a long summer of violence and murder. At first York acted sympathetically towards Devon, who several times appeared at council meetings during March and April.[66] But at the same time, York and the other magnates were growing increasingly concerned at the deteriorating state of law and order in Devonshire. The most serious offence was the disruption of the assizes at Exeter in April and the associated attacks on Bonville there by the earl's sons, Thomas and Henry, and his cousin, Sir Hugh Courtenay of Boconnoc.[67] Yet these disturbances were a direct consequence of the government's refusal to remove Bonville from the commission of the peace and its extraordinary decision to include not only Bonville but also the earl of Wiltshire (who had recently been dropped from the council along with the duke of Somerset) on a commission of 21 April to raise a loan in the county.[68] Although the earl of Devon was not directly involved in the attacks on Bonville, the government had little doubt that the responsibility lay squarely with Earl Thomas. Before he left for the west country, the council took heavy bonds for his future good behaviour.[69] When, in September, the sessions were again disrupted it was the earl himself who led a far larger body of men than had congregated in Exeter five months previously. But this was only after a summer's violence that had witnessed the murder of one of the earl's servants, John Hoye, by Bonville's bastard son.[70]

The king's recovery forced all men to reappraise their position. The avoidance of elections in the spring of 1455 indicates that Somerset and Wiltshire were aware of the extent of hostility towards their régime, but they appear not to have recognised the immediacy of the threat.[71] Events moved fast and, not surprisingly, several lords who were not closely identified with the king's Court found themselves at the first battle of St Albans under Henry's banner. Devon was one of these. Bonville, on the other hand, avoided the battle although he was represented there by his pursuivant. That the earl was still considered by York to be sympathetic to his cause is suggested by the fact that when letters were sent by Duke Richard and his allies to the king at Watford on the eve of the battle they were handed personally to Earl Thomas.[72] Furthermore, according to 'Bale's Chronicle' the earl, along with the earls of Salisbury and Warwick, 'kept the roialte and sport' as they accompanied the king to London from St Albans.[73] This *rapprochement* with the Yorkists was not destined to last long. Enjoying the good lordship of the duke of York now involved forging an association with the Nevilles and this proved impossible for the earl. It must have been shortly after St Albans that Bonville's relations, the Haringtons, themselves clients of the earl of Salisbury, began to sing the praises of their lord. The date of the marriage of Lord Bonville's grandson (another William, aged about fifteen) to Salisbury's daughter, Catherine Neville, is not known but it probably occurred before the end of the year. On 1 December Bonville acted as a feoffee of Eleanor, widow of the earl of Northumberland who was killed at St Albans, but herself a Neville as Salisbury's sister.[74] This demonstrates that his connection with the Neville family was well established by this time. The drift of events must have become clear before long to Earl Thomas and he quickly left London for the west country. His fears were fully justified. During the 1455 parliament Bonville was appointed one of the keepers of the sea and one of the triers of petitions for Gascony.[75] By December he was closely identified with the ruling faction and commissioned to assist in the suppression of Devon's outrages in the south-west, a partisan appointment made in defiance of a parliamentary request that Bonville, as well as the earl, should be placed in custody.[76]

Devon's hostility towards the Nevilles (if not to York personally) was deepened by developments in the ecclesiastical arena. Early in October 1455 the canons of Exeter received permission to elect a new bishop to replace Edmund Lacy, who had died in September. They chose John Hals, who had been provided to the see by Calixtus III at the special request of King Henry. His credentials for the post were irresistible: of local lineage and the son of a justice of the king's bench, he had been a canon and prebendary of Exeter since 1438. More significant, however, were his crown connections. He had been in royal service since the late 1420s and one of Queen Margaret's chaplains since 1446.[77] His candidature must have been happily received by the cathedral chapter, which was of a distinctly royalist hue. But the choice of Hals was wholly unacceptable to the Nevilles. During York's first protectorate the chancellor (Salisbury) had persuaded the council that it should make available to his son, George, aged about twenty-one, whichever bishopric should next fall vacant.[78] When York was again in power the Nevilles induced Hals to decline his newly-gained bishopric. Pope Calixtus could only be prevailed upon to endorse the new election after being informed by letter that Neville, despite his youth, was a suitable person for so remote and disturbed a see. Remote it might be, disturbed it certainly was, but above all it was valuable and although Neville was debarred from carrying out many of his spiritual and pastoral duties he was able (from March 1456) to enjoy its considerable revenues and mobilise them in the interests of his family.[79] The earl of Devon's attacks on leading canons such as Henry Webber in November, when the election of Neville took place, had a variety of motives, but the prospect of the temporalities moving into the hands of one of the most powerful families in England and one to which his greatest enemy had attached himself by marriage must have reinforced his conviction that the only solution to his problems lay in adopting a strategy whereby he would meet his adversary face to face and destroy him on the battlefield.

As has been suggested, the violence of the last few months of 1455 and the early part of 1456 was qualitatively different from what went before. The duration of earlier campaigns could be measured in terms of days rather than the two months or more of Devon's retinue operations in 1455. Certainly, many elements that were present in the 1455 disorders were equally characteristic of earlier troubles: the occupation of Exeter, the disruption of the sessions, attacks on the king's commissioners, robbery and assault had all been ingredients of local turbulence since the late 1440s. Lives had been lost and armies assembled before, but by October 1455 no quarter was to be given to the enemy. It was Radford's assassination that marked the change.[80] The enormity of this crime horrified contemporary opinion. It was not just Radford's eminent and respected position in local society, enhanced by his membership of Bonville's council, that gave the deed its peculiar flavour; rather was it the assault on accepted modes of behaviour and contemporary mores. Sir Thomas Courtenay (the earl's eldest son) had given his word as a knight and a gentleman that Radford would not be harmed, and he had grossly betrayed this trust.[81] Radford was godfather to another of the Courtenay sons, Henry. The funeral (which involved the mutilation of the body) was accompanied by the singing of lewd songs. All legal processes, particularly the inquest, had been usurped by the murderers. The element of mockery shocked even the hardened sensibilities of the age. The venom manifest in the execution of the crime shows that the Courtenay family felt betrayed by Radford's connection with Bonville. Whether or not Radford's very considerable wealth motivated the assailants cannot be known but they certainly felt no compunction about seizing it after his death. After a long and distinguished career Radford died a rich man. He had recently (January 1455) enfeoffed Bonville and others of land worth £400 and the earl's troops plundered goods of his to the value of several hundred pounds. Indeed, the cash and valuables seized by Devon from all sources — valued in the indictments at over £2,500 — doubtless financed the campaign. There are few references in the small number of the earl's ministers' accounts that survive from this period to expenses related to the war: the reeve of Tiverton paid out a small sum for the repair of guns in 1455-56 and another small sum to repair the 'great gun' the following year.[82] The war was financed out of the profits it generated, its booty.

The scale of the earl of Devon's 'grevous riotes' alarmed parliament, which had visions of 800 cavalry and 4,000 foot soldiers rampaging through the county.[83] Professor Lander rightly attached importance to these events, 'which seem to have influenced to a greater extent than is usually realised the action taken in parliament'.[84] They can only be described in terms of civil war, but to what degree the deaths at St Albans — which marked in many ways the culmination of the Neville-Percy vendetta — helped mould Devon's attitude towards dealing with Bonville it is not possible to say. The 'battle' of Clyst, as has been mentioned, was preceded by what amounts to a formal declaration of war. Innocent people suffered and agrarian life was disrupted by the violence. Little income was forthcoming from the manor of Bishops Clyst, for instance, where 'no-one dared occupy the land for fear of the servants of the earl of Devon' and where 'the bailiffs and tenants were in peril of death because of the quarrel between the earl and Lord Bonville'.[85] Although this community lay at the centre of events and cannot be taken as typical of rural experience during the wartime months, a wide area of south-east Devonshire was nevertheless subjected to frequent sorties, burnings, ransackings and assaults. As to casualties, no sound figures survive. 'Benet's Chronicle' states that twelve men were killed and many wounded on either side at Clyst.[86] Small as these numbers are, they do not appear insignificant when compared with the sixty or so who lost their lives at St Albans.[87]

An analysis of the social composition of the earl's adherents in both 1451 and 1455 demonstrates that the political pressures that forced Earl Thomas to adopt the extreme course of civil war at the same time deprived him of yet more of his traditional support. In other words, his desperate measures in 1455 exacerbated a trend that had been evident over the previous two decades and more.[88] It is worth stressing that the 1451 campaign was associated with York's attempts to gain his rightful place in the king's counsels and its immediate objective was to remove the rapacious courtier, the earl of Wiltshire, whose recent acquisition of property in the south-west was causing widespread resentment. In 1455, however, Earl Thomas was acting in isolation and was no longer seen to be favoured by any major grouping. There was little to be gained from an association with him and much to be endangered by it. He was embarking on an ill-advised policy of terrorisation and violence in pursuit of a private feud and he made little attempt to conceal his motives.[89] The social make-up of his followers reflects his growing loss of credibility. The gentry element (that is, gentlemen and above) as a proportion of the whole fell from 19% in 1451 to 9% in 1455. This drop was particularly marked amongst the upper ranks of this group (esquires and above): in 1451 Devon had been accompanied by a lord, but in 1455 the only representatives of the upper stratum of local society were close members of his own family. The earl's main body of support came from the small farmer and this contingent remained constant: yeomen and husbandmen together formed 50% of the 1451 army and 49% of the 1455.[90] There was a striking rise in the proportion of artisans, textile workers and those in service occupations (servants, grooms, etc.) from 27% in 1451 to 40% in 1455. Most of this latter group (76%) were drawn from Exeter, Tiverton and other smaller towns mainly in the south-east of the county. This increase suggests that he was more dependent in 1455 than he had been in 1451 on the somewhat less stable elements in local society. The buoyant economy of south-east

Devonshire, whence the bulk of the earl's support came, would have created considerable disruption and social tension; this situation would have been aggravated by the existence, even within this prosperous area, of manors displaying all the classic symptoms of depression.[91] From this sometimes grim, desperate and unstable world the prospect of enjoying the spoils of war would have appeared irresistible.

Devon's imprisonment shortly after his surrender to York just before Christmas 1455, and the preparations being made to try him for treason in January, ensured that Henry VI's resumption of power in February 1456 came as a considerable relief to the earl. A speedy conversion from York to Lancaster brought with it valuable dividends. The projected trial was abandoned.[92] Although the government issued directives aimed at stemming the tide of violence that persisted unabated in Devonshire well into the new year, they came to nothing and in September the earl was restored to the bench of J.Ps.[93] In February 1457 he and his sons were pardoned for the murder of Radford along with all their other offences.[94] In July he was granted the keeping of the forest and park of Clarendon.[95] The increasing polarisation of English political life in the late 1450s prompted King Henry — or more precisely the queen — to consolidate support from all quarters, even from the earl of Devon, and this ensured that what Earl Thomas had been fighting for decades to achieve at last became a reality. The government was prepared to do nothing effective about reducing the level of disorder in the west country and was also prepared to reopen the channels of royal patronage to the Courtenay earls of Devon. At some point during the year 1456-57 the new alliance between the crown and the Courtenays was sealed in a spectacular fashion: the earl's eldest son, Sir Thomas Courtenay, married Queen Margaret's cousin, Marie, daughter of Charles, count of Maine.[96] Earl Thomas did not for long enjoy his newly-acquired good fortune, for he died at Abingdon in February 1458.[97] His executors included some of the core members of the queen's circle, William Booth, archbishop of York, John, earl of Shrewsbury and the chief justice, Sir John Fortescue.[98] Considering these connections, it seems highly unlikely that any truth lies behind the Yorkist slur to the effect that the queen had poisoned the earl of Devon.[99]

The new earl remained an unflinching supporter of the queen. After the Yorkist victory at Northampton, he gathered his tenants and moved north to join her.[100] After Wakefield (at which both Bonville's son, Lord Harington, and his grandson, William Bonville the younger, were killed) his forces formed part of the royal army that defeated Warwick at St Albans. Here Lord Bonville himself perished. The circumstances of his death made him a martyr to the Yorkist cause. He and Sir Thomas Kyriel had been given the custody of the king's person during the battle and King Henry had undertaken to spare their lives, but at the instigation of the queen, the earl of Devon and the duke of Exeter, a mock trial was held before the child prince of Wales and they were both executed.[101] Devon did not long survive this callous killing of his old adversary: after Towton he 'was seke and myght not voyde a waye, and was take and be heddyd'.[102] It is difficult to judge the impact of these events on the people of Devonshire. Certainly men from the county were involved in the fighting, but the great battles were all fought far away from the west country. The level of local disorder remained high and caused various governments some anxiety, especially in 1456, 1460 and 1461. The local civil war in 1455 had convinced men that only by taking the law into their own hands and solving disputes by violent means could their interests be safeguarded. The drift of national affairs after 1458 served to reinforce this attitude. This failure to use the courts deprives the historian of a major source of evidence upon which to make an assessment of the scale of violence in Devonshire. It is equally difficult to observe exactly how men responded to the changes in the local balance of power brought about by the varying fortunes of York and Lancaster. The ascendancy of the Court party enabled the earl of Devon to influence local appointments: for instance, the escheator of Devonshire and Cornwall selected in November 1459 was his receiver, John Anlaby.[103] A similar pattern prevailed during the period of Yorkist control of the administration after Northampton. The sheriff of Devon, John Dinham, was closely related to Bonville's friend, Lord Fitzwaryn. The scale of gift-giving indicates at least the city of Exeter's conception of the balance of power in the county. In the years between the king's resumption of power in 1456 and the battle of Northampton, the city receiver was authorised to distribute gifts of unprecedented generosity to the crown's leading local supporters. No expense was spared in gratifying the duke of Exeter (who inherited large estates in the county in 1457) and his wife: she was given a present worth twenty pounds in the summer of 1456 and he received from the city fathers silver valued at £26 13s. 4d.[104] The city registered its respect for the new earl of Devon and his distinguished wife not only with gifts of wine but also (for her) a quantity of damask.[105] The ascendancy of the Court faction in Devonshire was reinforced when the earl of Devon and his countess stayed at Dartington as the guests of the duke and duchess of Exeter at some point during the year 1457-58, thus publicly sealing the political bond between them.[106]

This powerful local alliance of a 'ducal hothead' and the unprincipled murderer of Radford — a combination hardly designed to induce a sense of security in the area — pushed those who were implacably hostile to the earl of Devon firmly into the Yorkist camp. During the first short period of Yorkist control of the king and his administration in the months after Northampton and, again, during the first months of Edward IV's reign, county officials were drawn predominantly from the affinities of Bonville and his friends Lord Fitzwaryn and Sir Philip Courtenay. Of the fifty-one commissioners whose remit lay exclusively within Devonshire during the period from July 1460 to February 1461 and from March to June 1461, nearly a quarter can be shown to have been overtly hostile to the earl of Devon in 1455-56. More striking is the fact that of this relatively small group of fifty-one, one-third were closely related (or became so within the first year or so of Edward's reign) to Sir Philip Courtenay or Fitzwaryn. In other words, during the first months of his reign, Edward was dependent for the good governance of Devonshire on an affinity and kindred group centred on these two magnates. The large number of children within this group of marriageable age attracted suitors from among the most important local families, thus reinforcing the position of the affinity as the major political bloc in the county. Although this situation was not destined to last, for a short time at least Fitzwaryn's circle maintained a dominance in Devonshire not unlike that enjoyed in the 1380s by Edward Courtenay, earl of Devon. But for the remaining representatives of the comital family, 1461 marked the beginning of the end. It was quite impossible for the last earl's brothers to form a coherent political grouping about themselves and it is significant that they remained unmarried at a time when the marriage market in Devonshire was brisk indeed.[107]

NOTES

1. DRO, Exeter city receiver's roll, 34–35 Henry VI (1455-56). Clyst is about three miles south-east of Exeter.
2. Huntingdon Library (USA), Battle Abbey Muniments, external affairs, folder 32, no. 937. I am indebted to Dr Ralph A. Griffiths for making photocopies of these documents available to me.
3. Charles Ross, *The Wars of the Roses* (1976), pp.29,132; J.R. Lander, *Conflict and Stability in Fifteenth-Century England* (3rd.ed., 1977), p.78.
4. M. Cherry, 'The Courtenay Earls of Devon: The Formation and Disintegration of a Late-Medieval Aristocratic Affinity', *Southern History,* I (1979), 71-97.
5. Ibid., pp.94-97.
6. DRO,CR536; BL, Add. Ch., 64,325.
7. See the relevant entries in J.C. Wedgwood, *History of Parliament, 1439-1509, Biographies* (1936), pp.20, 621-22, 721.
8. *PPC,* VI, 315.
9. *CPR, 1436-41,* p.532.
10. *CPR, 1441-46,* pp.54, 410.
11. Ibid., p.355.
12. *CPR, 1436-41,* p.133. Bonville's remit was as steward of the duchy within the county of Cornwall.
13. *CPR, 1435-41,* p.396; *PPC,* V, 175.
14. *PPC,* V, 158, 173-75.
15. Ibid., pp.159-60, 166.
16. Ibid., pp.112-13; see above pp. 81–82.
17. Ibid., p.240.
18. Above p. 82.
19. G. du Fresne de Beaucourt, *Chronique de Mathieu d'Escouchy* (Paris, 1863; reprinted 1968), I, 88.
20. This matter had first been brought before the 1445 parliament and judgement postponed. *RP,* V, 148; see also *CP,* I, 231 note b, 248.
21. There were two periods during the decade when an exceptionally large number of cases involving Devonshire gentry were brought before the king's bench, namely, late 1446 and late 1449. PRO, KB27/742, 754.
22. AN, K68/18 m.35. I am indebted to Anne Marshall for this reference.
23. *HMC, Hastings MSS.,* I(1928), 1.
24. PRO, C53/189 m.1,3,4,9,28; 190 m.12,29,35,36,41-47.
25. For Sir Philip Courtenay's Luttrell connection, see H.C. Maxwell-Lyte, *A History of Dunster* (1909), I, 118-19, and M. Cherry. 'The Courtenay Earls of Devon', pp.95-96. For Rodney, see Wedgwood, op.cit., pp.720-21.
26. These were William Carent, Sir John Chideock and Sir William Stafford, sheriffs of Somerset and Dorset in 1446-47, 1447-48 and 1441-42 respectively. For Stourton, see *CP,* XII, part 1, pp.301-2, and for his position in the council, R. Virgoe, 'The Composition of the King's Council, 1437-61', *BIHR,* XLIII (1970), 60-61.
27. For Hille, see *CPR, 1436-41,* p.560; *CPR, 1446-52,* p.45. For Noreys, see Wedgwood, op. cit., p.637.
28. The properties are listed in E.A. and G.S. Fry, 'Dorset Feet of Fines, 1327-1485', *Dorset Records* (1910), p.322.
29. J. Pym Yeatman, *History of the House of Arundel* (1882).
30. Trevelian's posts (many of which he held jointly with Bodulgate) are given in Wedgwood, op.cit., pp.873-74.

31. These were sheriffs in 1443–44, 1444–45 and 1445–46 respectively. For Cheyne's as-
     sociation with Bonville and his circle, see e.g. *CFR, 1437-45*, p.133; *CPR, 1436-41*,
     p.540. For those of Bluet, see *CPR, 1441-46*, p.137; *CPR, 1446-52*, p.91; *CCR, 1441-
     47*, p.148. For Broughton's connection with Harington, see PRO, E163/7/31 part 1.
32. This sample is taken from the chancery returns of M.P.s to which are appended the
     lists of attestors: PRO, C219/15/2-16/3 (Devonshire returns). Only very rarely do the
     names of knights appear on these lists.
33. Coplestone was the earl's receiver in the late 1420s and the early 1450s: BL, Add. Ch.,
     64, 324; DRO, CR 521. Radford was in Bonville's service by the late 1440s: PRO,
     SC6/1117/7.
34. A detailed study of this group is being prepared by the author.
35. Carminow (Devonshire) was the earl's cousin and Hille was Carminow's father-in-
     law. Denbold was portreeve of the earl's borough of Okehampton. E.H. Young,
     'Okehampton', *Devonshire Association Parochial Histories of Devonshire*, I, 63.
     Henderston was later employed by the earl: DRO, CR 493. Serle was a long-serving
     M.P. for the earl's borough of Plympton and Werthe was amongst the earl's sup-
     porters in the 1450s.
36. Boeff was steward in 1447–48: DRO, CR 523.
37. PRO, C219/15/4, part 1, m.18.
38. This was the Floyer family, for whom see DRO, CR 493 and 494.
39. BL, Add. Ch., 64,714.
40. PRO, KB9/267, m.42B; C67/40, m.13.
41. BL, Add. Ch., 64,717; DRO, CR 493. See also Wedgwood, op. cit., pp.112, 931.
42. Amongst those returned to this parliament were Calwodelegh, Dauney, Henderston,
     Hobbys, Holand, Hilling and Wyse.
43. R.A. Griffiths, 'Duke Richard of York's Intentions and the Origins of the Wars of the
     Roses', *Journal of Medieval History*, I (1975), 197.
44. Ralph Flenley (ed.), *Six Town Chronicles* (Oxford, 1911), p.106.
45. G.L. and M.A. Harriss, 'John Benet's Chronicle', *Camden Miscellany, XXIV* (4th. ser.,
     IX, 1972), p.203. There is another account of the incident in 'Worcester's Annals' in J.
     Stevenson (ed.), *Wars of the English in France during the Reign of Henry VI* (RS, 1861-64),
     II, 769.
46. The earl of Devon and the duke of Norfolk are recorded as having led 3,000 men
     between them in December 1450. 'Benet's Chronicle', p.203.
47. R.L. Storey, *The End of the House of Lancaster* (1966), ch. 5.
48. PRO, KB9/267 m.44.
49. Lord Cobham's feud with Wiltshire dates from January 1451, when he attacked one of
     the earl's servants, Robert Cappes. PRO, KB27/761, m.42, 50; 762, m.30.
50. PRO, KB9/267, m.42B. See also Storey, op. cit., p.92.
51. 'Benet's Chronicle', p.205.
52. The social composition of the earl's adherents in 1451 and 1455 is discussed belo p.137.
53. Storey, op.cit., pp.98-99.
54. Only the most important of the west-country leaders ended up in prison. Sir Hugh
     Courtenay of Boconnoc was placed in the Marshalsea and Cobham in Berkhamstead:
     PRO, KB9/268, m.90; *RP*, V, 248. The exact date of Devon's internment in
     Wallingford Castle is difficult to establish. York remained at liberty (although in dis-
     grace) and it seems likely that the earl was not immediately imprisoned. 'Benet's
     Chronicle' (p.208) states that he was placed in Wallingford 'shortly before Christmas
     1452'. More problematic is the date of his release. 'Benet's Chronicle' gives it as soon
     after Somerset's arrest in November 1453 (p.211), but he had been summoned to
     attend parliament on 20 February 1453 and was appointed one of the triers of petitions
     in that parliament. *RP*, V, 227.

55. *CPR, 1448-52,* p.525
56. Ibid., p.526; *CPR, 1452-61,* p.18.
57. Ibid., p.91.
58. PRO, E101/410/9.
59. PRO, KB9/15/1, m.24, 29d; C219/16/2, part 1.
60. James Gairdner (ed.), *The Paston Letters* (1897), I, 264.
61. This commission was made in conjunction with his appointment to lead a new campaign to Gascony in September 1453: *CPR, 1452-61,* p.166; Stevenson, op.cit., II, 422.
62. *Paston Letters,* I, 268.
63. Ibid., p.290.
64. PRO, KB9/105, m.46.
65. *RP,* V, 249-50.
66. *PPC,* V, 116-73, 355-56.
67. PRO, KB9/16, m.76.
68. *CPR, 1452-61,* p.148.
69. *CCR,1447-52,* p.512.
70. PRO, KB9/274, m.36; Hoye had recently acted as bailiff of the earl's hundred of Hayridge: DRO, CR 523.
71. C.A.J. Armstrong, 'Politics and the Battle of St Albans, 1455', *BIHR,* XXXIII (1960), 13-17.
72. *RP,* V, 282; Armstrong, op.cit., p.22.
73. 'Bale's Chronicle' in Flenley, *Six Town Chronicles,* p.142.
74. *CCR, 1451-61,* p.98.
75. *RP,* V, 279.
76. *PPC,* VI, 267-70; *RP,* V, 332.
77. A.B. Emden, *A Biographical Register of the University of Oxford to 1500* (3 vols., Oxford), II, 856-57; John Le Neve, *Fasti Ecclesiae Anglicanae, 1300-1541,* IX (1964), 2,3.
78. *DNB,* XL, 252-56.
79. The pope insisted, however, that Neville should not be consecrated until he reached the age of twenty-seven.
80. It is not intended here to give a detailed account of what is probably the best-known private war of the mid-fifteenth century. The events are well covered by Storey, *End of the House of Lancaster,* pp. 165-75; G.H. Radford, 'Nicholas Radford, 1385(?) — 1455', *TDevonA,* XXXV (1903), 251-78, and her 'The Fight at Clyst in 1455', *TDevonA,* XLIV (1912), 252-65.
81. Three contemporary accounts of the murder survive: PRO, KB9/16, m.50; SC8/138/6864; *Paston Letters,* I, 351 (also printed in N. Davis [ed.], *Paston Letters and Papers of the Fifteenth Century,* II [Oxford, 1976], 126-27).
82. BL, Add. Ch., 64,714, 64,717.
83. *RP,* V, 285.
84. J.R. Lander, 'Henry VI and the Duke of York's Second Protectorate, 1455-6', *BJRL,* XLIII (1960-61), 44-69, and in his *Crown and Nobility, 1450-1509* (1976), p.84.
85. Quoted in N.W. Alcock, 'An East Devon Manor in the Late Middle Ages, II: Leasing the Demesne', *TDevonA,* CV (1977), 150-51.
86. 'Benet's Chronicle', p.216.
87. Armstrong, op.cit., p.50.
88. The data is taken from the indictments drawn up against the earl and his adherents. The sample consists of 210 persons from the 1451 campaign (PRO, KB9/267, m.42B, supplemented by the more carelessly compiled KB9/105/1, m.11) and 351 persons from the 1455 campaign (PRO, KB9/16, m.64-69 and SC8/138/6864).
89. See, for instance, the arguments he adopted when trying to persuade the mayor of

Exeter to join him against Bonville, as transcribed in Radford, 'The Fight at Clyst', pp.259-60.

90. Compare the similar proportion of tenant farmers who supported Egremont in 1454: R.A. Griffiths, 'Local Rivalries and National Politics: The Percies, the Nevilles and the Duke of Exeter, 1452-55', *Speculum,* XLIII (1968), 599.

91. For the buoyant local economy, see H.S.A. Fox, 'The Chronology of Enclosure and Economic Development in Medieval Devon', *Econ HR,* 2nd ser., XXVIII (1975), 181-202; for a depressed pocket within this area, see Alcock, op.cit.

92. *Paston Letters,* I, 378.

93. *CPR, 1452-61,* pp.304-5.

94. Ibid., pp.358, 393, 398.

95. Ibid., p.362.

96. Thomas Courtenay II, earl of Devon (d. 1461) is generally thought to have died unmarried. *CP,* IV, 327. Lady Radford was the first to notice a reference to the countess in the Exeter city receiver's account for 1457-58: 'The Fight at Clyst', p.264. The identity of the countess appears in DRO, CR 621 and the date of the marriage in PRO, E101/410/19. I am indebted to Dr Griffiths for this reference.

97. PRO, C139/169, m.38.

98. *CCR, 1454-61,* p.357.

99. J.S. Davies (ed.), *An English Chronicle of the Reigns of Richard II, Henry IV, Henry V and Henry VI* (Camden Soc., LXIV, 1856), p.75.

100. J. Gairdner (ed.), 'Gregory's Chronicle', in *Historical Collections of a Citizen of London* (Camden Soc., new ser., XVII, 1876), p.209.

101. 'Davies's Chronicle', pp.107-8.

102. 'Gregory's Chronicle', p.216.

103. He was the earl's receiver in 1458-59: DRO, CR 494.

104. DRO, Exeter city receivers' rolls 34-35 Henry VI (1455-56) and 35-36 Henry VI (1456-57).

105. 37-38 Henry VI (1458-59)

106. 36-37 Henry VI (1457-58).

107. See J.A.F. Thomson, 'The Courtenay Family in the Yorkist Period', *BIHR,* XLV (1972), 230-46.

7. Urban Patronage and Patrons in the Fifteenth Century

Rosemary Horrox
Beverley

Studies of medieval patronage have multiplied in the past few years and no one would now dispute its central role in late-medieval politics. To date, however, the emphasis has been on patronage of the nobility and gentry by the king or other nobles; the towns as recipients of patronage have received less attention. Urban patronage is in many ways analogous to the patronage of individuals, with formal grants underpinned by less tangible expressions of good lordship, such as backing in disputes with a third party. However, towns offer the rare chance to see the relationship from the point of view of the patronised rather than the patron. Surviving town accounts record the lobbying and expenditure entailed in securing patronage, a process which for individuals must be assumed but rarely can be demonstrated. Moreover, urban patronage provides the context in which to understand the growing use of outsiders as borough representatives in parliament. This paper examines the role of patrons and patronage in provincial towns in the fifteenth century. London, whose size always made it something of a special case, is not included, though it does conform to some of the trends outlined below.

Towns in the fifteenth century sought two main categories of grant, both in the gift of the king. The most common were grants giving financial help: remission of fee farms, favourable assessment for taxation, grants of murage and pavage. In addition, many towns sought royal permission to acquire land in mortmain, the revenues to be used to offset town expenses. These financial grants usually embody an account of the poverty and decay of the recipient town. It was of course in a town's interest to emphasise its problems when seeking help from the king, but there seems little doubt that the crescendo of financial complaint from towns in the fifteenth century was a sign of genuine economic distress.[1] Royal grants were usually little better than temporary palliatives. It was rare, for instance, for the king to grant a permanent reduction in a fee farm. Remissions were normally for a few years to help with a particular problem, such as refortifying the town. The *ad hoc* nature of royal help may not have worried the towns, whose accounts show that they tended

to manage their own financial affairs on a similar short-term basis.
Certainly for a town in economic difficulties the king must have seemed
the most obvious source of help, and urban decay inevitably gave an edge
to the towns' need for his favour.

The other major preoccupation of towns in this period was their
demand for increased local autonomy. The second half of the century has
been called the classic age of borough incorporation.[2] A few leading
towns, among them Hull, Southampton and Lincoln, went further and
acquired county status. One manifestation of this independence was an
emphasis on civic ceremonial. The 1404 charter which made Norwich a
county also allowed the mayor to have a sword borne before him, the
point erect, in the presence of all but the king himself.[3] Lesser privileges
were sometimes granted separately and were obviously valued. In 1406 the
mayor of Faversham was authorised by letters patent to have a mace
carried before him throughout the liberty of the Cinque Ports.[4] There is
evidence that towns saw local autonomy as a panacea for their economic
problems, although their faith in it was probably ill-founded.[5] A few
towns flourished after incorporation, notably Southampton, but it cannot
plausibly be claimed that incorporation played a direct part in the towns'
success.

Royal patronage of towns seems to have remained at a fairly constant
level throughout the century. Fluctuations tend to be short-term and pre-
dictable. The beginning of each reign saw a marked rise in urban
patronage as towns sought the confirmation of their charters. Such confirmations were usually routine but still involved expenditure and some
anxiety for the towns concerned. A few towns, such as Canterbury, seem
to have presented their charters for confirmation at the beginning of every
reign.[6] Others, no doubt for reasons of expense, renewed them less
regularly. A change of dynasty, for obvious reasons, brought a spate of
renewals. Henry IV's early patent rolls include many *inspeximi* of town
charters.[7] Within each reign parliamentary sessions were usually followed
by a crop of grants to towns. These were not only the result of petitions
presented within parliament itself, but reflect the opportunity taken by
many burgess members to deal with town business outside parliament.
After Henry IV's accession, for instance, Canterbury gave the task of re-
newing its charter to the two burgesses chosen for Henry's first
parliament.[8]

It is rarely possible to claim an increase in urban patronage as part of a
conscious royal policy towards towns in general. The nearest approach to
deliberate patronage of towns is provided by royal progresses, when kings
would often make grants to towns *en route*. The progress which Richard
III undertook after his coronation is a particularly clear example. The
journey was marked by a series of grants to towns, notably to Woodstock,

Gloucester, York and Lincoln. Richard's refusal to accept the traditional gifts of money on this progress was also aimed primarily at towns.[9] The motivation behind such progresses, however, seems to have been to court general public approval. There is no indication that fifteenth-century kings sought a special relationship with towns *per se*. The most that can be said is that a king might favour a particular town for political reasons and that towns, like people, might receive patronage as a reward for past service. In 1405 the burgesses of Ludlow were freed from all tolls and customs during the minority of the earl of March for their good service in resisting the Welsh rebels.[10]

At first sight the relationship between king and towns, even seigneurial towns, seems a close one in the fifteenth century. Virtually all grants are framed as a grant direct from king to town. The formula common in the early stages of urban development, whereby the king would make a grant to a town in the form of a grant to its immediate lord, had almost entirely vanished by the beginning of the fifteenth century.[11] In return, the king looked to the towns for money, for men in time of war and for general political support. The immediacy of this relationship is, however, largely illusory. Towns still relied on noble and gentry support to secure royal patronage. The lobbying which accompanied any request for royal favour was a fact of life for all but the king's closest supporters. It is, however, a comment on the standing of fifteenth-century towns that only London enjoyed anything like a direct relationship with the king. This is reflected in the status of mayors. In formal terms the mayor was the king's representative within his town, but of all fifteenth-century mayors only those of London were on a footing of any familiarity with the king.[12]

This was not simply because the king was geographically remote. Towns in the south-east, such as Canterbury or the Cinque Ports, which received regular royal visits, relied as much on the help of intermediaries at court as a town like Hull which might receive only one or two royal visits in a century. It is rather an indication that towns, even leading ports like Hull and Southampton, were still not regarded as of major political importance. The money and men they offered were welcome, and kings normally remained on good terms with them. But for political control the king looked to the nobility, and to the gentry within his household.

Towns were therefore in a vulnerable position. They needed continuing royal favour to obtain economic help and preserve their liberties, but their political muscle was slight. Their obvious solution was to find influential supporters who could press their claims at court and generally uphold their interests. This need for help increased in the course of the century. Not only did many towns find themselves in growing economic difficulties, but the dynastic struggles of mid-century increased the dangers of political miscalculation and made influential friends more desirable. The result was what has been described as an obsessive search for lordship.[13] That search and its implications form the subject of the rest of this paper.

Many towns still had an immediate lord, to whom they naturally looked for support. This is most evident in the case of manorial towns, such as Stamford or Warwick, but there were other forms of urban lordship. Some towns which were not truly manorial nevertheless had a lord with sufficient influence within the town to make him their obvious patron, like the de la Poles in Hull. Elsewhere urban lordship could be financial: the Westmorland interest in Grimsby rested solely on their control of the fee farm.[14] With all forms of hereditary lordship, however, towns were at the mercy of wide variations in ability and standing between generations. No town of any importance could afford to rely solely on its immediate lord. Local noblemen and leading gentry were courted assiduously. In the East Riding the lordship of the earls of Northumberland was sought by both Hull and Beverley, simply on the strength of their standing in the county.[15] Their holdings within the two towns seem to have been limited to a house in Hull.[16] The more lords a town could obtain, the greater its chances of compensating for fluctuations in the support of any individual lord. Towns, therefore, had no qualms in calling upon the help of lords who were the rivals of each other; indeed, they may have done so as a matter of policy. Exeter consulted both the Courtenays and Bonvilles.[17] Hull kept communications open with the Nevilles as well as with the Percies.[18]

Towns were not, however, looking only for lordship. Much of their activity was directed at securing useful contacts within the royal establishment. They were even prepared to go to expense for little more than nebulous goodwill. Town account books show the extent to which towns attempted to make use of casual visitors, even if their connection with the town was negligible. A visitor of some standing could be sure of a gift of food or wine, and towns were swift to exploit occasions which brought influential people into the vicinity. Even funerals were sometimes used in this way: Shrewsbury gave wine to the gentry attending the funeral of a son of Sir Christopher Talbot in 1443-44.[19] A more common occasion for the exercise of civic hospitality was a session of a royal commission. A commission sitting within a town would usually be feasted at the town's expense and towns were also prepared to send gifts to commissioners meeting nearby. The Beverley accounts include a payment to ministers of the king at the sessions of the peace at Weighton, ten miles away.[20]

A similar hope for goodwill lies behind the towns' generous payments to royal messengers. At Hull 6s.8d. seems to have been their usual payment but it could be as high as £2, depending on the status of the messenger and the importance of his message.[21] These payments are a useful reminder of the indirect benefits conferred by royal service. In 1450 Hamo Sutton, a yeoman of the crown, received one mark, almost a month's wages, for carrying a privy seal writ to Hull.[22] Messengers of noblemen benefited in the same way. An entry in the Rye accounts is unusually explicit:

> Expenses upon a certain pursuivant for that he carried a seal of the arms of the lord duke of Buckingham with him, and in reverence for the said seal a pleasant and joyous countenance was extended to him, 2½d. Expended upon the said pursuivant when we had him to supper, for the reverence of the said duke of Buckingham and for the honour of the town, 4d.[23]

Payments were also made to the minstrels of the king and his noblemen. The accounts of southern boroughs record many such gifts, usually made for the 'honour of the town'. The minstrels clearly had a recognised circuit, with their rewards fixed by custom.

Normally, however, town expenditure had a more specific aim. Towns backed up gifts to their lord with presents to his family, affinity and household servants. In 1460 Beverley not only gave wine to the earl of Northumberland but, on various occasions, to his mother and four of his leading retainers. It also paid a reward to one of his servants.[24] The circle of the duke of Suffolk benefited in the same way in Hull. In 1448–49 the town gave 26*s*.8*d*. to William James, the duke's chamberlain, and spent 28*s*.6½*d*. on a dinner for the ducal council.[25]

Towns were prompt to make use of local men within the royal household. In the 1440s Hull relied heavily on the help of Henry Bromflete, at that time a king's knight. In the 1480s it looked to Marmaduke Constable of Flamborough, a knight of the body of Richard III and Henry VII.[26] Many towns in the south-east turned to Sir John Scot, Edward IV's controller of the household, for help at court in the 1460s and 1470s. Rye, for instance, paid 9*s*. for fish given to him for expediting a grant of forfeited land within the town. Lydd and New Romney also made him gifts of fish.[27] Most town accounts include similar payments to royal servants with local interests. It is a reminder that the position of the household as the link between the king and the provinces was not only of value to the king but was exploited by local communities also.

Many towns had a more permanent link with the king in the form of a royal official within the town. The records of the Cinque Ports are full of references to attempts to win the friendship of the warden and of the constable of Dover castle.[28] In 1464 the ports looked to their warden to obtain royal confirmation of their new charter. In 1476 Philip Lowes, the new lieutenant of Dover, was paid £20 for his labour to the king on behalf of the ports.[29] The presence of royal officials within a town was not, however, an unmixed blessing. They could also be a threat to borough independence. The Cinque Ports banned all officials of Dover castle from membership of the Brodhull, the council of the ports, unless one were chosen as mayor of his town.[30] Southampton also suffered from the interference of royal officials. The town's charter of 1451 found it necessary to redefine parts of the 1445 charter because of the 'crafty ways and artful guise of certain of [the king's] officers who unjustly exercise their office within the said town'.[31] This conflict between urban independence and outside help is discussed in more detail below.

The most formal manifestation of the towns' search for support was their practice of retaining counsel, almost invariably lawyers with strong local connections. In return for his annual fee the lawyer was expected to give the town the benefit of his advice free. Thus, in 1455 the borough of Barnstaple paid Nicholas Radford 26s. 8d. for his fee and consulted him several times without additional payment — the accounts include the horse-hire of men riding to visit him.[32] If, however, the counsel was called upon to travel on the town's behalf or to undertake particularly complicated business it was customary for him to receive an additional reward as well as his expenses. In 1440 John Portington received his fee of 40s. from Hull and, when he visited the town for discussions, was given the cost of his accommodation and horse-hire and an additional reward of 20s.[33] It seems likely that in most towns the number of counsel retained in this way was fixed. This was certainly the case in Ipswich, where in 1490 John Yaxley, a serjeant at law, was promised the position of one of the counsel of the town at the next vacancy.[34] In addition, a few towns went to the trouble of paying a retainer to royal officials within the chancery or exchequer. The most elaborate example is provided by the Cinque Ports, which had three attorneys: in the chancery, in the exchequer and in the courts of king's bench and common pleas.[35] Ipswich retained two attorneys, one in the exchequer and one in the courts.[36] Most towns, however, preferred to avoid the expense of permanent attorneys: Hull no longer retained an attorney in London after the early 1430s.[37]

There was another category of town counsel: men who were not formally retained but who helped the town in return for gifts and *ad hoc* payments. This was true of royal clerks as well as lawyers. In the early fifteenth century Canterbury made considerable use of John Stopynden, a chancery clerk who rose to be clerk of the rolls, but he does not seem to have been formally retained as the town's attorney.[38] In many cases these were men with local connections whose national standing had become too high for them to be retained. There was a definite point beyond which it was not considered proper for a royal official to be feed by other bodies. On the exchequer side this was on appointment as a baron of the exchequer. In the early 1440s Hull retained Peter Ardern, then a serjeant at law, as counsel. When Ardern became a baron of the exchequer his annual fee was stopped, although he continued to receive gifts from the town.[39] At Beverley John Holme's career followed a similar pattern; a Beverley man by birth, he remained the town's leading adviser after his promotion.[40] For lawyers the crucial step was appointment as justice of common pleas or king's attorney. Thomas Yonge, recorder of Bristol, resigned in 1467 when he became a justice of common pleas. A more interesting example is John Portington, another of the Hull counsel. Portington continued to receive his fee when he was made an assize judge but, again, it stopped immediately he became justice of common pleas.[41]

The second half of the century saw a shift away from the formal retaining of counsel, other than the recorder, in favour of a greater reliance on less formal contacts. The Hull accounts show this particularly clearly. In 1440 the town first appointed a recorder and also had three retained counsel. In 1451 the retiring recorder was replaced by one of the counsel, who was not himself replaced. The same thing happened in 1460, and in 1473 the fee to the one remaining counsel was stopped, leaving the recorder as the only lawyer feed by the town. This remained the situation for the rest of the century.[42] A similar development is suggested by the Exeter freemen's lists, which show that from the 1480s men ceased to be made freemen for their good counsel.[43]

This reduction in feed counsel can partly be explained by the emergence of the recorder as the main legal agent in many towns. Recorders had begun to appear by the late fourteenth century: Coventry had one by 1399, and most towns of any size acquired them in the course of the fifteenth century.[44] This, however, is not the whole story. Beverley had no recorder, but there the formal retaining of counsel stopped between 1450 and 1460. The motive may have been partly financial. *Ad hoc* payments were more flexible. Although a town would still need to spend heavily on advice if it found itself in some dispute, the cancellation of annual fees meant that in a period free of disputes the town could save money. Most important, however, was the fact that towns recognised that informal contacts with men in high places were more valuable than permanent links with men setting out on their career. For a town in dispute with the king, 20s. spent on the chief justice offered more return than a 13s. 4d. fee to a local lawyer. A town which retained counsel had to spend money on national figures in any case, and under these conditions the formal retention of counsel became a less attractive proposition.

In turning to lawyers, on whatever basis, towns were not simply buying legal advice. They were much more interested in the contacts which the lawyers could offer. Nicholas Radford, recorder of Exeter and counsel of Barnstaple in the 1440s, was an influential local figure and a member of Lord Bonville's council.[45] Alexander Hody, counsel for

Bridgwater and Exeter, was steward of the earl of Salisbury.[46] His various commitments obviously kept him busy. In 1447, during Exeter's dispute with the bishop, the mayor wrote to his colleagues to explain a delay: 'The cause of so long tarrying in making of the answers hath been for right great business that Alexander Hody hath had about his own matters'.[47] Still in the south-west, Thomas Yonge, counsel of Exeter and later recorder of Bristol, was attorney of the earl of Shrewsbury and the duke of York.[48] One of the Coventry recorders, Henry Botiller, was retained by Lord Zouche as one of his learned council and as steward of his lordship of Weston in Arden, and he also acted for the de la Poles.[49]

What these contacts could mean in practice to a town is suggested by an Ipswich incident of 1493. The earl of Oxford as admiral of England ordered the arrest of a ship in the Ipswich roads. The Ipswich bailiffs refused to act and sent their charter, on which they based their refusal, to the earl. Oxford discussed the matter with his advisers and they all agreed that Ipswich was in the right. The earl's counsel on this occasion were James Hobard, then attorney general, Robert Drury, John Yaxley and Thomas Appleton. Hobard had begun his career as attorney for Ipswich in the exchequer. Yaxley has already been mentioned: he was a foreign burgess of Ipswich and prospective counsel for the town. Appleton had served on Ipswich commissions. It is not surprising that the town carried its point.[50]

These various allies and contacts were utilised by the towns in three main ways. Individual advisers were constantly called upon for help with town business. In 1449 Beverley sent men to Henry Vavasour at York to have his answer concerning a letter of the king to the inhabitants of Beverley requesting money.[51] A few years later Lydd was sending men to consult with the lieutenant of Dover: 'For counsel to be had, to know how we should be ruled when the king's men come hither to the vicar', a reference to the town's demand for a resident vicar. The same town paid half a mark to John Clerk, steward of the archbishop of Canterbury, for his 'counsel and good advice on our charters and franchises'.[52] Examples of this kind can be multiplied indefinitely. It is, however, on major issues, often disputes with another body, that a town mobilised all its support and the scale of urban lordship-hunting becomes fully apparent.

Exeter's dispute with Bishop Edmund Lacy, in the 1440s is well known. The town accounts for this period show that Exeter, as well as employing all its counsel on the matter, made gifts to the sheriff of Devon, the king's receiver in Devon, various local gentry, Sir John Fortescue and the justices of assize. The town also held several meetings with the earl of Devon and Sir William Bonville to discuss the affair. Meanwhile, in London the mayor, John Shillingford, was lobbying the chancellor and justices.[53] Even this example cannot compare with Hull's activity in the 1450s. Throughout this decade the town was in dispute with the admiral concerning its claims to the admiralty of the Humber, the quarrel finally coming to a head in 1460 when Hull shut its gates against the admiral, Lord Egremont. In a single year, 1451-52, Hull sent gifts to Northumberland and Buckingham; Lords Poynings, Roos, Beaumont, Egremont and Clifford; the bishop of Carlisle and an unspecified suffragan bishop; Sir Ralph Percy, brother of Egremont; Sir John Neville, son of the earl of Salisbury; John Portington; certain esquires of the duke of Buckingham; and the head of the Constable family of Flamborough. In the same year lobbying in London by two of the town's counsel cost over £16.[54]

This range of support could see a town through most of its problems. For a major exercise of royal patronage, however, such as a new charter, a town normally needed a single strong patron at court rather than a range of lesser supporters. It is no accident that Hull's major charter, one of the earliest incorporation charters, dates from 1440 when the town's patron, Suffolk, was in the ascendant at court.[55] At the same period Lincoln enjoyed the support of Ralph, Lord Cromwell and the town received a number of financial exemptions from the king while Cromwell was treasurer. One of the town's petitions is warranted *per dominum Crumwell*.[56] In some cases, the king himself was the patron, almost invariably because a town had built up a close relationship with him before his accession. York's relationship with Richard III is well known, and Scarborough also benefited from his accession. Stamford and Ludlow, both duchy of York manors, received important charters immediately after Edward IV's accession.[57] Such special relationships were usually short-lived. Cromwell's successor as treasurer had no connection with Lincoln and the town ceased to receive favourable treatment. After the fall of Suffolk, Hull received no major patronage until well into the next century: the duke's son and heir was a nonentity and the whole family fell from favour under Henry VII. Some of Richard III's urban grants were actually cancelled by Henry VII, although his act of resumption claimed to exclude grants to bodies corporate. Richard's grant of county status to Scarborough did not outlive him.[58]

All this activity cost money. Some urban historians have tended to be dismissive of the gifts of wine and the like which appear in every town account book. Furley, the historian of Winchester, contrasts them with 'justifiable' expenditure, such as repairs to town property. But such gifts served an explicit political purpose.[59] For the same reason, it is impossible to distinguish them, as Furley tries to do, from what he calls 'business expenditure', such as payments to counsel for their advice or the costs of men riding on town business. This distinction was not made by the towns themselves. Although the terminology of town account books varies, these two elements usually form a single category, generally headed *precepta maioris* or *expensae forinsecae.*[60]

The level of town expenditure in this category seems to have remained remarkably constant throughout the fifteenth century, although the totals for individual years can vary quite widely. The type of expenditure familiar in the fifteenth century seems, moreover, to have become established in the course of the previous century. Earlier accounts are relatively rare. One of the earliest is the first surviving Hull account, for 1320-23. There is no indication that this was an innovation and the keeping of accounts must have developed as soon as a town acquired control over a source of income, in Hull's case in the first decade of the century when the town held land for the first time. Expenditure on support in some form must have begun almost immediately. The 1320-23 account shows that Hull was already making payments to influential royal ministers and rewarding individuals for help with town business, although the range of recipients was less wide than in the fifteenth century.[61] Hull in 1320 was still a royal town, under the authority of the king's keepers. It is reasonable to suppose that as immediate royal ties loosened, the town began to look to a wider range of local dignitaries for support. The pursuit of lordship was, paradoxically, a measure of growing urban independence and as such was probably well established in most major towns before the end of the fourteenth century. The surviving fourteenth-century Beverley and Winchester accounts show a type and level of expenditure which do not differ greatly from those of the next century.[62] There is, however, some indication that the range of support sought by towns widened in the course of the fifteenth century, with more payments to peripheral figures and a greater willingness to give presents for no immediate return beyond general goodwill. Most of these payments involved only small sums and their effect on the general level of expenditure is slight.

For most large towns in the fifteenth century an average year's expenditure on *precepta maioris* seems to have been about £12, although it could drop to as little as £4. In an exceptional year, as at the height of Hull's dispute with the admiral, expenditure could be as high as £30. This does not include fees to retained counsel, which could add anything from £2 to £8 depending on the numbers retained. Nor does it take into account parliamentary expenses. Borough members were expected to lobby on their town's behalf and their costs should be included in any assessment of expenditure on lordship. On the basis of the Hull accounts such towns were spending between 12% and 15% of their income on acquiring and utilising outside support.

These figures, however, represent expenditure which could be set against the town's regular sources of income. Extraordinary payments were normally met by some form of levy on leading citizens and so do not feature in the town accounts at all but have to be picked up from corporation act books or their local equivalent. What constituted an extra-ordinary payment depended to some extent on the wealth of the town. Many smaller boroughs met all their parliamentary expenses by levy, whereas richer boroughs could absorb them in their regular accounts.[63] The cost of the customary gift to the king on a royal visit was almost always raised from the burgesses, even in wealthy towns.[64] So, in many cases, were the costs of obtaining a new charter. In 1440 Hull paid £230 for its charter, well over a year's income. The costs have no entry in the chamberlains' rolls and were met by contributions from burgesses.[65] The cost of this charter may have been exceptional, as £130 went in a single payment to the earl of Suffolk. Towns with less demanding patrons may have escaped more lightly, although too few comparable lists survive for any standard rate to be arrived at.[66] However, since Canterbury spent £36 on a confirmation of its charter in 1461 it is not unreasonable to suggest a cost of at least £100 for a new charter.[67] Letters patent were cheaper. Early in the next century Hull paid £32 for new letters patent, and fifteenth-century confirmations seem to have cost around £10 each in total.[68] In all these cases the wages of the town's own agents and the payments for enrolling the grant are relatively insignificant. Most of the money went on buying support, whether the customary payments to royal officials to expedite each stage of the process or the gifts to the town's particular supporters.

The type of backing discussed so far was provided by men outside the town. Even the local men among them, like John Holme of Beverley, were set outside borough affairs by their national office. Urban govern-ment in the fifteenth century shows two clear strands. On the one hand, there were the 'insiders', local men who held town office and were respon-sible for its day-to-day government. On the other, there were the 'outsiders', men with local interests who advised the town but played no direct part in its government.[69] This was never an absolutely rigid distinc-tion. Broadly speaking, it becomes less true the larger the town. The great trading towns, in particular, always numbered among their active burgesses men with interests beyond the town itself which could be put at the town's disposal. Richard Anson of Hull is typical of this class. He followed the traditional burgess career of chamberlain, alderman and mayor, but he also held royal office in the port and had connections with the duke of York through which he acquired office in the forfeited Stafford lordship of Holderness in 1460.[70] A few men managed to hold an even wider range of outside interests without surrendering their position in the town. Piers Curteis of Leicester is perhaps the most striking example, combining the roles of active burgess, duchy of Lancaster official and royal household man.[71] In general, however, a burgess with important outside interests inevitably played a reduced role in local affairs. Christopher Browne of Stamford, an important merchant and a member of Lady Margaret Beaufort's council, was alderman, the Stamford equivalent of mayor, three times. On the last occasion, in 1502, however, he exercised the office by deputy because of his commitments to Margaret Beaufort and in the following year had to be urged by his fellow town councillors to find himself a house in the town so that he could legitimately remain on the town council.[72] Browne is on the very borderline between the town and its outside advisers.

If men like Christopher Browne provided a personal link between the two elements in urban government, many towns also had an institutional link in the form of a local guild. Guilds are traditionally divided into two: the trade and craft guilds on the one hand, and social and religious guilds on the other. But one should also distinguish between the purely local religious guilds, with a completely urban membership, and those which drew in the gentry and nobility of the surrounding area. Membership of the great guilds, such as Corpus Christi at York or Boston, Holy Trinity at Coventry or Holy Cross at Stratford, made common ground between the burgesses and their influential allies.[73] Not all members took an active part in guild activities and some joined only for the spiritual benefits entailed. The practice of enrolling the dead as guild members is an extreme illustration of this attitude. Enough evidence survives, however, to show that many members of the local nobility and gentry did attend guild functions. In 1424 the feast of the Palmers' Guild at Ludlow was attended by Edmund, earl of March, Lord Talbot and William Burley.[74] The Beverley town accounts show that when the earl of Northumberland attended the guild plays he would spend the day at the house of one of the townsmen.[75] In most towns it seems to have been one guild, out of several, which enjoyed a wider membership, such as the guild of St Katherine at Stamford. Towards the end of the century its members included the abbots of Crowland, Bourne and Spalding, Lady Margaret Beaufort, Cecily, Lady Wells and Sir Richard Sapcotes.[76] The advantages offered by this link between burgesses and patrons are so evident that it is likely that most major towns had a comparable guild.

The dependence of towns on the good offices of outsiders also needs to be borne in mind when considering the growth of urban autonomy in the fifteenth century. Most urban histories stress the efforts of boroughs to keep local government in their own hands by excluding the influence of royal officials and local gentry. This interpretation is usually based on town legislation. Virtually every town for which records survive was passing ordinances against livery and maintenance in the mid-fifteenth century.[77] It is, however, not unduly cynical to suggest that such legislation merely shows that external influence was a reality, not that it was ever excluded. The fact that such ordinances were regularly re-enacted, sometimes with royal backing, implies that they were not proving effective.[78]

More important, it seems that such ordinances were never designed to stop outside influence altogether, but only to keep its manifestations within limits acceptable to the town. Ipswich passed two ordinances on the subject. In 1455 it was decided that any burgess or foreigner who *purchased* a message or letter from any lord or lady for an office in the town should be permanently excluded from office. In 1474 the ordinance was modified. Men were now to be excluded if they presented letters of support from two knights or esquires, perhaps an indication of growing gentry influence within the county.[79] Neither ordinance prevented a burgess enjoying outside backing; their aim was the more limited one of preventing outside manipulation of elections. Elsewhere the background to similar ordinances suggests that they were motivated by faction fighting within the town; hence the common insistence that burgesses should not wear livery. In 1504 Gloucester included its ordinance against liveries in a group of ordinances concerned with the regulation of taverns and bawdy houses, implying that the problem was seen as one of public order rather than of political autonomy.[80]

The fact that towns sought only to limit the abuses of maintenance is hardly surprising. There is every reason to believe that towns genuinely valued the right to govern themselves. But they could hardly hope to exclude outside influence entirely when they themselves constantly looked to outsiders for help. In practice, a compromise had to be reached. The towns' attitude to borough elections shows their position particularly clearly. Towns welcomed influential support and were willing to elect men who could offer useful contacts. There is a famous York example of this: Thomas Wrangwish was considered the best candidate for mayor because he had the support of the duke of Gloucester.[81] But towns were not prepared to countenance direct interference in local elections. York simply ignored the efforts of Henry VII and the earl of Northumberland to dictate their choice of recorder.[82] Grimsby, which came under the influence of Sir Thomas Burgh in the 1480s, drew the line when Burgh's supporters tried to rig a mayoral election in 1491. The town's response was to draw up a set of rules: burgesses were to swear to uphold the mayor and only to accept a mayor elected by the majority of the burgesses; differences between burgesses were to be settled by arbitration and they were to seek no maintenance but that of the mayor, to whom they would report any offence by John Missenden or any other gentleman or yeoman — Missenden was a Burgh retainer.[83] These ordinances neatly seek to outlaw the two unacceptable aspects of maintenance: interference in elections and the threat to public order.

Such compromises did not always work. At times they failed completely, as when Gilbert Debenham was able to dominate Ipswich and
Colchester in the 1460s.[84] Few towns suffered such complete outside
control, but it may be assumed that most found it difficult to enforce the
line between acceptable and unacceptable lordship as thoroughly as they
might wish. The lords to whom towns looked for support were not
prepared to help solely in return for money or gifts. They also expected to
be able to intervene in town affairs in their own interests or those of their
servants. Such interference could be relatively trivial. In 1454 the mayor of
Hull, at the instance of the council of the duchess of Suffolk, respited a
fine due from Thomas Mouteney for occupying a plot of land outside the
town without licence.[85] Patrons' intervention in town affairs could, however, pose a more serious threat to the town's freedom of action. In 1464
Coventry was forced to back down over a dispute in the town between
William Bedon and William Huet. The mayor adjudged Huet to be in the
wrong and had him imprisoned, but Huet 'by the means of his friends
laboured unto my lord of Warwick'. He was accordingly released on the
payment of only minor damages to Bedon. The Leet Book, putting a
flattering gloss on the mayor's capitulation, comments that he was 'laying
rightwiseness apart and following mercy'.[86] A degree of outside interference was the price towns had to pay for outside help.

The towns' dependence on outside help provides the context in which
to understand changes in borough representation in parliament in the
fifteenth century. It is well known that the century saw an increasing
number of gentry and lawyers returned for boroughs. The usual
explanation is that the nobility and gentry had seen the advantages of
being represented in the commons and manipulated borough elections
accordingly. Towns acquiesced either because they had no choice or, a
slightly more positive view, because they welcomed the help with parliamentary costs which gentry members sometimes offered.[87] The implied
assumption is that any gentry or lawyer representative was forced on the
town from outside and the towns' acquiescence was a sign of weakness.

This assumption needs to be modified. The increase in the number of
gentry and lawyer members coincides with the towns' own growing
awareness of the value of influential supporters. When it is remembered
that from the towns' point of view the main duty of their parliamentary
representative was to act as their attorney and undertake town business, it
is clear that towns would welcome the support of well connected lawyers
and gentlemen, just as they looked to such men to carry out their business
outside parliament.[88] It is a fallacy to argue, as Patricia Jalland does, that
the only person who could represent borough interests was what she
defines as a 'true burgess': a man who held town office and who was

neither a lawyer nor the servant of a local dignitary.[89] Indeed, the reverse
is more likely to be true. Her own analysis of Hull returns underlines the
point. Hull, like York, had kept elections firmly in its own hands and
returned its own burgesses to parliament. Between 1450 and 1470 Hull
elected ten men on eight occasions. By far the most common choice was
William Eland, who was chosen six times. Eland, on Jalland's definition,
was not a true burgess. He was a lawyer, and steward of the archbishop of
York's manor of Beverley. Although he lived in Hull he was never
chamberlain, alderman or mayor. Jalland professes herself unable to
understand how a town with such a strong burgess tradition could con-
sistently choose someone who was not a true burgess.[90] Hull, however,
clearly had no doubts about Eland's usefulness. He was, in fact, retained as
town counsel from 1447 to 1460, when he was made recorder, a position
he held until 1487. Throughout this period he was engaged on extensive
business for the town, quite apart from his duties as parliamentary representative.[91] The next most common choice was Richard Anson, elected
three times in ten years (he died in 1460) and Anson, as we have already
seen, had connections outside the town.

If an independent borough like Hull rated outside contacts so highly in
choosing its representatives, it is hardly surprising to find smaller
boroughs doing the same. Many of the men traditionally cited as examples
of outside influence on elections had been helping the town for some years
previously. For instance, in the parliament of 1478, when the crown was
exerting itself to influence elections, the Dover candidates were obviously
the choice of the lieutenant of Dover. Roger Appleton was surveyor of
Eltham and counsel to the lieutenant of Dover; Thomas Hexstall was clerk
of Dover castle and receiver of the duke of Gloucester.[92] But Hexstall also
had a long history of service to the Cinque Ports; Lydd was paying him
for his help in borough business by the mid-fifties.[93] The representatives
of Ipswich in the same parliament were both Howard men, James Hobard
and John Tymperley; Hobard had been retained by Ipswich from 1460 as
attorney in the exchequer and as counsel.[94] Such connections can only be
verified when fairly full town records survive, but they may be suspected
in many other cases. Humphrey Harvey, chosen for Wells in 1483, is cited
by Houghton as an example of a complete outsider. Harvey was a lawyer
and counsel to the dean and chapter; his father was recorder of Bristol.[95]
This is exactly the sort of background utilised by towns. The fact that
Harvey is not mentioned in the convocation book is not conclusive
evidence that he had no prior connection with the borough: counsel rarely
show up in act books but only in town accounts, where payments to them
are noted.

This is not to argue that borough elections were never subject to outside
interference, for they undoubtedly were, as the example of 1478, cited

above, demonstrates. Equally, there were certainly a number of boroughs, such as the smaller duchy of Cornwall boroughs, which can be regarded as rotten boroughs. But it is too simple to equate the choice of an outsider with external pressure in every case. Often the so-called outsider had a tradition of service to the town and may well have been the town's own choice. At the very least, the existence of such links would have made the town more willing to accept an outsider pressed upon them by a third party. Even where there was no tradition of service towns might be willing to rate an outsider with useful contacts more highly than their own burgesses. In the reign of Richard III Salisbury chose John Musgrave, a northern esquire of the body recently planted in Wiltshire by the king. Musgrave can have had no previous connection with the city but the record suggests that he was their own choice. He was coupled with the city's mayor, a neat balance of local representation and important contacts.[96]

In considering the choice of outsiders as parliamentary representatives, it is worth bearing in mind the analogy offered by fifteenth-century recorders. Most leading towns acquired a recorder in the course of the century. They were a town's leading counsel and represented it in its business with other bodies. The requirements for a good recorder were much the same as for counsel, and indeed many recorders began their career as counsel for one or more towns. Very few fifteenth-century recorders resided in the towns they represented but had to be summoned for consultation as necessary.[97] Most, moreover, had strong noble or gentry connections. Some were themselves members of leading local families, like Miles Metcalfe at York or Robert Constable at Hull.[98] Many combined their work for the town with other consultancies. Among the Hull recorders, William Eland was counsel of Hugh Hastings and steward of the archbishop of York; Edmund Thwaites was a Northumberland retainer.[99] The recorder was a town's main representative in the outside world, but even here towns valued important contacts more highly than residence in the town or freedom from other interests.

The range of support sought by towns seems to undermine any attempt to ascribe political views to a given town. Manorial towns are perhaps a special case: a town like Stamford, which was part of the duchy of York, was inevitably 'Yorkist' in the 1450s. But in more independent boroughs, although the views of neighbouring lords carried some weight, they were tempered by the town's cautious appraisal of its own interests. Towns were prepared to defy their patron on occasion. Hull looked to the Percies for support but was still prepared to challenge the claims of Lord Egremont as admiral. It has already been suggested that towns consciously hedged their bets in looking for support. The Cinque Ports, for instance, were prepared to make cautious overtures to Jack Cade as an insurance policy.[100] The principle on which towns acted comes over clearly in their records: they always supported the *de facto* king and in addition gave more modest help to anyone who asked for it and could not reasonably be refused. Hence the not unfamiliar sight of towns supporting Lancaster and York simultaneously.

This attitude is understandable when one remembers how much towns stood to lose by the withdrawal of royal favour. Since most of the patronage which towns sought lay in the king's gift, the loss of royal favour meant at best the refusal of further grants, at worst the suspension of existing liberties. The punishment which Edward IV meted out to Canterbury in 1471 for its support of Lancaster is an obvious example.[101] The town had made the basic mistake of allowing the political enthusiasms of its mayor to become town policy. Few corporate towns made the same misjudgement. In Hull one of the leading burgesses of the 1450s, Richard Anson, was a Yorkist who was executed after Wakefield, but the town was never drawn into supporting similar views.

Most fifteenth-century towns, if they were careful, could hope to avoid outright royal displeasure. But this was only the first stage in protecting their interests. They were still dependent on influential support to secure royal grants or to provide backing in disputes with other parties. The towns' need to secure the goodwill of eminent local or national figures was not a fifteenth-century development, although the range of support which they sought seems to have widened in the course of the century. It is, moreover, in the fifteenth century that the most obvious manifestation of their dependence emerges: the use of outsiders to represent them in parliament, a phenomenon paralleled within the towns by a shift away from retained counsel in favour of *ad hoc* payments to national figures. This is in one sense a reflection of urban weakness. The growing economic difficulties of many towns and the risk of political disaster posed by the conflicts of mid-century made towns more anxious to secure strong patrons. But this does not mean that the use of outsiders was forced upon them against their will. Towns chose to turn to outsiders as recorders and legal advisers, appointments in which they had a free hand. The growing number of gentry and lawyer borough members reflects the towns' assessment of the most useful type of representative as much as the anxiety of the nobility and gentry to be represented in the commons. Such appointments were one element of the search for support which features so largely in fifteenth-century urban affairs.

NOTES

1. R.B. Dobson, 'Urban Decline in Late Medieval England', *TRHS*, 5th ser., XXVII (1977), 10-12. I am most grateful to Professor Dobson for his comments on this paper.
2. M. Weinbaum, *The Incorporation of Boroughs* (Manchester, 1937), ch. IV. Compare S. Reynolds, *An Introduction to the History of English Medieval Towns* (Oxford, 1977), pp.113-14, for a reminder that in some respects incorporation merely acknowledged existing liberties.
3. *CChR, 1341-1417*, pp.421-23.
4. *CPR, 1406-8*, p.162.
5. C. Platt, *Medieval Southampton: the port and trading community, A.D. 1000-1600* (1973), p.165. D. Palliser, 'A Crisis in English Towns? The Case of York, 1460-1640', *Northern History*, XIV (1978), 116-17, suggests that the bureaucracy and ceremonial trappings of independence actually increased towns' economic difficulties.
6. City of Canterbury MSS., *HMC, 9th Report* (1883), pp.137-45.
7. *CPR, 1399-1405, passim.*
8. M. McKisack, *The Parliamentary Representation of English Boroughs during the Middle Ages* (Oxford, 1932), p.139.
9. BL, Harleian MS.433 ff.111, 115; MSS. of the Corporation of Gloucester, *HMC, 12th Report*, Appendix part IX (1891), pp.403-4; *The Royal Charters of the City of Lincoln, Henry II to William III*, ed. W. de G. Birch (Cambridge, 1911), pp.107-56; *Christ Church Letters*, ed. J.B. Sheppard (Camden Soc., new ser., XIX, 1877), p.46; J. Gairdner, *History of the Life and Reign of Richard the Third* (Cambridge, 1898), p.112. The Lincoln grant was not made until the end of 1484 but can probably be associated with the king's visit of the previous year; compare the visit and later grant of Henry VI: F.Hill, *Medieval Lincoln* (Cambridge, 1965), p.272.
10. *CPR, 1401-5*, p.485.
11. The exceptions tend to be grants of markets: e.g., *CPR, 1401-5*, p.105; *CChR, 1341-1417*, p.430.
12. C. Ross, *Edward IV* (1974), pp.354-55, who suggests that even this was a late development.
13. Dobson, 'Urban Decline', p.15.
14. Grimsby MSS., *HMC, 14th Report*, Appendix VIII (1895), pp.247, 251-52; E. Gillett, *A History of Grimsby* (Oxford, 1970), pp.50-58; A. Rogers, 'Parliamentary Elections in Grimsby in the Fifteenth Century', *BIHR*, XLII (1969), 213.
15. Kingston upon Hull Record Office (KHRO), Chamberlains' rolls BRF 2/357 *et seq.*; Beverley Borough Records, Keepers' account rolls, *passim*. I am most grateful to the archivist of Kingston upon Hull, Mr G.W. Oxley, for his help and to Beverley Borough Council for allowing me access to their archives.
16. R. Horrox, *The Changing Plan of Hull, 1290-1650* (Hull, 1978), pp.27-28.
17. *Letters and Papers of John Shillingford, mayor of Exeter, 1447-50*, ed. S.A. Moore (Camden Soc., new ser., II, 1871), pp.146, 150.
18. See, for example, KHRO, BRF 2/365-68. Beverley adopted a similar policy: Keepers' account rolls 1460.
19. Shrewsbury MSS., *HMC, 15th Report*, part X (1899), p.28.
20. Keepers' account rolls 1433/4. Town accounts are a useful, if patchy, source for the activity and composition of royal commissions.
21. KHRO, Chamberlains' rolls, *passim*. There was, however, considerable local variation: Beverley paid a similar rate to Hull, the Cinque Ports much less. Probably the distance travelled by the messenger was taken into account.
22. KHRO, BRF 2/364.

23. Corporation of Rye MSS., *HMC, 5th Report*, part I (1876), p.490. Buckingham was warden of the Cinque Ports at this date.
24. Keepers' account rolls 1460.
25. KHRO, BRF 2/363.
26. KHRO, BRE 2 f. 12; BRF 2/358, 360, 377, 381, 383, 384, 388.
27. Rye MSS., p.493; Corporation of Lydd MSS., *HMC, 5th Report,* part I, p.524; Corporation of New Romney MSS., ibid., p.547. Scot's home was Brabourne, Kent.
28. Rye MSS., pp.491, 492; Lydd MSS., pp.517, 518, 520; New Romney MSS., pp.539, 541, 543.
29. *A Calendar of the White and Black Books of the Cinque Ports, 1432-1955*, ed. F. Hull (HMC joint publication, V, 1966), pp.51, 71.
30. Ibid., p.27.
31. Platt, *Medieval Southampton*, p.167.
32. Corporation of the Borough of Barnstaple MSS., *HMC, 9th Report* (1883), p.205.
33. KHRO, BRF 2/357.
34. Nathaniel Bacon, *The Annalls of Ipswiche*, ed. W.H. Richardson (Ipswich, 1884), p.160.
35. *Calendar of Books of the Cinque Ports*, pp.48-49.
36. *Annalls of Ipswiche*, pp.118, 130, 174.
37. KHRO, BRF 2/344 *et seq.*
38. City of Canterbury MSS., *HMC, 9th Report* (1883), pp.138-39.
39. KHRO, BRF 2/360 *et seq.*; *CPR, 1446-52*, p.179. Serjeants at law were a popular choice as counsel or recorder: *The Coventry Leet Book*, ed. M.D. Harris (EETS, original ser., 134, 135, 138, 146; 4 parts in 1, 1907-13), p.527. In the long term this assured towns of contacts among the justices: E.W. Ives, 'Promotion in the Legal Profession of Yorkist and Early Tudor England', *Law Quarterly Review*, LXXV (1959), 358-59.
40. Keepers' account rolls, 1437-38, 1445, 1449-50.
41. J.C. Wedgwood, *History of Parliament, 1439-1509, Biographies* (1936), pp.981-82;
42. KHRO, BRF 2/356 *et seq.*
43. *Exeter Freemen, 1266-1967*, ed. M.M. Rowe and A.M. Jackson (Devon and Cornwall Record Soc., extra ser. I, 1973), pp. 38, 50, 51, 52. Men continued to be made freemen for political reasons, and indeed the practice seems to have increased in the sixteenth century: R.B. Dobson, 'Admissions to the Freedom of the City of York in the Later Middle Ages', *EconHR*, 2nd ser., XXVI (1973), 12; *Rolls of the Freemen of the City of Chester, I. 1392-1700* (Lancashire and Cheshire Record Soc., LI, 1906); C. Platt, *The English Medieval Town* (1976), p.229.
44. *The Records of the Guild of the Holy Trinity, St Mary, St John the Baptist and St Katherine of Coventry*, II, ed. G. Templeman (Dugdale Soc., XIX, 1944), p.7.
45. Wedgwood, op.cit., p.707n.
46. Ibid., pp.460-61.
47. *Shillingford Letters*, p.3.
48. Wedgwood, op.cit., pp.981-82.
49. *Records of Holy Trinity*, II, appendix II; *CIPM, Henry VII*, III, no. 1144; *CPR, 1467-77*, p.96.
50. *Annalls of Ipswiche*, p.166.
51. Keepers' account rolls 1449-50. Hull also looked to Vavasour for support: in 1445 he came to Hull on royal business and was paid 20*s.* to speak well to the king on the town's behalf: KHRO, BRF 2/362A; see also ibid., 363. Vavasour was an usher of the chamber: *CPR, 1441-46*, p.98.
52. Lydd MSS., pp.520, 523.
53. *Shillingford Letters*, pp.143-54.

54. KHRO, BRF 2/365. See also Canterbury's expenditure on its dispute with the prior of St Augustine's: Canterbury MSS., pp. 133–37.

55. J.R. Boyle, *Charters and Letters Patent granted to Kingston upon Hull* (Hull, 1905), pp.34–45. For the role of Suffolk, see below.

56. SC8/121/6024, cited by Hill, *Medieval Lincoln*, p.280.

57. A. Rogers, 'Late Medieval Stamford: a study of the town council, 1465-1492', in *Perspectives in English Urban History*, ed. A. Everitt (1973), p.17; *CChR, 1427-1516*, pp.155-61, 164–67. Peterborough may also have benefited from its Yorkist connections: *Peterborough Local Administration: parochial government before the Reformation*, ed. W.T. Mellows (Northants Record Soc., IX, 1939), p. xxxii.

58. *RP*, VI, 336; *The History of Scarborough*, ed. A. Rowntree (1931), p.134. His grant to Lincoln was also cancelled: Hill, *Medieval Lincoln*, p.285.

59. J.S. Furley, *City Government of Winchester from the records of the XIV & XV centuries* (Oxford, 1923), pp.37, 117.

60. At the end of the century Beverley began to distinguish between town expenses and expenditure *super magnatos*. The latter, a new category, includes presents and entertainment for influential men: Keepers' account rolls 1494.

61. KHRO, BRF 2/340.

62. Keepers' account rolls 1344, 1366, 1386; Furley, *City Government of Winchester*, pp.113-17.

63. McKisack, *Parliamentary Representation*, pp.90, 92-93, 96, 98.

64. E.g., *Annalls of Ipswiche*, p.146; Hill, *Medieval Lincoln*, p.272; *Coventry Leet Book*, p.34. £100 seems to have been the standard gift.

65. KHRO, BRE 2 f.12-v. Ipswich also financed charters by levy: *Annalls of Ipswiche*, p.151.

66. Coventry waived about £100 owed to the town by the duke of Clarence in return for his help in securing the restoration of the town's franchises in 1472: *Coventry Leet Book*, pp.381-82, 855-56.

67. Canterbury MSS., p.140. Coventry levied £100 for a new charter in 1445: *Coventry Leet Book*, p.221.

68. KHRO, BB 3 f.29v. Most town accounts underestimate such costs by including only the wages of their agents; the rest was presumably raised separately as in Hull.

69. Rogers, 'Late Medieval Stamford', pp.28, 31.

70. Wedgwood, op.cit., pp.12-13; *CPR, 1452-61*, p.624. Anson's patron seems to have been the earl of Warwick rather than York himself: *CFR, 1452-61*, p.199.

71. Wedgwood, op.cit., pp.244-45.

72. Rogers, 'Late Medieval Stamford', p.29.

73. *The Register of the Guild of Corpus Christi, York* (Surtees Soc., LVII, 1871); D.M. Owen, *Church and Society in Medieval Lincolnshire* (Lincoln, 1971), p.127; *The Register of the Guild of the Holy Trinity, St Mary, St John the Baptist and St Katherine of Coventry*, ed. M.D. Harris (Dugdale Soc., XIII, 1935); *The Register of the Guild of the Holy Cross, the Blessed Mary and St John the Baptist of Stratford upon Avon*, ed. J.H. Bloom (1907).

74. *VCH, Salop*, II (1973), 136. See also *Stratford-upon-Avon, Corporation Records, The Guild Accounts*, ed. W.J. Hardy (Stratford, 1886), for the involvement of the Warwickshire gentry in the business of the guild.

75. Keepers' account rolls 1423: the earl and countess spent the day at the house of William Thixhill, barber. In 1457 Queen Margaret and her train watched the Coventry plays from the house of Richard Wode, grocer: *Coventry Leet Book*, p.300. Casual noble visitors were often entertained in private houses; in 1440 the earl of Northumberland had dinner at the home of the mayor of Hull: KHRO, BRF 2/357.

76. Rogers, 'Late Medieval Stamford', p.34.

77. There is a useful list in Winifred Haward, 'Gilbert Debenham: a medieval rascal in real life', *History*, XIII (1929), 308n. See also *Coventry Leet Book*, p.294, and examples from Ipswich, Gloucester and Grimsby below.

78. Many royal letters against livery and maintenance in towns were almost certainly issued at the towns' own request; see, for instance, BL, Harleian MS. 433 ff. 115v (Southampton), 127v (Gloucester).

79. *Annalls of Ipswiche*, pp.113, 135.

80. Gloucester MSS., pp.435-37.

81. *York Civic Records*, I, ed. A. Raine (Yorkshire Archaeological Soc., XCVIII, 1938), p.68.

82. Ibid., pp.124, 131-33, 141-42, 148-52. Coventry, however, submitted to Henry's choice of Richard Empson as recorder: *Coventry Leet Book*, p. 537. This was not a Tudor innovation. Henry VI forced his choice of recorder on Salisbury and York had previously accepted Edward IV's recommendation of Miles Metcalfe: *VCH, Wiltshire*, VI, 99; *York Civic Records*, p.19.

83. Gillett, *History of Grimsby*, pp.61-62.

84. Haward, op.cit., pp.309-12.

85. KHRO, BB 3A f.38v.

86. *Coventry Leet Book*, pp.328-32; and compare the letter of the duke of Gloucester to Southampton in favour of one of his servants: Southampton MSS., *HMC, 11th Report*, Appendix III (1887), p.102.

87. J.S. Roskell, *The Commons in the Parliament of 1422* (Manchester, 1954), p.141; McKisack, *Parliamentary Representation*, pp.113-15; K.N. Houghton, 'Theory and Practice in Borough Elections to Parliament during the later fifteenth century', *BIHR*, XXXIX (1966), 138-39.

88. McKisack, *Parliamentary Representation*, pp.120, 134-39, for members acting as attorneys, but see p.116 where it is argued that outsiders would not be prepared to act in this way.

89. P. Jalland, 'The Revolution in Northern Borough Representation in Mid-Fifteenth-Century England' *Northern History*, XI (1975). For a slightly different definition of 'true burgess' as one engaged in trade, see Roskell, *Commons in 1422*, pp.126-27, 130.

90. Jalland, op.cit., p.37 and Table II.

91. KHRO, BRF 2/362B-386.

92. Houghton, op.cit., p.136n.

93. Lydd MSS., pp.520, 521; see also New Romney MSS., p.543; Rye MSS., p.492.

94. Ross, *Edward IV*, p.344; *Annalls of Ipswiche*, pp.118, 122.

95. Houghton, op.cit., p.135.

96. McKisack, *Parliamentary Representation*, p.64. For Musgrave's position in Wiltshire, see R. Horrox, 'The Extent and Use of Crown Patronage under Richard III' (Cambridge Ph.D. thesis, 1977), pp.155-56.

97. Coventry tried to secure resident recorders, but seems to have failed: *Coventry Leet Book*, pp.525-28.

98. Metcalfe was one of the Metcalfes of Nappa, his brother Thomas was chancellor of the duchy of Lancaster under Richard III, and Miles himself was second justice at Lancaster and deputy-steward in the north parts: *Testamenta Eboracensia*, IV (Surtees Soc., LIII, 1868), pp.9-10; Wedgwood, op.cit., p.588; R. Somerville, *History of the Duchy of Lancaster*, I (1953), 391-92, 426, 473. Constable was the fourth son of Sir Robert of Flamborough and a serjeant at law. At the time of his appointment his eldest brother Marmaduke was head of the family and knight of the body to Henry VII: J. Foster, *Pedigrees of Yorkshire Families*, III (1874), *sub* Constable of Flamborough; *CCR, 1485-1500*, no. 875; *CPR, 1485-94*, p.111.

99. For Eland, see *Testamenta Eboracensia*, III (Surtees Soc., XLV, 1864), pp.193n, 279; for Thwaites, ibid., p.308.
100. Lydd MSS., p.520.
101. C.F. Richmond, 'Fauconberg's Kentish Rising of May 1471', *EHR*, LXXXV (1970), 683. The Cinque Ports and Coventry also had their liberties suspended: ibid.; *Coventry Leet Book*, pp.369-70. Coventry seems to have been threatened with the same fate in 1425: ibid., p.98n.

8. Patronage and Promotion in the Late–Medieval Church

Robert W. Dunning
Victoria County History of Somerset

By implication there is something sinister about patronage and connexion in the fifteenth-century political scene, something a little above and beyond the law. In almost any century, indeed, it has a slightly pejorative sense. Yet in church affairs patronage has been part, and an essential part, of the system of clerical appointment in every century until the present. What essential difference is there between:

> Mekely besecheth your hyghnesse your humble subjet and feithfull liegeman Robert W., scoler, that it may please your excellent grace to yeve and graunte unto hym the next place that schalbe voide . . . within your collage callyd kyngs hall . . .

as set out in a letter-book for all to copy;[1] and the present means of acquiring a crown living in the Church of England, which involves filling in a complicated form issued by the lord chancellor's department? The only, if rather subtle, difference is that some influence is needed to obtain the lord chancellor's form in the first place. But anyone, provided he is ordained in the Church of England, could answer advertisements in the *Church Times* for a vicar for St John's, Rhosnesi, in the Wrexham Team Ministry in the diocese of St Asaph, or for the living of Redenhall with Harleston and Wortwell in the diocese of Norwich, in the gift of the Cambridge University Board of Electors to Livings.[2] Patrons have sought clerks and clerks patrons since the church was organised as it is; what is worth studying, among other things, is the way in which favours have been distributed and the income of the church diverted from the support of the parish priest or the diocesan bishop to the indirect financing of public service and private administration. The creation of a network of interest in ecclesiastical affairs was an important factor in the armoury of many political figures, no less important than influence in secular courts and local government institutions.

It has long been clear that medieval kings regarded episcopal appointments as a means both to reward their servants and to pay them for continuing service at no cost to the exchequer.[3] If in the case of poorer sees the rewards were minimal, at least something of an assurance was implied that men with a pastoral vocation remained, and the Chicheles of this world moved on as soon as they could.[4] An analysis of crown livings below the episcopal level might show much more variety, but prebends in royal free chapels such as St Stephen's in Westminster or St Martin's le Grand were likely to be filled almost exclusively by civil servants whatever the religious inclination of the sovereign, and the more distant collegiate churches like Tamworth, Hastings or Bridgnorth were equally almost the exclusive perquisites of crown officials — just as, of course, similar institutions, and especially cathedral chapters, were at the disposal of diocesan bishops. There was essentially no difference between episcopal and royal government: a benefice was a convenient means of providing an official with a living.

There must, of course, have been wide variations in practice due to the natural inclinations of patrons. In 1464–65 Thomas Kempe, bishop of London, ran his estates through laymen only,[5] while at the same time Thomas Bekynton, bishop of Bath and Wells, appointed canons of Wells as receiver-general and as auditor.[6] Similar variety could be found on secular estates. Dr Rawcliffe has shown how Humphrey, duke of Buckingham employed no clerics in his administration; that Duke Henry had one cleric, a Cambridge graduate, as his councillor at Brecon; but that Duke Edward employed at least eleven, most of them graduates, as councillors, receivers, surveyors, chancellor, treasurer, or some other office in that magnificent household.[7] But policy must have depended on the amount of patronage (in a clerical sense) available. Dr Jack demonstrated how the Lords Grey of Ruthin used their twenty advowsons to advance the careers of younger sons, to reward senior estate staff, and to provide for the relatives of trustworthy employees. The Staffords had three times the number of livings if patronage of religious houses be included; and analysis of what might be called secondary patronage — how livings were given to those with more tenuous connexions or were offered by other patrons for Stafford benefit — might be a rewarding, but would certainly be a complicated, business.[8]

The Courtenays, earls of Devon, provide a rather less formidable study along these lines, for they had a much less grand array of livings in their gift.[9] As a family in the late fourteenth century their advowsons were concentrated in Devon and Cornwall, with important outliers such as Sutton Courtenay in Berkshire, Waddesdon in Buckinghamshire, and Crewkerne in Somerset. In Devon there was the valuable divided benefice of Tiverton, the prebendal church of Chulmleigh, the four prebends in Exeter Castle and a few parochial livings. It is clear from a study of appointments to all these that they were regarded as sources of family benefit, but there was, perhaps, a distinction between the richer and the poorer ones, and between men appointed to them whose immediate services were required, and men whom it might well be expedient to reward. The distinction is best made by looking at those clergy known for their close connexion with the earl's household and their fellows at the same time; and then by a study of the incumbents of one of the richest Courtenay livings.

The list of liveries of the earl of Devon for the year 1384-85 includes eight clerks then on the Courtenay payroll.[10] They were, incidentally, ranked with the ladies, after the esquires and before the lawyers. Two of the eight were described as canon, one as prebendary, five as parson and one, perhaps the most important, was not described at all. The last was John Redeclyf, then steward of the earl's household.[11] Also among the group was Thomas Kerdyngton, receiver-general of the Courtenay estates a decade later.[12] Both held very modest Courtenay livings, Redeclyf from 1383 a portion at Tiverton, and from 1386 until 1407 the church of Northill;[13] Kerdyngton from 1391, but only briefly, the church of Landulph.[14]

Much more significant in terms of influence were the two canons, Hugh Brydham and William Pouton. Brydham was a senior cleric by 1384 and was probably related to an old family receiver-general, Baldwin Bryggham.[15] Before 1371 Hugh was appointed to the earl's living of Sutton Courtenay, which he exchanged for the archdeaconry of Totnes in Exeter Cathedral.[16] He exchanged the archdeaconry for livings outside Devon in 1385,[17] but though he soon returned to Exeter diocese, his value to the earl was probably not so great. William Pouton was another Courtenay creation, for his earliest recorded living was a portion of Waddesdon, which he exchanged for a canonry at Exeter, an exchange which of itself required Courtenay connivance if not initiative.[18] Thus in 1384, when the earl issued his liveries, both Brydham and Pouton could represent the Courtenay interest in the cathedral chapter, a position achieved indirectly but nevertheless surely.

Patrick atte Wode was described on the livery roll as prebendary, for he held one of the prebends in the chapel in Exeter Castle.[19] His later career included appointments to the rectory of St Thomas at Winchilsea in which Archbishop William Courtenay was involved.[20] Nothing else is known about his activities in Devon. Of the other three clerks receiving the earl's livery, William Cullompton was a portioner at Tiverton, the main Courtenay home;[21] Roger Daumarle was a relative, perhaps a younger son, of Sir John Daumarle, one of the earl's knights;[22] and John Hoper was probably the incumbent of Bondleigh.[23] Their ecclesiastical rewards were not significant — in fact, Daumarle's only appearance in the episcopal registers was in 1413 when he was excommunicated for his part in a clandestine marriage ceremony.[24]

So these eight clerics, clearly those at the time who were closest to the Courtenay household, had between them an extremely modest share in the family's ecclesiastical patronage. And there were many others in the area, men who held a single, small Courtenay living, who stayed in Devon or Cornwall obscurely all their lives, appointed for some reason which will never be known, though perhaps ready to serve their patron in some modest way whenever called upon to do so. But there were others, drawn to the richer pickings, whose role in relation to the Courtenays is more obvious: men of influence in national affairs whose position made them potentially valuable allies in local and national affairs, but men who could not be offered what might seem the strait-jacket of a household livery.

On 7 March 1391-92 Nicholas Bubwith, an up-and-coming Yorkshire-man, later successively bishop of Salisbury and of Bath and Wells, exchanged his obscure Cornish living of Southill for the equally obscure Devon chantry of Sticklepath.[25] Sticklepath was then occupied by Walter Dolbeare, a canon of Lichfield. Neither living would have demanded personal residence and that was clearly the main attraction to both parties — but how was the matter arranged, and to what purpose? The patrons were in both cases no ordinary landowners, but the earl of Devon on one side and Thomas, earl of Stafford and lord of Tonbridge, on the other. There is no evidence that Dolbeare was of any service to the earl of Devon; and perhaps the whole episode was simply part of the traffic in livings which was a common feature of the period. Local men of standing were likely to prove more useful. Earl Edward played a vital initial part in the careers of the brothers John and Baldwin Shillingford which by implication was more successful for the family. The brothers began their careers by holding a portion of the Courtenay living of Waddesdon in succession.[26] Baldwin remained in Exeter diocese for most of his life, but John was potentially of greater value to his patron as an advocate in the court of arches and a royal commissioner of appeals from the court of the constable and the marshal between 1382 and 1406. He was also on Archbishop Courtenay's council at Blackfriars in 1382 to condemn the views of Wycliffe, and on another at Oxford in 1399 to advise Richard II on the papal schism. The third Courtenay protégé was nearly a disaster. Master Laurence Stephan joined Wycliffe as one of his preachers, and spent the summer of 1382 in Cornwall on a mission.[27] A few months later he made his peace with Archbishop Courtenay, and also presumably with his bishop, and after some years of respectable obscurity was given a Courtenay prebend at Chulmleigh.

The support of promising local graduates is a theme running through Courtenay patronage in the later middle ages. Thomas Hendyman was a native of the diocese of Exeter, fellow and later rector of Exeter College, Oxford, a distinguished theologian, and for two terms chancellor of his university. Certainly in his later years he held five Courtenay livings, including for six months the most valuable of all, the first portion of Crewkerne.[28] Master Walter Robert, a bachelor of canon law, followed him at Tiverton, preceded him at Sampford Courtenay, and ended at Northill in succession to the old household steward, John Redeclyf.[29] Was there some ulterior motive in supporting men like these, and from where had the initiative come? Was it a diocesan bishop wanting to encourage higher standards among his clergy or a landowner seeking to extend his influence; or was it simply a natural reaction to a local man's importunate request?

Waddesdon, Tiverton and Crewkerne have figured often enough already to suggest that certain livings were commonly available to the most prominent men among the Courtenay connexion. The three portions of the rectory of Crewkerne were filled by a succession of such men from the fourteenth century until the early sixteenth, and illustrate better than most the consequences of noble patronage combined with the attraction of a more than adequate income.[30] The living had been divided into three portions in the late thirteenth century, and ranged in value according to a local estimate from over £66 for the first portion to £20 for the third.[31] Robert Pyll, appointed to the first portion by Sir Hugh Courtenay in 1328, was licensed to be absent from his cure in his patron's service in the 1330s, and in 1342 was one of Courtenay's executors.[32] Walter Colles, rector in 1422-28, had already been supported at Oxford by the fruits of Devon livings, including a portion of Tiverton.[33] His potential value to the Courtenays was his position as official of Bishop Lacy's peculiar jurisdiction in Devon. Colles was later to become king's clerk, for a short time constable of Bordeaux, and in 1442 an envoy for peace talks with the French.[34] Colles exchanged Crewkerne with the Courtenay-supported Thomas Hendyman in 1427, when the living was temporarily in the hands of the crown during Earl Thomas's minority, though the late earl's trustees actually established their claim to the patronage.[35] Six months later Hendyman exchanged it with another of his own kind, John Odelond or Wodeland, a canonist and later a prebendary of Exeter.[36] Odelond occupied the first portion for the next forty-four years, doubtless proving something of a frustration to successive patrons. He was eventually followed by John de Combe at the presentation not of a Courtenay earl, but of the grantee of the attainted earl's lands, the duke of Clarence. But John' de Combe was a west-countryman, possibly even a native of Crewkerne; and he was successively canon, precentor and treasurer of Exeter, and vicar-general to Bishop Courtenay of Exeter.[37] Courtenay influence was thus still exercised even in the absence of the rightful patron.

The holders of the second portion of Crewkerne make the same points even more strongly, beginning with Benedict Paston in 1338. Two years later he was quite specifically described as the earl of Devon's clerk.[38] But even before that he was official of the bishop of Exeter's peculiar jurisdiction in Cornwall, by 1340 he was a regular member of Bishop Grandisson's household, and was later the bishop's chancellor and official principal.[39] About 1361 Crewkerne was added to the collection of Philip Courtenay, the then earl's teenage son;[40] and he was followed by William Pouton, the household clerk of the 1380s.[41] Then came Dr John Welbourn, who already had had a distinguished career in other parts of the country, including work as an advocate in the court of arches, and who served as a royal commissioner for appeals under both Richard II and Henry IV.[42] Andrew Lanvyan, registrar of the bishops of Bath and Wells, was appointed by the Dowager Countess Anne in 1428 and held it with a Cornish living, but was soon replaced — under what pressure is not known — by John Courtenay 'having the first clerical tonsure', son of the late earl.[43] Then came Master Henry Hutchyn, whose first living had been Sampford Courtenay,[44] but he was succeeded by obscurer, evidently not local, men: John Mountagu, appointed by Archbishop Neville and other trustees; Thomas Normanton by Clarence.[45] The crown in 1479 appointed Richard Surland, then described as king's servant, a canon of St George's, Windsor, and from 1486 subdean of the chapels royal.[46] He was succeeded by another royal appointee, Christopher Plummer, successively chaplain to Queen Elizabeth and then to Henry VIII and Katherine of Aragon.[47]

The third and smallest portion of Crewkerne was still not beneath the attention between 1422 and 1427 of Master John Stafford, dean of St Martin's le Grand and treasurer of England.[48] For three years from 1443 it was held by Dr Thomas Kent, clerk of the council and under-constable of England, and after him came Dr William Hooper, a former rector of Waddesdon, commissioner for appeals from several courts, and pluralist extraordinary.[49] Thereafter, the academic quality of the incumbents falls away: William Sprygge, a Devon graduate, held it until 1478,[50] but after him the patronage was exercised by the crown in favour of much smaller fry. The Courtenays, broken on the wheel of political misfortune, no longer — even when they could — appointed men of distinction; and in 1504 the name of their candidate actually eluded the bishop's registrar.[51] Did they no longer concern themselves with the possibilities of patronage, or were they no longer acceptable patrons for men with their way to make?

The careers of two west-country clerics outside the orbit of Courtenay influence illustrate, if they do not typify, the possibilities of promotion and the importance of patronage to the individual. John Hody's origins are more precisely known than most, though his continued success seems to be closely linked not with his original, lay patron, but with a fellow cleric. Hugh Pavy's is not a name which first springs to the English mind as a flower of Henry VII's bench of bishops, but his rise can be charted with a fair degree of accuracy through his sister's marriage and his own connexions with Richard Beauchamp, bishop of Salisbury.

John Hody's origins are described in a rare, apparently early-sixteenth-century, family history:[52]

> Adam Hody was a bondeman to my Lorde of Awdely and heywarde of Wollavyngton, and he had 2 sonnys, John and Thomas. Thys John went to scole with a chawntery prest in Wollavyngton and fro that to Oxforde, and so he hadde lycens of the lorde of Awdely, and was imade a prest, and after that be fortune he was a chanon yn Wellys and Chawnceler yn Wellys . . .

The history goes on to record that Hody sent his nephews to school, how he bought their freedom from another Lord Audley; and how, of the two, John became chief justice of the king's bench in 1440, and Alexander was steward of the earl of Salisbury, member of Parliament, combatant at Wakefield, and killed somewhere between the actual fighting and the Yorkist attainder.[53] The next generation produced Sir William Hody, chief baron of the exchequer, among whose prized possessions were the letters of manumission his father and his uncle had acquired through the first John's generosity.

Lord Audley was probably responsible not only for Hody's education but for his first living, Woolavington (Somerset), in 1394 when in the gift of the crown through the confiscation of the property of the alien priory of Goldcliff (Mon.).[54] That was the first of twenty-six benefices which Hody was to acquire within the next forty years, several of which, with papal dispensation, he was able to enjoy together. Not all his appointments can yet be clearly accounted for. Hody was a lawyer, and was appointed chancellor to Bishop Totyngton of Norwich in 1408,[55] but he received no living in that diocese until after the bishop's death. He had two Dorset livings from Sir John Tiptoft, acquired either through his crown appointment at Wimborne or through the Somerset connexions of Tiptoft's wife.[56] Equally they and some of his other livings may have been pawns in the benefice transfer market. But one theme runs through his impressive list of livings. At the very outset of his career Hody entered the service of Thomas Polton, the archdeacon of Taunton and commissary-general of Bishop Erghum of Wells.[57] By 1400 Hody was his official, his deputy as judge in the courts of the archdeaconry. By 1401 Hody and Polton held adjoining livings under the northern slopes of Dunkery Beacon in west Somerset.[58] But far more important than his diocesan posts to any client was Polton's position as papal chaplain and diplomat.[59]

To Polton's influence must surely be due Hody's papal dispensation to hold an incompatible benefice with the precentorship of Wells in 1411.[60] To him was almost certainly due (for they came within five months of Polton's return to the *Curia* as king's proctor) a dispensation to hold two incompatible benefices for life and release from the obligation as precentor to reside at Wells,[61] followed a few months later by papal appointment to a prebend at Exeter.[62] By now the links with Polton may have been even closer: the release from obligation to reside was a formal one, allowing the recipient to study at a university or to visit the *Curia*. It seems quite possible that Hody accompanied Polton first to the council of Constance in 1416 and then back to Rome, where Polton served as the king's proctor until 1423.[63] So close were their links, at any rate, that in 1417 Hody gave Polton his rectory of Brightwell in exchange for Polton's prebend at Wells.[64]

Hody was certainly back in Somerset in 1424, when he was acting as vicar-general for the newly-appointed bishop, John Stafford, but after Polton's translation from Chichester to Worcester in 1426 Hody returned to his service; he appears as the bishop's chancellor, and was duly rewarded with two Worcestershire livings in the bishop's gift.[65] He was, as might have been anticipated, supervisor of the bishop's will after Polton died at Basle in 1433.[66] After that Hody acquired only two more livings, both by exchange, the last the archdeaconry of Dorset. Hody's will has not survived, but his nephew John, who died only a year or so after him in 1441, wished to be buried near his uncle and benefactor, in the chantry chapel at Woolavington which had been the beginning of it all.[67]

Hugh Pavy, the second example, came from a quite different section of society. He was the son of a prominent Bristol merchant, William Pavy, successively bailiff, sheriff and member of the common council of the city: a man with the usual Bristol business connexions in Gascony, Brittany, Iceland and Ireland.[68] In 1454 he was styled 'gentilman' in a deed involving the Bristol merchant-prince William Canynges;[69] and Hugh himself was declared on papal authority to be of noble birth.[70] William Pavy's will shows that education was not just for the son destined for the church; he left 24 marks for the support of his youngest son at school for six years.[71]

Pavy seems to have gone to Winchester and then to Oxford, where he was admitted B.A. in 1450.[72] Thereafter, in contrast to Hody, his preferments were modest: only eight livings, beginning (oddly for a man ordained in Bath and Wells diocese) with the rectory of Dittisham in Devon in 1453. But the patrons of the living for that turn only were four Somerset men, Sir Walter Rodney, Richard Chokke, John Rodney and John Cogan. Richard Chokke was Pavy's brother-in-law.[73] Chokke himself had connexions with Bishop Bekynton of Bath and Wells as one of those laymen loosely attached to the bishop's household.[74] Pavy's next two livings were both in the bishop's gift; a prebend at Wells in 1454 and the rectory of Chelwood in 1456 were clearly enough the fruits of the connexion, and Chokke himself took possession of Chelwood as Pavy's proctor.[75] The next preferment, Shepton Mallet, came after Bekynton's death, but the bishop's support was not necessary: the patrons of Shepton were Pavy's brother-in-law, now Sir Richard Chokke, and his nephew John.[76]

In that same year Pavy's career took another, and significant, turn. Five days after admission to Shepton Mallet he was admitted in his absence to the prebend of Grimstone in Salisbury Cathedral, in the gift of the bishop of Salisbury, Richard Beauchamp.[77] The precise origin of the connexion between the two has not yet been discovered, but the Salisbury Chapter Act Book known as *Machon* records the fact that Bishop Beauchamp entered Salisbury in August 1468 surrounded by members of his household and the people of the country (*sui familiares ac incomitiva sua*).[78] On the next day there was a solemn high mass in the cathedral, and then, in a formal ceremony in the chapter house, Pavy was installed in his prebend in person. There is some evidence that Pavy thereafter divided his time between Salisbury and the bishop's household. He was with Beauchamp at Sonning in April 1471,[79] at Salisbury with him in December 1471.[80] In April 1472 he was appointed a canon residentiary,[81] and certainly until 1485 he was regularly in receipt of commons for a substantial part of each year.[82] A closer association with his bishop than these meagre scraps suggest was evident in his promotion to be archdeacon of Wiltshire in 1479,[83] in succession to Peter Courtenay, and his appointment as one of Beauchamp's executors in 1481.[84]

There was one more piece of promotion to come. In May 1485 Pavy, described as king's clerk, was granted custody of the temporalities of the bishopric of St. David's in succession to Thomas Langton, himself translated to Salisbury.[85] By whose influence had Pavy been promoted? Those who served with him as executors of Bishop Beauchamp would surely be more of a hindrance than a help: Bishop Morton, Richard Beauchamp of Bromham, known as Lord St. Amand, Sir Thomas Vaughan, Sir Roger Tocotes and John Cheyne, the late bishop's relatives and political associates, were well out of favour. Morton was in the Tower, Vaughan was dead, executed at Pontefract; Beauchamp, Tocotes and Cheyne were attainted, though Beauchamp, after his support for Buckingham, was given some of Tocotes's forfeited lands and was at the time described as king's servant.[86] The Chokke influence was no longer effective, for Sir Richard, Pavy's brother-in-law, had died two days before Richard III's coronation.[87]

The exact influences involved in Pavy's promotion may never be finally established, though it is clear that his appointment as keeper of the tem-

poralities of the vacant Welsh bishopric, preliminary to his appointment to
the see, was not a sudden move. The matter had been arranged as early as
December 1484, and was clearly connected directly with Thomas
Langton's move from St. David's to Salisbury and may have been due to
Langton's interest. A signet letter of 8 December 1484 had informed the
Salisbury chapter of the king's distinct preference for Langton.[88] On the
following day, again under the signet, a receipt was issued to Hugh Pavy
for the sum of £100, part-payment of 200 marks for the temporalities of
the bishopric of St. David's whenever they should fall to the crown.[89]
There was the inevitable delay between plan and execution. Formal licence
to elect Langton was given to the chapter at Salisbury on 19 December
1484,[90] and his translation took place on 9 February 1485.[91]

It was not, presumably, simoniacal to purchase custody of land; though
the price paid was high. The value of the Welsh estates was so small that
only a long tenure of the property could have made the transaction a
financial success. Yet no such long period was envisaged when Pavy was
appointed bishop on 2 May, for his consecration would have followed
within a short time in normal circumstances.[92] But times were not normal.
Pavy's consecration was postponed until 9 October, but he had to wait for
nearly a year for the formal restitution of his temporalities.[93] Whether the
delay was due to politics or to the complications of Pavy's pre-emption is
not known, nor yet whether he had to pay more than the original 200
marks for his rightful property. The delay can certainly be interpreted in
part as a sign that he was regarded as politically partisan by Henry VII; it
follows that his promotion was in some sense political, the reward of a
faithful supporter.

For the next eleven years Pavy spent a commendably long time each
year in Wales until a curious disappearance for nine months beginning
early in 1492 and then from the summer of 1494, when he retired to Long
Ashton in Somerset, the home of the Chokkes.[94] So he returned to the
neighbourhood of his native Bristol; and when he drew up his will the
first man named was his nephew, Sir John Chokke.[95] Then came his
clerical household from Wales: Master John Barret, Master William Johns,
Master John Denby, and Canon William Wilcok, men whom he had
chosen and rewarded, as he had been chosen and rewarded by Bishop
Beauchamp thirty years earlier.[96]

Analysis of the careers of medieval clergy is in many ways an unsatisfac-
tory business. Lists of benefices need not be as arid as they seem if patrons
are brought into the equation; but even then the vital questions usually
have to remain unanswered. It may, perhaps, be clear enough who is a
man dedicated to a parochial career and who to an administrative one; but

were those men content with one or two benefices simply unsuccessful, men who failed to attract a patron? In theory the heights of a clerical career were open to those of the humblest origins. Thomas Bekynton, son of a country weaver, found his background of no impediment; but the first steps in his rise are quite unknown and yet crucial. Who picked him from other village boys and prepared him for Winchester? Who paid his fees there and at Oxford?[97] This is the vital part of patronage. The Courtenays seem to have used some of their livings to start young men on their careers, and they cannot have been alone. There are, too, plenty of examples of parish incomes being used to the same end, with the active connivance of a sympathetic bishop. Episcopal and monastic households, too, offered essential beginnings, and conscientious parish priests were then, as in every age, the church's talent scouts.

Progress thereafter depended on connexion and the exercise of the patronage system. The results are evident enough. John Hody's twenty-six benefices were not unusual, but it is motive that needs to be discovered and understood. A patron had obligations towards the livings in his gift, and for some patrons pastoral responsibility was paramount. For others there were less spiritual considerations: the cost of estate management could be reduced, the possibilities of an extension of political influence in church courts and administration could become a reality. The exercise of patronage by the crown has for long been regarded as both normal, widespread and effective. No less widespread and normal, and effective on a more local and limited level, could be the patronage of the nobility and gentry. Their control of parochial livings, the essential leadership of the church, was vast, but it was never likely to be exercised for other than limited objectives.

NOTES

1. BL, Add. MS. 41503 f.141.
2. *Church Times*, 20 July 1979.
3. E.F. Jacob, *The Fifteenth Century, 1399-1485* (Oxford, 1961), pp. 271-73.
4. Henry Chichele was bishop of St. David's in 1408-14: [*The*] *Reg* [*ister of Henry*] *Chichele*, ed. E.F. Jacob, I(1938), xxix.
5. PRO, SC6/1140/25.
6. Richard Swan was receiver-general in 1459-65: [*The*] *Reg*[*ister of Thomas*] *Bekynton*, ed. H.C. Maxwell-Lyte and M.C.B. Dawes (Somerset Record Soc., XLIX, 1934) no.1221; Lambeth Palace, CR 1132. Robert Tarry, B.Cn.L., was appointed joint auditor in 1444: *Reg. Bekynton*, I, no.70.
7. C. Rawcliffe, *The Staffords, Earls of Stafford and Dukes of Buckingham, 1394-1521* (Cambridge, 1978), pp.227, 229-31.
8. Ibid., pp.83-84.
9. See, in general, M. Cherry, 'The Courtenay Earls of Devon: the Formation and Dis-integration of a Late-mediaeval Aristocratic Affinity', *Southern History*, I (1979), 71-97; and infra. For the advowsons of the family in Devon and Cornwall, see the registers of the bishops of Exeter: [*The*] *Reg*[*ister of John de*] *Grandisson*, ed. F.C. Hingeston-Randolph (3 vols., 1894-99); [*The*] *Reg*[*ister of Thomas de*] *Brantyngham*, ed. F.C. Hingeston-Randolph (2 vols., 1902-6); [*The*] *Reg*[*ister of*] *Edmund Stafford*, ed. F.C. Hingeston-Randolph (1886).
10. BL, Add. Ch. 64320. See Cherry, 'Courtenay Earls of Devon', p.81 and n.
11. BL, Add. Ch. 64803.
12. BL, Add. Ch. 13972, 64321.
13. *Reg. Brantyngham*, pp.84, 97; *Reg. Edmund Stafford*, p.190.
14. *Reg. Brantyngham*, pp.113, 121.
15. BL, Add. Ch. 64317.
16. *Reg. Brantyngham*, p.16.
17. Ibid., pp.91, 117.
18. Ibid., p.84.
19. Ibid., p.78.
20. Ibid., p.94.
21. Ibid., p.339.
22. BL, Add. Ch. 64320.
23. *Reg. Brantyngham*, p.83.
24. *Reg. Edmund Stafford*, p.252.
25. *Reg. Brantyngham*, p.118.
26. A.B. Emden, *A Biographical Register of the University of Oxford to A.D. 1500* (2 vols., Oxford, 1957-59) (henceforward *BRUO*), III, 1689-90.
27. Ibid., III, 1772.
28. Ibid., II, 907-8.
29. Ibid., III, 1579; *Reg. Edmund Stafford*, p. 190.
30. *VCH, Somerset*, IV(1978), 29-30.
31. Ibid., p. 29.
32. *Calendar of the Register of John de Drokensford*, ed. E. Hobhouse (Somerset Record Soc., I, 1887), p.292; [*The*] *Reg*[*ister of*] *Ralph of Shrewsbury*, I, ed. T.S. Holmes (Somerset Record Soc., IX, 1896), pp.72-73, 106, 178; *Reg. Grandisson*, II, 940, 946, 953.
33. *Reg. Edmund Stafford*, p.214.
34. *BRUO*, I, 465-66.
35. [*The*]*Reg*[*ister of*] *John Stafford*, ed. T.S. Holmes (Somerset Record Soc., XXXI-XXXII,

1915-16), p.58. Hendyman had been a portioner of Tiverton in 1398-1404, incumbent of Sampford Courtenay (*Reg. Edmund Stafford*, pp. 207, 214), and vicar-general of Edmund Stafford: [*The*] *Reg*[*ister of Nicholas*] *Bubwith*, ed. T.S. Holmes (Somerset Record Soc., XXIX-XXX, 1914), p.413.

36. *Reg. John Stafford*, p.62.
37. *BRUO*, I, 473; R.G. Bartelot, *History of Crewkerne School* (Crewkerne, 1899), pp. 5-11.
38. *Reg. Ralph of Shrewsbury*, p.318; *Reg. Grandisson*, I, 305.
39. Ibid., II, 718, 728, 834, 930, 940, 1207.
40. *Cal. Papal Petitions*, p.374, where Philip was said to be thirteen; *Reg. Ralph of Shrewsbury*, p.766.
41. *Proc. Somerset Arch. Soc.*, CXIV (1969-70), 92; BL, Add. Ch. 64320.
42. *BRUO*, III, 2226.
43. *Reg. John Stafford*, pp. 60, 95.
44. *BRUO*, II, 978. His appointment to Crewkerne is not recorded there, as he is named John in *Reg. John Stafford*, pp. 185-86, though the correct name is given in *Reg. Bekynton*, p.246.
45. *Reg*[*ister of Robert*] *Shillington and* [*Richard*] *Fox*, ed. H.C. Maxwell-Lyte (Somerset Record Soc., LII, 1937), pp. 2-3, 40.
46. *CPR, 1476-85*, p.165; *Regs. Stillington and Fox*, p.82; *BRUO*, III, 1817.
47. *Reg*[*isters of Oliver*] *King and Hadrian* [*de Castello*], ed. H.C. Maxwell-Lyte (Somerset Record Soc., LIV, 1939), p.137; *Letters and Papers of Henry VIII*, I,95; *BRUO*, III, 1487.
48. *CPR, 1416-22*, p.440.
49. *Reg. John Stafford*, p.284; *BRUO*, II, 1037-38 (though Crewkerne is not there included), 1958-59.
50. *Reg. Bekynton*, pp. 232-33; *CPR, 1476-85*, pp. 99-100, 500; *Regs. Stillington and Fox*, pp. 111, 139.
51. *Regs. King and Hadrian*, p.100.
52. *Somerset and Dorset Notes and Queries*, XVIII (1925), 127-28.
53. Ibid. Alexander is there said to have been beheaded. J. Wedgwood, *History of Parliament: Biographies of the Members of the Commons House, 1439-1509* (1936), p.460, is less certain. Wedgwood's reference to him as steward of the earl of Salisbury in 1432-55 is not otherwise substantiated, though he occurs in office in 1443: *Somerset Record Soc.*, XIV, 197.
54. *CPR, 1391-96*, p.369. For Hody's career, see *BRUO*, II, 941-42.
55. *BRUO*, II, 942; J. le Neve, *Fasti Ecclesiae Anglicanae, 1300-1541*, ed. J.M. Horn et al., *Monastic Cathedral* (1963), p.24
56. She was Philippa, widow of Sir Matthew Gournay: J. Hutchins, *History and Antiquities of Dorset*, IV(1873), 72, 491.
57. *HMC, MSS. of Wells Cathedral*, II, 34.
58. Hody held Wotton Courtenay, Polton Luccombe.
59. *BRUO*, III, 1494-95: papal chaplain in 1394, abbreviator of papal letters by 1401, prothonotary apostolic by 1414.
60. *Cal. Papal Letters*, VI, 300.
61. Ibid., pp.463, 505.
62. Ibid., p.471.
63. *BRUO*, III, 1495.
64. *Reg. Bubwith*, p.294.
65. *BRUO*, II, 942.
66. *Reg. Chichele*, III, 493-94.
67. *Somerset Mediaeval Wills, 1383-1500* (Somerset Record Soc., XIX, 1903), p.336.
68. *The Mayor of Bristowe is Kalendar*, ed. L.T. Smith (Camden Soc., 1872), pp. 39-40; *Trans. Bristol and Gloucestershire Arch. Soc.*, XXVI (1903), 131; *Little Red Book of Bristol*,

ed. F.B. Bickley (Bristol, 1900), II,50; *Great Red Book of Bristol*, ed. E.W.W. Veale (Bristol Record Soc., IV, VIII, 1933, 1938), I, 125, 128-29, 131, 253-55; II, 52, 57; *Overseas Trade of Bristol*, ed. E.M. Carus-Wilson (Bristol Record Soc., VII, 1937), pp. 79-80, 86, 118, 125.

69. 'Calendar of Deeds collected by G.W. Braikenridge', ed. F.B. Bickley (Bristol Record Office TS), no.245.

70. *Cal. Papal Letters*, XI, 94.

71. *A Calendar of Wills . . . in the Great Orphan Book of . . . Bristol, 1379-1674*, ed. E.A. Fry (1897), p.132.

72. *BRUO*, III, 1438.

73. Richard Chokke had married Joan, Hugh's sister: *Great Orphan Book*, p.132.

74. R.W. Dunning, 'The Administration of the Diocese of Bath and Wells, 1401-91' (Bristol Ph.D. thesis, 1963), p.359.

75. *Reg. Bekynton*, p.267.

76. *Regs. Stillington and Fox*, p.8.

77. Salisbury, Diocesan Record Office, Dean and Chapter, Register Machon, p.19.

78. Ibid.

79. Ibid., pp.54-55.

80. Ibid., p.78.

81. Ibid., p.88.

82. Salisbury, Diocesan Record Office, Dean and Chapter Accounts, 1471, 1476-77, 1480, 1484-85; Register Machon, *s.a.* 1472-75, pp. 89ff.

83. Le Neve, *Fasti, Salisbury* (1962), p.14.

84. P.C.C., 4 Logge.

85. *CPR, 1476-85*, p.527.

86. Ibid., p.416.

87. Ibid., p.360; E.Foss, *A Biographical Dictionary of the Judges of England* (1870), p.164.

88. BL, Harleian MS.433 p.273. For this and other references to this source, I am indebted to Mr. W.E. Hampton. Langton's possible influence is suggested by Dr. Rosemary Horrox.

89. Ibid., p.198.

90. *CPR, 1476-85*, p.488.

91. Le Neve, *Fasti, Salisbury*, p.2.

92. Ibid., *The Welsh Dioceses* (1965), p.55.

93. Ibid.

94. *The Episcopal Registers of the Diocese of St. David's, 1397-1518*, ed. R.F. Isaacson (Cymmrodorion Record Soc., 1917), II, 458-711, especially pp.668, 690, 702, 704, 708.

95. *Somerset Mediaval Wills, 1383-1500*, pp.330-32.

96. Ibid.; *Reg. St. David's, passim*.

97. Bekynton remembered in his will the patrons and benefactors to whom he owed his promotion: Humphrey, duke of Gloucester, William of Wykeham, Master John Elmer, and Walter Thurston: A.F. Judd, *The Life of Thomas Bekynton* (Chichester, 1961), p.163.

Index